Football, Fandom and Consumption

Modern football is an industry and capitalism is its engine. However, this book argues for a more nuanced understanding of contemporary football culture and the (self-)identity of football fans.

Drawing on original ethnographic research conducted with fans at all levels, from international to lower league, the book explores the tensions between fans as consumers and 'traditional' football cultures, arguing that modern football fans are able to negotiate the discourses of capitalism and tradition operating upon them to enact their own power and identity within football culture.

Featuring case studies of Norwich City, MK Dons and Chelsea fans, this is fascinating reading for anybody with an interest in sport and society or cultural studies.

Oliver Brooks is Tutor in the School of Politics, Philosophy, Language and Communication Studies at the University of East Anglia, UK.

Critical Research in Football

Series Editors:
Pete Millward, *Liverpool John Moores University, UK*
Jamie Cleland, *University of Southern Australia*
Dan Parnell, *Manchester Metropolitan University, UK*
Stacey Pope, *Durham University, UK*
Paul Widdop, *Leeds Beckett University, UK*

The *Critical Research in Football* book series was launched in 2017 to showcase the inter- and multi-disciplinary breadth of debate relating to 'football.' The series defines 'football' as broader than association football, with research on rugby, Gaelic and gridiron codes also featured. Including monographs, edited collections, short books and textbooks, books in the series are written and/or edited by leading experts in the field, whilst consciously also affording space to emerging voices in the area, and are designed to appeal to students, postgraduate students and scholars who are interested in the range of disciplines in which critical research in football connects. The series is published in association with the *Football Collective*, www.footballcollective.org.uk.

Available in this series:

Fan Activism, Protest and Politics
Ultras in Post-Socialist Croatia
Andrew Hodges

Football, Fandom and Consumption
Oliver Brooks

Football, Fandom and Consumption

Oliver Brooks

Routledge
Taylor & Francis Group
LONDON AND NEW YORK

First published 2019
by Routledge
2 Park Square, Milton Park, Abingdon, Oxon OX14 4RN

and by Routledge
52 Vanderbilt Avenue, New York, NY 10017

Routledge is an imprint of the Taylor & Francis Group, an informa business

British Library Cataloguing-in-Publication Data
A catalogue record for this book is available from the British Library.

Library of Congress Cataloguing-in-Publication Data
Names: Brooks, Oliver (Lecturer) author.
Title: Football, fandom and consumption / Oliver Brooks.
Description: Abingdon, Oxon, New York NY : Routledge, [2019] |
Series: Critical research in football | Includes bibliographical references and index.
Identifiers: LCCN 2018046359 | ISBN 9780367142650 (hardback) |
ISBN 9780429030987 (master ebook)
Subjects: LCSH: Soccer–Social aspects–England. | Soccer–Economic aspects–England. | Soccer fans–Psychology–England. | Consumption (Economics)–Social aspects–England. | Capitalism–Social aspects–England.
Classification: LCC GV943.9.S64 .B77 2019 | DDC 796.334041–dc23
LC record available at https://lccn.loc.gov/2018046359

ISBN: 978-0-367-14265-0 (hbk)
ISBN: 978-0-429-03098-7 (ebk)

Typeset in Goudy
by Deanta Global Publishing Services, Chennai, India

Mute, Baz and Roo—Thank you for the support.

Contents

Preface viii

1 Introduction: #YouAreFootball 1

2 The people's game? 10

3 Changing formation 35

4 Norwich City: 'The best pies in the league' 46

5 MK Dons: Fear and loathing in Milton Keynes 71

6 Chelsea: 'Champions of Europe' 96

7 'IN-GER-LAND': Ethnography in the pub 122

8 Conclusion: They think it's all over 149

Appendix A 157
Index 158

Preface

This book endeavours to develop a more nuanced understanding of contemporary football culture. As such, the research adopts a consumer-oriented cultural studies approach to analyse the ways in which modern 'consumer' fans negotiate their position within football culture and the power operating upon them as they do so. Drawing on data from ethnographic research I argue that modern fans engage in processes of complex discursive negotiation, constructing their identities at the juncture of the hegemonic discourses that surround football culture: capitalism and tradition, but also their individual understanding of how they are *expected* to enact fandom.

I argue that modern fans are able to negotiate the discourses of capitalism and tradition operating upon them to enact their own power and identity within football culture. As such, this book seeks to advance debates about collective identity formation and the scope of representation within contemporary football culture. In doing so, this research contributes to football scholarship's long tradition of making perceptive social commentaries, drawing on football culture to contribute to wider debates concerning capitalism and collective identity formation.

Chapter 1

Introduction

#YouAreFootball

As I exited the tube at Fulham Broadway to conduct my pilot study with Chelsea fans (27 September 2011), employees of Barclays Bank approached me. As the official sponsor of the Premier League, Barclays had just started its '#YouAreFootball campaign,' an initiative started by the bank to 'thank real football fans' (Barclays 2011) by giving them the opportunity to win match day tickets and recoup travel expenses. To be in with a chance of winning tickets, I was asked to tell Barclays what football meant to me to 'help them celebrate the passion of real fans' (Barclays 2011).

Barclays (2011) emphasise the centrality of the fan to football culture as suggested by the branding of their campaign '#YouAreFootball,' a slogan that along with their rationale of engaging with the individual passions of fans, positions fans as active agents within football culture. Taking the Barclays campaign into account, this idea of an active, participatory fandom seems constitutive of Barclays' (2011) conception of a 'real football fan,' yet there is a slight caveat to this. To identify as a 'real fan,' and to take part in the competition, participants had to be in possession of a match day ticket. While the campaign would seem to acknowledge the constitutive role of the fan within football culture, it is required that the fan is active *in consumption*, 'buying into' football's culture of capitalism and supporting its affiliated industries.

The bank's definition of the 'real football fan' works with the assumption that fans accept contemporary football's culture of capitalism, 'real' fans acknowledging their position as consumers within the culture. Barclays' (2011) conception of the 'real football fan' looks to naturalise the game's[1] modern capitalism and the relationship of producer and consumer between fan and football club, however the concept of the 'real football fan' is shrouded in conflicting discourse within football culture. Indeed, while Barclays (2011) clearly recognise modern football as a developed capitalist industry, there is significant opposition to the game's modern capitalism and the subsequent consumer fan identities that have developed as a result of this process.

Explaining my research to 'Richard' (19 June 2012), a contact I made conducting research in 'MG's,' a popular sports bar in Norfolk (UK), he questioned its significance and representativeness:

> Your research is looking at those that can afford to go to football matches, not fans. The real fans can't afford to go to games anymore and have been put off by the circus surrounding it these days. Real football fans don't go to matches anymore so I don't think there's much point (in you) going to matches (to conduct research)—it'll all be the same thing.

Barclays (2011) use rhetoric that alludes to the active consumerism of fans within football culture yet 'Richard' denies their fandom, positioning them as passive consumers, 'your research is looking at those that can afford to go to football matches, *not fans* (emphasis added).' Similarly, while Barclays implore consumer fans to 'share their passions' about football, 'Richard' denies consumer fans' individuality and subjectivity. He suggests that their fandom will be figured by their relationship of consumerism to their clubs and thus my ethnographic observations within the stadium will 'all be the same thing.' This book operates against the assumption that football culture has historically operated free from capitalism and subsequently looks to understand the individual pleasure and motivations of modern consumer fans, exploring how they understand the way in which they are positioned within football culture, how they articulate their fandom and negotiate the ways in which they are narrowly represented.

Fundamentally 'Richard' (2012) mobilises the concept of the 'real football fan,' in opposition to Barclays (2011) and the concept of the consumer fan. He argues that 'real fans don't go to matches anymore,' insinuating that they have become both economically and ideologically disenfranchised; 'real fans can't afford to go to games anymore', they are 'put off by the circus surrounding it these days' ('Richard' 2012). This notion refers to the cultural changes that have happened within football culture since the early 1990s, said to mark football cultures' assimilation with modern capitalism, when the Football Association (FA) made concerted attempts to attract new demographics to the sport: women, families and the middle-class (see Fynn & Guest 1994; Lee 1998; King 2002; Imlach 2005). To achieve this, the terraces were removed, and an all seating policy was introduced while ticket prices were increased concomitant with the game's embourgeoisement, to assimilate football with wider leisure industries. 'Richard' encapsulates the idea that this cultural reorientation of the game precipitated alterations in the physical experience of watching live football matches but also, significantly, the 'type' of fan that these changes attracted. Fundamentally he argues that as consumers, contemporary fans cannot be considered 'real,' with individual fan identities.

A tension is apparent within football culture. While the game has developed through different phases of capitalism, 'Richard's' (2012) understanding of modern football culture as 'capitalist football culture' is demonstrative of a large counter discourse that decries the loss of the traditional experience of attending football matches and the traditional fan identities of the working-class men that occupied the terraces. This tension is reflected in the way in which Barclays (2011) and 'Richard' mobilise the concept of the 'real football fan.' As suggested, while Barclays emphasise the centrality of consumer fans within the culture, framing their fandom as active consumerism, 'Richard' juxtaposes their passive consumption to the knowing abstinence of the 'traditional fan' (see Ingle 2005), framing consumer fans as hollow, ersatz and corporate dupes.

The way in which 'Richard' (2012) creates opposition between consumer fans and traditional fans emphasises the centrality of both capitalist and traditional discourse to contemporary football culture, indicating that he has an understanding of the cultural developments that have happened within the game, yet it is clear that he recognises the aura that continues to be associated with traditional football culture and the identity of the traditional fan.

'Richard's' (2012) response to my research is indicative of much of the literature surrounding football culture. Like 'Richard' both popular and academic texts proficiently identify the commercial and economic changes that have happened within football culture as the game has developed through different phases of capitalism, yet these texts predominantly focus on the ways in which these changes have affected the fandom and identity of 'traditional fans.' I argue that many contemporary texts, particularly those written by self-identified traditional fans, pundits and former players, seem dramatically overpowered by an emotional sense of loss (Bale 1998; Brimson 1998; Burgess 2005; Conn 2005; Ingle 2005). Similarly, while more rigorous academic critiques such as King's (2002) work demonstrate appreciation of the complexities and contradictions of football's modern capitalism, much of the empirical work surrounding football culture still refers to a 'traditional fan experience' as a starting point for research, positioning the authentic 'fan' in opposition to an imagined disingenuous modern 'consumer' of football (see Brown 1998; Williams 2000; King 2002; Pearson 2012).

'Richard's' (2012) quotation encapsulates the idea of loss associated with traditional fan identities within modern football culture. He rejects the identity of consumer fans for reflecting the processes of the game's modern capitalism. This is indicative of the popular literature, not taking into account the legitimacy or nuances of consumer fan identities or the influence of capitalism on the game's early development. Similarly, while the academic literature makes a significant contribution to the new agenda for football scholarship (see Guilanotti 2002; King 2002; Pearson 2012), it similarly ignores the identity of consumer fans, helping to create a binary between the 'authentic' traditional fan and the 'disingenuous' consumer fan.

If, as I suggest, agents of the game's modern capitalism act with an agenda of naturalising the relationship of consumption between fan, club and affiliated industries, then I argue that both popular and academic literature surrounding football culture naturalises the 'traditional' relationship between working-class fans and football culture, helping to maintain the aura (see Benjamin 2008) associated with traditional fan identities. 'Richard's' (2012) response to my research and his 'othering' of consumer fans is indicative of this in which he demonstrates his identification with the traditional discourses surrounding football culture. Indeed, his disregard for my research seems indicative of his disregard for the identity of consumer fans, 'Richard' discrediting their role within football culture.

Taking this into account, consumer fans appear to be trapped within discourses of representation, with their identity as consumers explicitly constructed by both agents of the game's capitalism and the game's tradition. Barclays (2011), as an agent of the game's capitalism, look to reward fans for 'buying into' the capitalism of the sport. This is the genius of the capitalist system, with its discourse permeating into the products that embody its hegemony. The relationship of consumption between fan and club is naturalised by agents of the game's modern capitalism in which fans are encouraged to self-identify as consumers. Marcuse (1991: 9) encapsulates this idea outlining the way in which capitalism encourages identity formation thorough patronage:

> People recognise themselves in their commodities, they find their soul in the automobiles, hi-fi sets, spirit level home, kitchen equipment. The very mechanism which ties the individual to his society has changed and social control is achieved in the need that it has produced.

Barclays (2011) in their campaign suggest that consumption legitimates the identity of the fan, making them 'real.' Indeed, as I suggest, the opportunity Barclays (2011) provide fans to describe their passions and enact their identity can be considered as a reward for their consumption: the bank providing fans with a platform to enact identity through the purchase of match tickets. On the other hand, agents of the game's tradition, self-identified traditional fans, pundits and academics, negatively frame fans as consumers, 'othering' them in relation to the concept of the 'traditional fan' indicative of a time when football culture was (wrongly) considered to be free from capitalist interest. The consumer fans that have replaced the traditional fans within the stadium are presented as the embodiment of these processes, depersonalised and denied subjectivity.

While both agents of the game's modern capitalism and agents of the game's tradition disseminate discourse that looks to naturalise the relationship between fan and football culture, it is of note that despite being aware of both discourses 'Richard' (2012) identifies with the discourse associated with traditional football culture. While the businesses and institutions responsible for the game's modern capitalism disseminate discourse to naturalise the fan's position as consumers within the culture, self-identified traditional fans largely disseminate the discourses associated with the game's traditional culture. The personal accounts of the traditional fans construct their identity in opposition to the game's modern capitalism, presenting a cause and effect relationship, in which capitalism is presented as the cause of their exclusion from contemporary football culture (see Bale 1998; Brimson 1998; Burgess 2005; Conn 2005). This creates a dichotomy of 'them and us' in which agents of the game's modern capitalism are positioned in opposition to self-identified 'real' football fans.

I argue that these emotional, individual narratives of fandom are more accessible than the discourse disseminated by major corporations. The individual narratives of traditional fans successfully expand upon the romanticised and nostalgic images of the terraces popularised within popular culture both by 'Hooly lit' and 'Hooly film'[2] (see Brimson 1998), while similarly tapping into anti-consumerist discourse epitomised by Marcuse (1991). In doing so these texts appeal both to the popular imagination of the wider audience, while helping to generate support for the traditional fan's claims of authenticity, positioning them as underdogs in opposition to the collective hegemony of capitalism and its embodied consumer fans.

In documenting the ways in which the game's modern capitalism has affected the identity of the 'traditional fan,' a binary is created between the 'good' traditional fan and 'bad' agents of capitalism. In doing so, football's capitalism is presented as fundamentally negative, exclusively associated with the game's modern era. I argue that this has twofold significance in relation to the way in which football culture is studied and analysed. While traditional fans have a platform within football culture to disseminate counter discourse to the game's capitalism, consumer fans, framed as embodied agents of the game's capitalism, have limited representation within football culture. As I suggest, consumer fans are positioned both positively as consumers by football's governing bodies and negatively as consumers by self-identified traditional fans, trapped in discourses of representation without a platform to articulate their own fan identity. Second, while football is both a cultural phenomenon and a culture of contestation, it seems significant that cultural studies approaches, particularly consumption-oriented cultural studies approaches to football culture, are rarely enacted (see King 2002; Sandvoss 2003).

While consumption-oriented cultural studies accept capitalist orthodoxy (see Fiske 1986; 1992; Barker 2004; Sandvoss 2005; Lash 2007), the different phases of football's capitalism are ignored and disavowed by self-identified traditional fans. Indeed, their identity is framed in opposition to the game's modern capitalism and its consumer fans. Adopting a consumption-orientated cultural studies approach to football culture would take the game's capitalism as a natural starting point and, as suggested, self-identified traditional fans are loath to accept this.

The traditional fan's critiques of football's modern capitalism and the 'othering' of consumer fans work with the assumption that commodities carry embedded ideological meaning that serves the interest of capitalism.[3] However, it is significant that contemporarily this perception of identity formation within capitalist society has been challenged. Barker (2004) argues that first it should not be taken for granted that commodities necessarily carry ideological meaning that supports the capitalist system. Indeed, he suggests that commodities, alternatively, may encourage resistance and transgression (Barker 2004). Second, he suggests that it needs to be recognised that consumers are active in consumption, attributing their own meanings to the commodities that they consume (Barker 2004). In other words, Barker (2004) argues that consumers do not passively accept the meanings that critics have suggested are invested within texts but are capable of creating their own meanings through the interplay of texts and their individual consumer needs.

It is the way in which traditional fans exercise power over consumer fans limiting the boundaries of football culture that has encouraged me to adopt a consumer-oriented cultural studies approach to my research. Subsequently I take the capitalism of the sport as the starting point, with the following chapter outlining the way in which the game has progressed through different phases of capitalism. In the acknowledgement of capitalist orthodoxy, consumer–oriented cultural studies as a discipline looks to examine the idiosyncrasies of identity, exploring the individuality and creativity of collective formations of people by analysing the ways in which they can oppose, challenge and find pleasure in capitalist texts. Sandvoss (2005: 9) encapsulates this notion describing contemporary fandom as a practice in which individuals emotionally engage with the products of capitalism. Barclays' (2011) campaign seems to work with this premise. Taking football's capitalism as the starting point, the campaign asks fans about their identification with their club and their passion for the game that has been enabled through their purchase of match day tickets. As suggested, the rhetoric of the campaign frames the process as active consumption, concomitant with the premise of consumer-oriented cultural studies in which it is taken for granted that fans construct meanings and their identity from their engagements with capitalist texts. While consumer-oriented cultural studies accepts that production remains in the hands of dominant multi-national corporations, a premise concomitant with 'late capitalist' theory (see Mandel 1975; Jameson 1997; Targ 2006; Harvey 2014), it argues that meanings are created, managed and negotiated at the level of consumption.

My research adheres to this idea, with the findings of my ethnographic research indicating that the fans of the three clubs selected for analysis[4] are aware of the discourses operating on them both within football culture and in capitalist society more generally, challenging the idea that they are merely 'corporate dupes.' Indeed, my argument is that the fans' levels of engagement and understanding of these discourses produce different expectations of how they *should* identify as fans.

Rather than being trapped within discourses of representation, my argument is that consumer fans engage in processes of complex discursive negotiation, constructing their identities at the juncture of the hegemonic discourses that surround football culture: consumerism and tradition. Fans from each club enact unique hybrid identities in which they self-identify as consumer fans while similarly looking to authenticate their fan identity by enacting rituals associated with traditional football culture. My research indicates that these complex articulations of identity differ in relation to the unique culture of their club and their individual identification with the discourses of traditional football culture, producing unique expectations of what it means to be a modern football fan. While the hegemonic discourses surrounding the culture, tradition and capitalism work to create a binary between the traditional fan and the modern consumer, my research suggests that in practice this is not the case, with the fans drawing upon both discourses in their enactment of fan identity, challenging the simplistic binary that has been created.

At no point am I suggesting that the pervasiveness and power of capitalism should be ignored or even accepted, however my argument is that by effectively denying the fandom of consumer fans, positioning them as 'others' to be feared, we are effectively denying ourselves the opportunity to understand their negotiations of capitalism or consider their individual motivations for fandom upon which consumer-oriented cultural studies thrives (see Jameson 1991; Fiske 1992; Hills 2002; Barker 2004; Sandvoss 2005).

Consumer-oriented cultural studies as a discipline examines the idiosyncrasies of identity formation to assess the creativity and individuality of consumers, offering readers examples of ways in which we as consumers can oppose, challenge and find pleasure in products of capitalism, providing us with opportunities to further consider our position with the system. As Barker (2004) indicates, consumer-oriented cultural studies look to analyse how texts carry meanings that articulate collective identities and their objective and subjective position within society. Taking football culture as the 'text,' this book looks to develop a more nuanced understanding of contemporary football to situate it with consumer-oriented cultural studies to understand the individual pleasure and motivations of consumers, exploring how consumer fans understand the way in which they are positioned within the culture, how they articulate their fandom and negotiate the ways in which they are narrowly represented.

To accomplish this, I draw upon the moral values of participatory research. From a philosophical stance the principles underlying participatory research are based on the recognition of human subjectivity and the social construction of reality (Reason & Rowan 1981). Again, I argue that this is largely unique in contemporary football culture with my research adopting a scholarly approach rarely applied to football culture, while focusing on a 'type' of fan that is largely denied subjectivity.

This book seeks to advance debates about collective identity formation and the scope of representation within modern football culture. In doing so, this book contributes to football scholarship's long tradition of making perceptive social commentaries, drawing on football culture to contribute to wider debates concerning capitalism and collective identity formation. This book not only helps to address the power imbalance within contemporary football culture, but also assimilates football scholarship with consumer–oriented cultural studies, endeavouring to assess the pleasures and 'exceptional readings' audiences conduct with capitalist texts (Sandvoss 2005: 48), ensuring that consumer fans are given the chance to play their part within football culture and that their voices are heard.

Notes

1 'The game' is a term that will be used throughout the book. 'The game' is used as an umbrella concept to capture the idea that live football is an 'event' that extends beyond the action on the pitch. The participants suggest that they have different motivations for attending live matches; pleasures are found in club catering, in socialising with like-minded people, meeting family, drinking and in purchasing merchandise. It is this wider idea of football as an 'event,' as a leisure industry, that I draw upon in use of the term.

2 There has been a range of texts documenting the culture and hooliganism of the terraces such as *Congratulations You Have Just Met the ICF* (Pennant 2003), *Good Afternoon Gentlemen* (Gardner 2012) and *Running with the Firm* (Bannon 2013). The popular image of the terraces is similarly fictionalised in film: *The Football Factory* (2004); *Green Street* (2005); *The Firm* (2009). My research indicates that these texts influence the participant's expectations of fandom.

3 Marx in the 1850s, Adorno in the 1940s and Althusser in the 1970s have made such arguments.

4 Norwich City, Milton Keynes Dons and Chelsea were selected as case studies. Norwich City was selected as 'a family club;' Milton Keynes was selected as a 'franchise' football club; Chelsea was selected as a 'tourist attraction' club.

Bibliography

Adorno, T (2001) *The Culture Industry: Selected Essays on Mass Culture*. London. Routledge.

Althusser, L (1984) *Essays on Ideology*. London. Verso.

Bale, J (1998) 'Virtual Fandoms: Futurescapes of Football.' Cited in Brown, A *Fanatics: Power, Identity and Fandom in Football*. London. Routledge.

Bannon, J (2013) *Running with the Firm*. London. Ebury Press.

Barclays Bank (2011) *You Are Football*. Barclays Bank [Website] Available from: https://www.youarefootball.barclays.co.uk/ (Accessed 30 September 2011).

Barker, C (2004) *The Sage Dictionary of Cultural Studies*. London. Sage.

Benjamin, W (2008) *The Work of Art in the Age of Mechanical Reproduction*. London. Penguin.

Brimson, D (1998) *The Geezers Guide to Football: A Lifetime of Lads and Lager*. London. Mainstream Publishing.

Brown, A (1998) *Fanatics: Power, Identity & Fandom in Football*. London. Routledge.

Burgess, C (2005) What on Earth has Happened to Football? *The Guardian* [Website] Available from: http://www.theguardian.com/football/2005/feb/09/sport.comment (Accessed 16 November 2012).

Conn, D (2005) *The Beautiful Game? Searching for the Soul of Football*. London. Yellow Jersey Press.

Fiske, J (1986) Television, Polysemy and Popularity. *Critical Studies in Mass Communication* 3 (2) 391–408.

Fiske, J (1992) 'The Cultural Economy of Fandom' Cited in Lewis, L *The Adoring Audience*. London. Routledge.

Fynn, A & Guest, L (1994) *Out of Time: Why Football Isn't Working*. London. Simon & Schuster Press.

Gardner, B (2012) *Good Afternoon Gentlemen*. London. Blake.

Giulianotti, R (2002) Supporters, Fans and Flaneurs: Taxonomy of Spectator Identities in Football. *Journal of Sport and Social Issues* 26 (1) 25–46.
Harvey, D (2014) *Seventeen Contradictions and the End of Capitalism*. London. Profile Publishing.
Hills, M (2002) *Fan Cultures*. London. Routledge.
Imlach, G (2005) My *Father and Other Working-Class Football Heroes*. London. Yellow Jersey Press.
Ingle, S (2005) Football Fans are Idiots. *The Guardian* [Website] Available from: http://www.theguardian.com/football/2005/sep/02/sport.blueprintforabetterfootball (Accessed 23 October 2011).
Jameson, F (1991) *Postmodernism or the Cultural Logic of Late Capitalism*. London. Verso.
Jameson, F (1997) Culture and Finance Capitalism. *Critical Inquiry* 24 (1) 246–265.
King, A (2002) *The End of the Terraces: The Transformation of English Football in the 1990's*. London. Leicester University Press.
Lash, S (2007) 'Power After Hegemony: Cultural Studies in Mutation?' *Theory, Culture and Society* 24 (3) 55–78.
Lee, S (1998) 'Grey Shirts to Grey Suits: The Political Economy of English Football in the 1990's' Cited in Brown, A *Fanatics: Power, Identity & Fandom in Football*. London. Routledge.
Mandel, E (1975) *Late Capitalism*. London. Humanities Press.
Marcuse, H (1991) *One Dimensional Man: Studies in the Ideology of Advanced Industrial Society*. London. Routledge.
Marx, K (1932) *Economic and Philosophic Manuscripts of 1844*. Moscow. Progress.
Pearson, G (2012) *An Ethnography of English Football Fans: Cans, Cops and Carnivals*. Manchester. Manchester University Press.
Pennant, C (2003) *Congratulations You Have Just Met the ICF*. London. Blake.
Reason, P & Rowan, R (1981) *Human Inquiry: A Sourcebook of New Paradigm Research*. London. Wiley.
Sandvoss, C (2003) *A Game of Two Halves: Football Television and Globalisation*. London. Routledge.
Sandvoss, C (2005) *Fans*. Cambridge. Polity.
Targ, H (2006) Late Capitalism, Neoliberal Globalisation and Militarism. *New Political Science* 9 (2) 15–26.
Williams, J (2000) 'The Changing Face of Football: A Case for National Regulation' Cited in Mitchie, J et al. *Football in the Digital Age: Whose Game Is It Anyway?* London. Mainstream Publishing.

Chapter 2

The people's game?

In his nostalgic text *My Father and Other Working-Class Football Heroes* (2005), Gary Imlach draws on his experience as an American Football commentator in the late 1980s to mid-1990s to celebrate the 'integrity' and 'authenticity' of English football. Imlach (2005: 213) describes the culture of American professional sport as a synthetic 'cash fuelled soap opera … an entirely indigenous phenomenon' without parallel in England. Perpetuating this juxtaposition, Imlach (2005: 213) creates a binary between 'commercialisation' and 'authenticity,' a romantic, idealised version of sports culture that he attributes to English football. In characterising American sport as decadent and excessive, 'pure commercialisation,' Imlach (2005: 213) draws on the history and tradition of English football to depict it as a pursuit of higher cultural importance and integrity, sport not as a multi-billion-dollar, multi-national industry but as a 'game of the people.'

A significant part of this binary relates to the role of the fan. American franchise culture dictates that teams can be uprooted at an owner's will; fandom, he argues, is merely an arbitrary choice following the logics of rapacious American consumer society in which fans are 'basically rooting for jerseys.' On the contrary football clubs are described as institutions with proud histories representative of the character of local communities, fandom governed by long standing familial lineage, geographical ties and indefinable emotional attachment (Imlach 2005: 213). This argument still holds much significance both in academia and to fans themselves in relation to traditional ideas about what football culture *should* be about.

It is ironic that during his time in America, football in England started to succumb to the influence of the 'transatlantic drift,' a cultural shift in which football clubs explicitly embraced commercialisation, professionalisation and rationalisation, transforming themselves from the cottage industries Imlach describes to fully fledged multinational businesses indicative of the *NFL* franchises that he had grown to loath. A significant body of intellectual response to these changes is highly nostalgic and melancholic, the past is idealised, the present is criticised and the future is feared (Carrington 1998; Williams 2000; King 2002; Burgess 2005; Conn 2005; Redhead 2007; Platts & Smith 2010). This literature echoes Imlach's (2005) lamentation of the *NFL* in which heightened commercialisation is said to sully the sport's 'purity of existence.' On returning to England in the late 1990s, Imlach (2005) documents his feelings of disorientation, his inability to embrace contemporary football culture and his prevailing desire for reorientation.

His recollections succinctly encapsulate the wider feeling of powerlessness and loss associated with football's modern era of capitalism, with the following quotation alluding to both the compromised purity of the 'traditional game' and, importantly, its alleged disenfranchisement of the male working-class 'traditional fan.' As he suggests: 'The stridency of the brash, relentless circus surrounding the game ... made it seem increasingly remote, *like someone else's sport*' (Imlach 2005: 213 My emphasis).

This quotation encapsulates the major opposition posited against modern football: that the game's contemporary capitalism has precipitated alterations in the physical experience of watching live football matches and subsequently the relationship between the game and its fans. This concern is raised by both academic and popular literature; how can fans maintain their undying devotion to a team when the clubs themselves are doing everything in their power to transform them into consumers (Fynn & Guest 1994; Bale 1998; Brimson 1998; Giulianotti 2002; King 2002; Ingle 2005: Barr 2009; Pearson 2012)? Indeed, Brimson (1998) suggests that having been re-positioned as consumers, 'traditional' fans respond in a manner befitting the natural conditions of capitalism, rejecting live football and refusing to 'consume' the sterile 'product' on offer. King (2002) argues that this protest is figured as necessary but fundamentally impossible; necessary as the 'traditional fan' experience is debased and disavowed by the changes within the culture but impossible as abstaining from live football merely aids the process of implementing a new middle-class crowd culture, attracting new demographics to the game and further disenfranchising the 'traditional fan.' As King's (2002) work demonstrates, some of the academic literature evaluates the nuances and complexities of football's modern capitalism (see Sandvoss 2003) yet many contemporary texts, particularly those written by self-identified fans, pundits and former players, seem dramatically overpowered by an emotional sense of loss (see Bale 1998; Brimson 1998; Burgess 2005; Conn 2005; Ingle 2005). Similarly, while more rigorous academic critiques such as King's (2002) work demonstrate appreciation for the complexities and contradictions of football's modern capitalism, outlining the way in which the game has progressed through different stages of capitalism, much of this work still refers to a 'traditional fan experience' associated with a time in which the game was considered to be free from capitalist interest.

Gilroy's concept of 'melancholia' (2004) seems pertinent to tease out the tensions and defining features of contemporary football culture. In *After Empire: Melancholia or Convivial Culture?* (2004), Gilroy argues that an insecure, melancholic mood has become part of the national infrastructure, product and symptom of neo-liberal consumer society. The concept of 'melancholia' provides an ideal framework to contextualise both the fear evoked by the perceived loss of the sport's traditional folk culture and the animosity directed at its new consumer fans, as well as explicating the referential and self-perpetuating relationship the two have on the culture.

Loss of identity, autonomy and the debasing of community have been discussed rigorously in relation to the establishment of neo-liberal capitalist orthodoxy (Marcuse 1991; Adorno 2001; Graham 2006; Schiel 2008). It is this sense of loss referenced by Gilroy (2004) that I argue is evoked by much of the literature surrounding modern football culture, decrying the loss of 'traditional' fan identities as a result of the sport's continued capitalism. With this being said, it is in this context of modern capitalism that Sandvoss (2005: 9) outlines his conception of contemporary fandom as the practices in which individuals emotionally engage with the products of capitalism. Indeed, it is significant that he uses the notion of consumption to explore his definition, with fandom at a basic level defined as 'a form of sustained affective *consumption*' (Sandvoss 2005: 9). With the products of capitalism and modern fandom defined symbiotically, Sandvoss (2005: 3) suggests that modern fandom has become reliant on the products of capitalism; indeed, he suggests that 'fandom mirrors conditions of popular culture.' It is the totality of capitalism and its constitutive role in modern life that has continued to evoke fear and scepticism, accounting for Gilroy's (2004) prevailing melancholy. Similarly, it is for this reason that I argue that such feelings of loss surround modern football culture, with contemporary fans acting as mirrors to self-identified 'traditional' fans, reflecting the developments that have happened within the culture.

Returning to Gilroy's 'melancholia' (2004: 15), he argues that societal melancholy is articulated in relation to key themes: invasion, war, contamination and loss. He uses the metaphor of WWII to explore this notion, arguing that an 'anti-Nazi war' has become a touchstone for the perceived decline of Britishness and the certainty that identity provided in the imperial period. With this in mind, the role of the 'Nazi' is played by 'folk devils' (see Cohen 2011, in this case the consumer fan, defined as a threat by wider society (traditional fans), while the feared decline of 'Britishness,' the idea of a stable way of life (traditional fan culture), is threatened and requires protection. The following quotation expands upon this idea:

> That memory of the country at war against foes who are simply, tidily and uncomplicatedly evil has recently acquired the status of an ethnic myth. It explains not only how the nation remade itself through war and victory but can also be understood as a rejection or deferral of its present problems. That process is driven by the need to get back to the place or moment before the country lost its moral and cultural bearing. Neither the appeal of homogeneity nor the antipathy towards immigrants and strangers who represent the involution of national culture can be separated from that underlying hunger for reorientation. Turning back in this direction is also turning away from the perceived dangers of pluralism and from the irreversible fact of multiculture.
>
> (Gilroy 2004: 97)

It is these stock themes of 'invasion,' 'war,' 'contamination' and 'loss' that I argue feature most prominently in critiques of modern football culture, again emphasising the game's assimilation with modern capitalism, but also how new consumer fans are treated with contempt, taking the role of the 'Nazi,' the 'other.' In the way in which much of the literature surrounding football culture fails to acknowledge the complexity of modern football and the heterogeneity of the modern fan, I argue that attempts are made to position consumer fans like the 'Nazi' as 'simply, tidily and uncomplicatedly evil' (Gilroy 2004: 15). The need of the traditional fan to engage in conflict with the game's new consumer fans can be assimilated to the ways in which the nation looked to remake itself through war and victory, with fans hoping to solidify their sense of identity by 'turning away from the perceived dangers of pluralism' (Gilroy 2004: 97), or the changes engendered by the games current era of capitalism to a time in which the culture was considered to be 'of the people.' The fear of the Nazi, like the fear evoked by new consumer fans, has led to an idealisation of the past, critique of the present and fear of the future.

It is my argument that ignoring the identity of modern consumer fans is not so much a protest against the modernisation of the sport and a rejection of its modern era of capitalism as it is a denial of the collective identity and centrality of consumer fans within football culture, bought about by the fear and sense of threat they pose to the identity of the traditional working-class fan. As I will explore in this chapter, football is not, and never has been, a culture associated with a single demographic or a sport free from capitalist interest. It is for this reason that I argue that it is possible to analyse the animosity directed towards modern consumer fans in relation to the wider social theme of melancholia, however up until its modern era it is notable that accounts of football culture have always made attempts to understand the motivations of fans and place them within wider social contexts. Previous studies analysing the game's fan culture have been celebrated for making vital contributions to the understanding of wider social change, with the broad range of literature surrounding hooligan culture in the late 1980s to mid-1990s frequently discussed as a symptom of the social discontent of the working-classes in Thatcherite Britain (Ward 1990; Armstrong & Harris 1991; Redhead 1991; Buford 1992; Giulianotti, Bonney & Hepworth 1994; Pearson 1999; Stott & Pearson 2007).

Developing a better understanding of contemporary football fandom will further improve our understanding of collective identity formation and fandom under modern capitalism, about how consumers exercise autonomy and experience constraint. To develop a more nuanced understanding of contemporary football culture and, as suggested, to contribute to consumer-oriented cultural studies that look to understand the agency and motivations of consumer, I argue that it is vital to analyse how consumer fans understand the way in which they are positioned within football culture, how they articulate and understand their fandom and how they negotiate the ways in which they are narrowly represented. As Sandvoss (2005) argues, in endeavouring to explore the ways in which fans assimilate products of capitalism to the particulars of their lives, cultural studies celebrate exceptional readings of texts to develop a greater understanding of the texts themselves. With this being said, this chapter documents the different stages of English football's capitalism, outlining its origin as a ritualistic leisure pursuit before its formal professionalisation, charting the formation of the bureaucratic system that defined football culture for nearly a century before the ideological shift that ushered in the game's modern capitalism.

'Futeball,' feudalism and the factory floor

For hundreds of years a barbarous form of 'futeball' flourished in feudal and pre-industrial villages, unregulated until its rules were officially codified in the latter half of the nineteenth century. Before this period of regulation, football resembled a primitive version of rugby; handling the ball was sanctioned, with the objective to ground it within the opposing goal area. Unlike contemporary football, participation was unlimited with historical accounts stipulating that whole villages would congregate to compete against each other in unsanctioned chaos (see Rafferty 1973; Holt 1989). Raffety (1973: 2) documents a vivid description of an early contest:

> The men at the parish assembled at the cross, the married on the one side and the bachelors on the other. When the ball was thrown up the game carried on from two o'clock until sunset. The game was this: he who at any time got the ball into his hands ran with it until overtaken by the opposite party and then, if he could shake himself loose from those on the opposite side who seized him, ran on, if not, he threw the ball from him, unless it was wrestled from him by the other party. The object of the married men was to hang it or put it three times into a small hole on the moor, which was the drool, or limit, on the one hand; that of the bachelors was to drown it or dip in three times in a deep place in the river, the limit on the other. The party who could affect either of these objects won the game.

Despite its 'warlike potential'[1] (Taylor 2007: 58), played strictly by 'the men' of the parish, 'futeball' was more than a simple leisure pursuit. As Raffety (1973: 2) insinuates, it was a ritualistic means through which collective identity and status were expressed within the community. Indeed Murray (1998: 2) indicates that contests were often celebrated as part of fertility rights or to punctuate the changing of the season. As suggested, Imlach (2005) associates football's 'authenticity' with its representation of local community and 'futeball' explicitly revolved around familial, geographical and community representation corresponding to the discursive images of 'traditional' football culture. Murray (1998: 2) argues that 'futeball' was also a pursuit through which class identities were established. Essentially 'futeball' was a popular game, the name referring to any ball game that was played on foot rather than horseback. Due to its simplistic, physical nature, 'futeball' was looked down upon by those who could afford more salubrious pursuits, a notion that feeds into the discursive association of traditional football culture with the working-classes. However, as Murray (1998: 3) indicates, it was not exclusively a game of the people and included among its aficionados countless clergymen, local dignitaries and individuals such as Oliver Cromwell, Walter Scott and Mary Queen of Scots. As suggested, both academic texts documenting the historical changes within football culture and those written by self-identified traditional fans describe traditional football culture as male and working-class (see Bale 1998; Brimson 1998; King 2002; Conn 2005; Barr 2009 Pearson 2012). Mary Queen of Scots' fandom problematises this gendered essentialism, while the literature similarly ignores the early endorsement of the sport by the middle- and upper-classes, particularly trivialising their role in regulating the sport and disseminating it in its regulated form to the working-classes.

As Britain changed from an agrarian to an industrial society around 1750, the change to football culture was profound. 'The people's game' played in the open fields of the countryside were adapted to suit the narrow streets and the unforgiving concrete of urban society. Leisure time once determined by sun, season and feudal obligation was replaced by restrictions decreed by the artificial lights of the factories and the demands of their owners. From being a communal ritual, football was transformed into a 'recreation indicative of industrial society,' disciplined and controlled (Murray 1998: 2). This early example of the influence of the middle-classes within football culture seems microcosmic of the changes that multi-millionaire entrepreneurs have facilitated in the game's modern era, yet this stage of football's foundational history, its early capitalism, is treated as a separate entity. This seems indicative of the wider attitude to contemporary football culture, particularly with texts written by self-identified traditional fans, keen to promote the simple opposition between the 'bad' artifice of the modern era and the 'good' tradition of the past, ignoring the links established by historical texts that contextualise the changes within football culture to the changes happening within wider society.

Football's embourgeoisement was indicative of the wider status of sport in industrial society. Improvements to roads and public transportation enabled contests to be played outside the locality of the village. Expanding transport networks provided the middle-classes with a greater sense of mobility, encouraging them to compete at national levels. These developments encouraged them to formalise rules and establish national standards. National rules were established initially for the bourgeoisie pursuits; horse racing in the middle of the eighteenth century, and golf and cricket soon followed, 1754 and 1788 respectively. It was in the mid-nineteenth century that the trend accelerated to wider leisure pursuits: mountaineering in 1857, track and field in 1866 and football in 1863, marking the inception of association football.

While popularised by feudal workers, the 'old boys' of the public school system facilitated football's codification. Before its standardisation, each public school contested the game with individual rules. The boys from Rugby School, with its expansive field, encouraged hard tackling and running with the ball, at Winchester where the field was narrow, dribbling was encouraged and there was no goal (Murray 1998: 3). With modernisations to transport networks and a growing culture of competition, it became necessary to establish common rules to enable interschool competition. The first serious attempt to create a national standard was enacted at Cambridge University. These rules provided the basis of the laws of association football that were formalised officially in 1863.

The 'old boys' of the public school gave the world the rules of association football but, importantly, they also fostered the spirit in which they intended it to be played. While football continued to operate on an amateurish level, like football's modern capitalism, I argue that association football operated with an ideological imperative. It is evident that the 'old boys' recognised the canonical power of football and were keen to exploit their power as facilitators to maintain their social privilege and bestow certain values upon the engaged masses. This notion is epitomised by an article published by *In the Field* (1964), cited by Murray (1998: 5):

> In the ethics of education, books and book learning are now universally admitted to be far from everything. Writers of the day, who have brought great wisdom to bear upon the subject, have even gone so far as to declare these to be only subordinate items of the great system by which the youth of a nation is so trained that when the time arrives it is prepared to command a division, lead a cavalry charge, bear the brunt of battle, the hardship of the field, or accept the responsibilities of developing upon the men whose hands is entrusted the government of the nation. The education of the playground, and the lessons learned from schoolfellows and college friends are, apart from the physical advantages gained in the former, of the highest practical value.

This highly loaded political statement is antithetical to the 'sport for sports sake' ideal associated with traditional football culture. The article reads as a class statement setting the rules and agenda by which the nation's self-appointed leaders would rule the association entrusted to their care. Sport was not just a leisure pursuit but also a mechanism for building character and discipline. In the latter part of the nineteenth century association football was disseminated among the working-classes in correlation with the Victorian ethic of self-help; it was particularly encouraged by industrial bosses, keen to promote healthy pursuits to the workers, engendering teamwork and camaraderie, providing them with an escape from the drudgery of routinised labour. As Devine (2012: 361) suggests:

> To the worker with magic in his feet, football offered a way out of the industrial system; to him for whom the magic was in the mind it offered a few hours of escapist release.

The notion that football provides an 'escape' from the 'real world' has permeated the sport's history and Rafferty (1973: 82) notes how the government promoted the value of football as a distraction from the perils of WWII. Similarly, the promotion of football helped to diffuse political anxiety in British society brought on by mounting threats to the country's industrial supremacy from Russia and the USA. In both the latter societies sport had generated widespread competition. In Russia gymnastics had become a vehicle for militant nationalism, while in the USA sport expressed the social Darwinist philosophy of American capitalism (Wagg 1984: 4). Industrial entrepreneurs exploited this premise and worker teams abounded by the 1880s, teams composed of employees from particular firms financed by paternalistic employers.[2]

While developing the culture of English football, it is vital to acknowledge that like the public school alumni, the entrepreneurs who sponsored football among their employees displayed a shrewd appreciation of their own self-interest. John Holding, the founder of Liverpool (1892), owned several pubs in the area and used the football club to promote his businesses and attract regular working clientele, while Samuel Hill-Wood, chairman of Arsenal (1929–1949) used his profile and position with the community to engender support for his political aspirations (Wagg 1984: 5).

The 'old boys' and industrialists did not dramatically financially re-structure football like the entrepreneurs of the modern era and the game still operated with an 'amateurish' sensibility, yet I argue that football was colonised by the middle-class establishment, operating with a capitalist imperative long before its modern era. The changes within the culture reflect the wider societal shifts from agrarian to industrial society, the improvements to national transport links, the wider embourgeoisement of sport and the initial realisation the game had value beyond simple competition. What once had been a chaotic free-for-all was by the 1870s studiously authenticated by a vigilant bourgeoisie. The football association founded in 1863 by a group of former public school boys was intended above all to provide the national ritual with a rule book and, significantly, a moral attitude, explicitly structuring the culture and agenda of English football. The way in which workers were encouraged to participate in the sport by industrial entrepreneurs is an early illustration of the way in which football culture has developed through different stages of capitalism.

The magic of the cup?

Until the FA Cup was established in 1871, teams engaged in 'friendlies' or 'ordinaries,' sporadically organised by club owners presumably when it became necessary to boost their public profile, or inspire or reward their work force. Significantly, these 'friendlies' attracted sizable crowds. It is often overlooked, but such contests were highly profitable. Ross (2005) cites the first officially recognised international match between England and Scotland to emphasise the idea that there was a sizable audience willing to pay to watch live football. Queen's Park answered a challenge from Charles Alcock, the secretary of the English FA, to represent Scotland in an event to celebrate St Andrew's Day. The West of Scotland Cricket Ground was selected to stage the contest explicitly for its ability to regulate and charge for attendance. Ross (2005: 15) suggests that fans reacted angrily to this and many 'hung from trees and climbed railings to gain a suitable vantage point,' yet the match was still played in front of a crowd of 4,000 paying spectators.

While friendly matches were popular, Crampsey (1990: 3) describes them as 'haphazard arrangements.' The sporadic nature of these contests had a dramatic effect on attendances and, significantly, gate receipts. Attendance fees were becoming a significant source of secondary income for the industrialists, but crowds became increasingly frustrated at their inability to stage contests on specified dates. Both academic texts and those written by self-identified traditional fans celebrate the amateurish tradition of football culture (Wagg 1984; Bale 1998; Carrington 1998; Conn 2005; Imlach 2005; Platts & Smith 2010), yet I argue that it was the consumer demands of the fans to watch more live matches that fundamentally lead to the process of the game's professionalisation.

The FA Cup was created in an attempt to regulate a set fixture list to alleviate the discontent of football's growing audience and capitalise financially on its popularity. It is poignant that the establishment of the Cup ushered in a further series of rationalisation, further distancing the game from its casual folk culture. Shin pads were introduced in 1874, the cross bar was implemented to the goal structure in 1875 and in 1882 touchlines structured the arena of play. Subsequently much of the literature written retrospectively by traditional fans laments the symbolic damage caused by the Cup to football's amateur legacy. Wagg (1984: 6) rebukes the 'milk and water players' of the era, citing the shin pad as an example of football's loss of 'brutish masculinity,' in which the allure of the prize associated with winning the competition damaged the 'integrity' and 'soul' of the game. These texts critique the formation of the Cup with a nostalgia influenced by the discontent harboured towards modern football culture, yet this discontent does not account for the ways in which fans actively sought these changes. As suggested, crowds were exasperated with the spontaneity of 'ordinaries' and the initial FA Cup contests attracted some of the biggest crowds in English history. In 1901 a crowd of 110,820 *paid* to watch Tottenham and Sheffield United contest the final at Crystal Palace (Murray 1998: 9).

Ross (2005: 15) claims that fans accustomed to unregulated 'ordinaries' resented paying to attend the more structured competition, a point that correlates with the contemporary arguments in which traditional fans claim to be economically excluded from attending live matches. It is my argument that this can be considered as a retrospective reaction to the game's contemporary capitalism, with the changes to the sport once again brought about by wider changes happening within Victorian society, particularly the fan's desire to watch more matches. Murray (1998: 8–9) suggests that in the early 1880s the Cup regularly attracted 50,000 paying spectators. Rather than resenting the financial determinant of regulated competition, he suggests that fans capitalised on the luxury of their shorter working week, the free Saturday afternoon they enjoyed in the late part of the century that effectively gave birth to the British weekend. He argues that football provided the working-man with an opportunity to realise a higher standard of living. It is significant that this argument has been used by Ken Bates (1994 cited by King 2002: 138), former chairman of Oldham, Chelsea and Leeds United, a rare example in which football's capitalist development has been linked to changes within wider society:

> The customer in any business pays for what he gets. I've been converted to all seating. I mean the working-class no longer go to Blackpool for their holidays, they go to Spain or Madeira and Phuket and the Caribbean, they go on cruises. They no longer have Blackpool rock and cloth caps and handkerchiefs on their head and their stockings rolled up while they're packing in to Brighton. And the other thing is that when they go to the pictures, the working-class, they don't go in and stand in the rain with water running down the back of their f***ing neck with their cloth cap and a muffler. They go into a warm place where they can sit down. Somewhere to hang their coats up. They can get a cup of coffee or ice cream or popcorn or whatever and they sit down for two or three hours comfort.

Like Murray (1998), Bates (1994 cited by King 2002) advocates the continued rationalisation and commercialisation of the sport and does not consider the changes to be detrimental to the culture or to the status of the working-class traditional fan. Instead, like Murray (1998), he links the changes that have happened within the game to the profound social and cultural changes that go back to the development of leisure time in the Victorian era and the development of affluence in the 1950s, in which the working-classes had more time and money to expend on leisure pursuits. In this context Bates (1994 cited by King 2002) suggests that rather than disenfranchise the fan, the changes to the culture simply look to address their needs and changing social status, epitomised by the way in which he assimilates the experience of attending matches to visiting the cinema or going on package holidays. Significantly, in his argument the fan is described both in mode of address and in categorisation of need as a 'consumer.'

Bates' (1994 cited by King 2002) argument mirrors the premise of consumer-oriented cultural studies in which it is taken for granted that we fulfil our need by engaging with products of capitalism (see Fiske 1986; 1992; Barker 2004; Sandvoss 2005; Lash 2007). Conversely the texts surrounding modern football culture broadly refute this assimilation, ignoring the early phases of the game's capitalism to create a binary between an idealised concept of the game's traditional folk culture and its modern era of capitalism, in which traditional football culture and the traditional fan are discussed as separate entities to modern football culture and consumer fans. Murray's (1998) work challenges this notion in which he astutely recognises 'traditional' fans as consumers, in which the changes to football culture correspond to their changing social status. Indeed Murray (1998) suggests that the fans' ability to pay to attend football matches became symbolic of a better quality of life.

Like 'futeball,' the Cup had a ritualistic and symbolic role in the development and assertion of self-identity. While it is fair to suggest that the changes were beneficial to the industrialists, improving worker morale and productivity, a notion that challenges the idea that football culture could ever be considered as a flat 'folk culture' free from capitalist interest, it is significant that the historical literature looks to outline the way in which changes to the culture correspond to changes within wider society, explicitly looking to understand the ways in which fandom relates to identity formation in Victorian society. While I argue that the changes to the culture described by Murray (1998) illustrate the game's early capitalism, literature analysing contemporary football culture largely fails to link the changes happening within football's modern capitalism to the life and identity of the consumer fan.

Professionalisation: The establishment of football's bureaucracy

The popularity of the FA Cup lead to the organisation of regional supplementary competitions organised to capitalise financially on the improved social status and leisure time afforded to the working-classes. However, the nature of knockout competition dictated that on defeat teams were eliminated, finding themselves dormant for months. Attempting to successfully navigate the early stage of the competition, it emerged that club owners tried to entice gifted players to join their teams with cash incentives. Crampsey (1990: 6) develops this notion:

> Players were being paid in England and many of those who were receiving money were Scotsmen. Their skill and straitened working circumstances made them prime targets for the great northern English clubs and the 'Scottish professors', as they were known, became the sporting equivalent of the seventeenth century mercenary soldier ... the financial incentive of English football exercised the same lure for Scots players as the West End did for English provincial theatre.

Despite being considered as an era of the game unsullied by capitalism, I argue that parallels can again be established with football's modern capitalism, particularly the role of entrepreneurs like Roman Abramovich and Sheikh Mansour who are accused of trying to 'buy success' for their respective teams, Chelsea and Manchester City, with squad investment from their personal fortune. Abramovich is reported to have spent £740 million since his takeover in 2003 (Kelso 2011) and Mansour is claimed to have invested a staggering £800 million since 2010 (Conn 2011). Evidently this level of investment is significantly greater than that of the nineteenth century industrialists, emphasising the need to recognise modern football as an industry of late capitalism, yet the ambition of the industrialists still combats the folk ideals of 'sport for sports sake,' again illustrating football's early capitalism.

Indeed, the different levels of involvement shown by the nineteenth century industrialists and modern football's entrepreneurs are indicative of different phases of capitalism as identified by Mandel (1975). Mandel (1975) describes early capitalism as 'monopoly capitalism,' a period characterised by the development of national markets and intra-society competition, while late capitalism has as its dominant features globalised markets and the rise of multinational corporations. Rather than viewing modern football culture as 'football's era of capitalism,' it is important to recognise that football, like society, has developed through different phases of capitalism.

In 1885, following complaints about competitors receiving cash performance-based rewards, a committee was established to punish proven transgression. After stringent investigation the FA legalised professionalism under a myriad of constraints, in correlation with the assumption that football should be more than mere business (see Taylor 2007). The FA demanded that attendance money should be equally distributed throughout the association, preventing the demise of teams who were unable to attract high attendances, the better players or challenge for competitive prizes. They introduced a maximum wage to prevent the rich teams monopolising the talent pool and the 'retain and transfer system,' which dictated that once a player had registered with a particular team he could not leave without explicit permission. This prevented gifted players leaving smaller teams in search of greater success (Taylor 2007).

Once again, these cultural developments precipitated significant alterations to the culture of the sport, particularly the identification of the fans and their experiences of fandom. The rules imposed upon professionalism served to create a strong sense of community. The equitable sharing of gate receipts served to limit the financial inequality between teams and the maximum wage regulation endeavoured to foster a relatively competitive playing environment. In conjunction with the 'retain and transfer system,' the maximum wage operated to restrict player flow. As wages were relatively commensurate across the country, players had little incentive to relocate for financial betterment. In comparison with the modern game, teams tended to be comprised of players from their locality, while the league overwhelmingly consisted of British players (see Taylor 2007). This contrasts significantly to the modern Premier League; Austin and Slater (2008) suggest that teams currently have an average of thirteen foreign players in their first team squad, whereas two decades ago there were only twelve players from outside the Commonwealth operating within the entire league. Again, I argue that this corresponds to the game's development through different phases of capitalism with English football embracing global capitalism and expanding into international markets (see Mandel 1975).

The regulation of the era is described explicitly in relation to fan identity, in which clubs fortified notions of national and local pride, widely understood by their supporters as representations of the local community (Crampsey 1990;

Devine 2012). The maximum wage and the 'retain and transfer system' not only meant that players were likely to sign for their local club, but that they were likely to represent them for the majority of their career. A sense of rationalised time underpinned the identification between fans and club, a premise that is incongruent with the modern game. In *The Culture of the New Capitalism*, Richard Sennett (2006) argues that the rise in bureaucratic institutions during the second half of the nineteenth century had a fundamental effect on the way that individuals began to conceptualise their lives. He argues that the average person, endowed with neither exceptional talent nor excessive ambition, makes sense of their life by believing that the accumulation of experience in their job not only makes them better at their specific task, engendering a sense of self pride and 'usefulness,' but also adds value to their worth as an individual within society, demanding the respect of others. This sense of security provided by bureaucracy in opposition to the volatility of modern capitalism enabled individuals to imagine their lives as a narrative, encouraging workers to plan their lives on a long-term basis. With football clubs prevented from transfer activity, Taylor (2007) describes how it was mandatory that they deployed business strategies that were long in duration. A successful club depended on investing time and effort into innovative training methods, nurturing talent over a number of seasons to gradually foster improvements on the pitch. It is argued that this process enabled rapport to develop based around a long-lasting sense of familiarity between the club, player and fan (Crampsey 1990; Devine 2012).

Taking this into account it could be argued that the bureaucratic system helped to foster community and, as Devine (2012: 362) stipulates, part of football's appeal lay in the fact that teams by their very nature reflected the individual character of their locality. Football again was more than ethereal entertainment or a leisure pursuit; it elicited great emotional investment, enthusiasm and local pride from fans based around the reciprocal assurance of their club that the long-term future of their team was assured. This sense of fandom corresponds to Imlach's (2005) concept of traditional fan identification, engendered by a sense of shared geography and imagined community. However, while it could be suggested that the bureaucratic period fostered specific conditions for fandom (see Crampsey 1990; Devine 2012), the historical literature particularly still acknowledges the active role of the fan within the culture. Indeed Hutchinson (1997: 39) suggests that while the wider culture of football was defined by bureaucratic regulation, the fan experiences of the late nineteenth century were idiosyncratic and developed organically. Using a case study of Newcastle United, he (Hutchinson 1997: 39) suggests that fans autonomously started to evaluate their relationship with their club to develop their own unique fan identities:

> During the late 1890s the Newcastle crowd had turned … into fans. It was a transformation that was taking place all over Britain and would become the foundation and the lifeblood of professional soccer throughout the next century. While once the paying customer plainly preferred just to stand and

> watch two sides play football of a certain quality ... Suddenly he was supporting a cause. The customers began to recognise and enjoy their own power to affect a match and create atmosphere. They had begun to use their voice.

Hutchinson (1997) acknowledges the way fans established their sense of identity not through their affinity to their team, but through active fandom. In a period of cultural stability football was still defined by different fan experiences and different fan identities unique to each club. It is my argument that parallels can be established with the game's modern capitalism. Like contemporary football culture, the period was still defined by strict regulation and the norms of early capitalism, engendering a specific form of identification between the fan and their team. Despite this highly structured, albeit different, form of regulation to contemporary football culture, Hutchinson (1997) identifies the ability of the fan to enact individual fan identities, unique to different communities.

The fall of football's bureaucracy

With the popular perception of the 1950s as a period of stability and contentment, much of the historical literature describes the decade as the utopian spell of football culture (see Murray 1998; Ross 2005), as Imlach (2005: 152) suggests:

> The 50s have been filled in the collective memory as football's heyday: black and white photos of Lowry paintings, with gapless terraces of endlessly repeating hatted heads with the occasional locked-out stick figure climbing over the fence.

The idea that the 1950s represented the final period in which 'ordinary working-class men' watched 'ordinary working-class men' challenge each other in the spirit of fair play and amateurism has gained much academic saliency (see Murray 1998; Ross 2005; Imlach 2005). As suggested, the strict legislation imposed by the FA upon the game's professionalisation is said to have encouraged passionate fan identification based on shared geography and imagined community. It is the abolition of these rules that are said to have dramatically altered the relationship between football and the 'traditional fan.' While the 1950s is said to represent a utopian football culture, the 1960s can be considered as the juncture in which the stability of the bureaucratic system and football culture started to evolve, with the foundations being set for its era of modern capitalism facilitated by the abolition of the maximum wage and the 'retain and transfer system.' It is significant that the historical literature emphasises the wider cultural context of the era, particularly the rise of leisure industries and global communication systems, to explain the changes in fandom, with hooliganism significantly considered in relation to wider social contexts.

In 1901 the wage cap for footballers was set at £4 a week, 'twice the average pay of a works foreman and four times that of a farm labourer' (Ewen 2010: 87).

Despite opposition from the Professional Footballers' Association and Trainers' Union, this had risen to only £10 by 1940. In 1958, the year of the World Cup, the PFA negotiated a rise to £20 but this was only marginally more than the national average wage (Ewen 2010: 87). Players were enticed by lucrative moves abroad but the 'retain and transfer system' prevented them from realising their ambition. In 1952 the English striker Tom Finney was denied the opportunity to sign for Palermo in Italy, which would have garnered him a £10,000 signing-on fee. The historical literature insinuates that this was beneficial for the 'character' of the game (see Ross 2005; Ewen 2010), yet with developments in global communication indicative of modern capitalism, players themselves were becoming increasingly aware of their limited opportunities and voiced frustration at the system.

In 1960 George Eastham challenged the 'retain and transfer system' when his club, Newcastle United, denied him the opportunity to move at the end of his contract. Despite multiple transfer requests, Newcastle to all intents and purposes owned Eastham (Murray 1998: 13). After a hiatus from the game, he appealed unsuccessfully to the Football League Management Committee; finally, his move was sanctioned but he remained aggrieved, taking his complaint to the High Court, an act of defiance that lead to the dissolution of the system. The Court found the law to be an unreasonable restraint on trade, advising that if a club did not wish to retain the services of a player at the end of his contract then he should be permitted to leave without a transfer fee.

As previously outlined, the 'retain and transfer system' is cited as a mechanism through which fans developed their identity and experienced a sense of communal representation via a 'reciprocal relationship' with their club (Crampsey 1990; Hutchinson 1997; Taylor 2007; Devine 2012). Certainly, with the communal emphasis of the bureaucratic period, attendance at live matches peaked, particularly after the Second World War. As Ross (2005: 65) illustrates:

> 1948–1949 was the highest watermark for football attendances in Britain. Documented evidence from the football league showed a total attendance in England of over 41 million.

The abolition of the 'retain and transfer system' and the eradication of the maximum wage cap in 1961 had a detrimental effect on attendance figures. This dramatically affected the financial stability of the game as Hutchinson (1997: 184) illustrates with Newcastle United:

> For years Newcastle had money to spend; there was no doubt about it … in the summer of 1960, Newcastle invested £6,000 in a big ultra-modern medical room, which was built on top of a swimming pool … But by 1962 the club had debts tolling £100,000; the average gate had dropped below 30,000.

Newcastle's relegation the previous season undoubtedly influenced their ability to attract fans, but declining attendances was a staple of 1950s/1960s football culture. The historical literature suggests that the dissolution of football's bureaucracy and its strong communal emphasis had detrimental effects on fan identity (Hutchinson 1997; Devine 2012), but Ross (2005: 75) similarly cites the social transition from a period of early to modern capitalism characterised by a growing leisure industry and new consumer choice as a major influence on the changing relationship between fans and the game. Ross (2005: 75) particularly emphasises the allure of television.[3] The premise that television has altered the relationship between football and fans is a common theme in both academic and popular texts with the idea that watching football in the home domesticates and 'feminises' football fandom, converting the fan into a passive, docile viewer (see Bale 1998; Brimson 1998; Weed 2008). I argue in accordance with Ross (2005) that television provides the fan with a greater extent of choice and experience, but in the 1960s it is fair to suggest that its novelty significantly affected attendance figures at live matches.

In the years after the Eastham case football suffered a palpable decline. The game slowly deteriorated into a deep malaise as wages and transfer fees spiralled out of control and attendances declined dramatically. Football became engulfed in a destructive oscillating cycle; clubs were left with little money to restore dilapidated stadia from the early nineteenth century, which further deterred fans from attending matches. Symanski and Zimbalist (2006: 6) developed this idea:

> The gradual decay of stadiums in England ... discouraged supporters and between 1950 and 1985 total attendance fell by more than half (41 million per season to 18 million) ... The audience for soccer became concentrated among young men on low income who were increasingly involved in violent confrontations with fans from rival teams.

As suggested, there is a vast body of literature focusing on football hooliganism (see Ward 1990; Armstrong & Harris 1991; Redhead 1991; Buford 1992; Giulianotti, Bonney & Hepworth 1994; Pearson 1999; Stott & Pearson 2007). While the literature largely deplores the violence of the era, much of the literature astutely recognises the complex mismanagement of the game by football's hierarchy engendering a specific fan experience in which they argue that fan identity was enacted by the way of a violent self-fulfilling prophecy. One of the most perceptive commentators on the issue is Stuart Hall (1978). Hall (cited by Ingham et al. 1978: 15–36) criticises the reactionary tendency of the British media to label the perpetrators as 'savages' in a 'verbal reduction of hooligans to the level of animals.' He suggests that branding fans as 'irrational' acted as a form of 'ritual degradation' to eschew the complex cultural problems and wider social issues that lay behind their action.

Andrew Hussey (2005) develops this proposition:

> It is easy to forget what a violent and unstable place Britain was in the early 1980s and how poor the conditions were for football fans during this period.

> Since the early 1970s English fans had been wreaking havoc in Europe and at home on each other. Their behaviour was received with platitudes and inertia from the media and the government. Those who ran the game, those who could do something about the bad grounds, the lousy security, the climate of hate and racism, invariably looked away. Everybody who attended a match during this period knew that something was deeply wrong.

Hussey's (2005) quotation is taken from an article outlining the Heysel disaster of 1985, involving Liverpool and Juventus fans. Hussey (2005) documents how both sets of supporters were separated by a matter of yards and flimsy chicken wire that was subsequently ripped down and turned into missiles. Terrified bystanders desperately stampeded, trying to escape the escalating conflict, but were enclosed by perimeter walls, one of which collapsed, killing 39 innocent spectators on the other side and maiming 600 more.

Hussey (2005), a Liverpool fan, like millions around Europe, watched the chaos unfold on television. He happened to be in a Parisian bar:

> As the match finished a window in the café was smashed. We walked out of the bar to face a small mob of locals. We tore into the pack. We weren't psychopaths or even normally football hooligans. But we fought as hard as we could. Even 20 years on, I find it difficult to explain this. How could anyone justify violence in the immediate wake of a televised massacre? The simple reason is that we refused to be ashamed of who we were. Many of those in Heysel that night have told me they felt the same emotion. Guilt was inextricably linked to defiance, which in turn created more violence.

To punctuate this idea Hussey (2005) cites Baudrillard's (1993) work on the Heysel disaster, published in *The Transparency of Evil*. Baudrillard (1993: 75–80) describes Heysel as a primitive but devastatingly effective form of 'interactive television,' attributing blame to Thatcher's conflict with coal miners, a battle he describes as 'state terrorism.' Baudrillard (1993: 75–77) suggests that Thatcher's actions were certain to lead to violence at public 'pseudo-events,' and therefore Heysel did not happen by chance, it was the result of disenfranchised individuals turning themselves into actors. He states that the nature of violence itself, crude, tribal and pointless, was a cultural reflex conditioned by society.

Hutchinson's (1997: 39) work echoes Baudrillard's (1993) argument that fans enacted their identity in relation to the cultural conditions of the period. In the bureaucratic era, Hutchinson (1997) argues that fans were vocal and passionate in accordance with the feeling of security they received from the game's communal emphasis. The Heysel disaster seems to punctuate the inverse of this with fans rampaging against the dissolution of the stability they previously enjoyed both within football culture and wider society. Their actions were destructive and deplorable but arguably enacted with the same intention of exerting their individual fan identity, displaying their affiliation to the game through affirmative action in response to their sense of betrayal from football's ruling bodies and government officials (see Baudrillard 1993; Hussey 2005). While hooliganism defined football culture until the late 1980s the literature still insinuates that the acts of violence perpetuated by the fans can be considered as unique rituals of identity formation.

Like contemporary football culture, the game's era of hooliganism is largely criticised and deplored by the existing literature but rather than looking to outlaw the hooligan, as is the case with modern consumer fans, it is significant that academic studies of hooliganism largely look to understand their actions, explicitly linking their behaviour to the wider social context and significantly framing the hooligan as active agents within football culture. As Baudrillard (1993: 75–77) suggests, hooliganism was seen as the result of disenfranchised individuals *turning themselves into actors*, the nature of violence a cultural reflex conditioned by society. I argue that this notion has two-fold significance.

First, I argue that parallels can be established between hooligans and traditional fans. As Baudrillard (1993) and Hussey (2005) suggest, hooligans felt a need to re-establish themselves as agents within football culture in response to their sense of betrayal by football's leading bodies and their inability to control the changes affecting them in wider society. Similarly, I argue that the contemporary discourses perpetuated by self-identified traditional fans operate with a similar agenda, with the fans making active attempts to emphasise their legitimate stake within the culture in response to the game's increasing assimilation with modern capitalism and its campaign to attract consumers. This is something, again, traditional fans have no sense of control over.

Second, it is of note that Baudrillard (1993: 75) describes hooligans as 'disenfranchised individuals.' I argue that this emphasises the scholarly tradition surrounding football culture, with the concept of the 'disenfranchised individual' discursively evoking the image of a specific 'type' of fan, the white working-class man, with contemporary studies (see Brown 1998; Williams 2000; King 2002; Pearson 2012) continuing to draw on the discourse surrounding 'traditional football culture' but also the discourse associated with the crisis of identity suffered by working-class men in modern capitalist society (see Hayward & Yar 2006; McDowell 2011; Syal 2013). I recognise that these studies make significant contributions to football culture yet the emphasis on a highly specific type of fandom indicates that the 'disenfranchised fan' can now be seen as the modern consumer.

By the mid-1980s football was nearing a crescendo of violence. Barnes (2007 cited by Mortimer 2012: 49) punctuates this by outlining a trio of disasters:

> The first was at Bradford city's Valley parade in May 1985, when 56 people were killed after a dropped fag-end set alight to 20 years of accumulated rubbish beneath a football stand. Eighteen days later 39 Juventus supporters were killed at Heysel ... Then in April 1989, 96 people were killed at Hillsborough ... The sport itself was despised and the people that followed it were considered canaille ... Football Stank. You couldn't give it away with

> a packet of Rice Krispies. The game was something to do with the dregs of society.

Beset with financial and cultural issues, football in England was on its knees. The trio of disasters and the plague of violence that consumed the game symbolised the end of football's bureaucratic era, ushering in the removal of the terraces, the cultural shift widely considered to represent the onset of football's modern capitalism. Once again this engendered a new set of social and cultural relations to the game, precipitating alterations to the identification of the fans and their expectations for fandom.

Harvey (2014: 9) argues that crises are essential to the reproduction of capitalism, as it is in crisis that the shortcomings of capitalism are addressed and confronted:

> Much gets torn down and laid waste to make way for the new. Once productive landscapes are turned into industrial wastelands. Old factories get torn down or converted and working-class neighbourhoods get gentrified.

The crisis of the late 1980s brought about the reorientation of football culture, with the game's ruling bodies finally confronting the issues that lead to the game's near collapse. It was clear that the game's early capitalist model was incongruent with the modern capitalism of wider society and the removal of the terraces can be seen to symbolise an attempt to bring football in line with more established leisure industries. The terraces, like the factories Harvey (2014) describes, were 'torn down,' traditional stadiums were 'converted' and football became 'gentrified.'

Modern football culture

From the early 1960s to the late 1980s football was considered 'damaged goods' (Baudrillard 1993; Hussey 2005; Barnes 2007) and many club chairmen became disillusioned with the game's deteriorating public image. This enabled a new generation of club owners such as Ken Bates (Oldham 1962–1968), David Dein (Arsenal 1983–2007) and Irving Scholar (Tottenham 1982–1991) to take over. These men were heavily inspired by the free-market philosophy of modern capitalism shaping western society and sought to radicalise football by encouraging investment and professional management. To recall the previously cited quote from Ken Bates (1994 cited by King 2002), these chairmen strived to change the perception of football, a measure to combat the tragic self-fulfilling prophecy that was enacted in its post war years and importantly to cater to the changing needs of the working-classes accustomed to the provisions of the expanding leisure industry. In doing so football culture started to attract new demographics: women, families and the middle-classes. Modern consumer fans.

Scholar was the first to initiate Bates' strategy, taking tentative steps to change the perception of football in the early 1980s, actively embracing commercialisation, rationalisation and professionalisation, characteristics that Mandel (1975) associates with modern capitalism. As soon as he became chairman of Tottenham in 1982, Scholar made the club property of a holding company and floated it on the stock exchange, generating £3.2 million in revenue. Using this capital, Scholar employed Alex Flynn of Saatchi & Saatchi to launch a multimedia advertising campaign to attract new fans to the club, implementing initiatives from more enlightened customer service industries (Horrie 1992: 100).

As teams like Tottenham looked to implement a business model owing to the logic of modern capitalism, the FA seemed to acknowledge both the financial opportunities and ideological changes engendered by this approach. With the backdrop of Tottenham's commercial success, the Football League agreed a deal worth £2.6 million with the BBC in 1983, to screen ten live games out of a season of 462 (King 2002: 59). The broadcasting of football marked a colossal evolution in the game's market worth and social status, something that has intensified to the present day. The sale of the 2012 television rights epitomises this idea, sold to Sky for £3.1 billion, giving them the privilege of televising 116 matches a season until 2016 (Sport on the Box 2012).

Despite the financial contribution television has made to modern football culture the literature debases the fan experience of watching football on television, juxtaposing the alleged passive experiences of 'arm chair fandom' to the kineticism associated with traditional terrace culture (see Bale 1998; Brimson 1998; Weed 2008). Hopcraft (2006: 188) describes the terraces as a 'privileged place of working-class communion.' When he describes the experience of being 'trapped for a couple of hours in a swaying crush of bodies, frequently forced off his feet in a delirious surge of mass movement, coming away with bruises and stains' he is not debasing it but rhapsodising a physical, emotional, quasi-religious experience that he suggests has been denied to fans in a post-Hillsborough football culture.

It is significant that Hopcraft (2006) refers to the Hillsborough disaster. While it brought an end to the dangers and violence of the 1980s it also symbolises the loss of the physical and emotional camaraderie nostalgically evoked by images of the terraces in contrast to the perceived sterility of new all-seater stadia, irrevocably associated with consumer fans and modern capitalism. The experience of the modern stadium is again described as passive consumption akin to 'sitting back' in an armchair and 'watching' rather than 'engaging' with the live spectacle (Bale 1998; Brimson 1998; King 2002; Hopcraft 2006). Wilson (2006) develops this premise:

> The past three World Cups have been increasingly supporter-friendly events and it has been noticeable that fans are becoming ever more sociable ... Now you see many more wives, girlfriends and families with children. The World Cup is being watched by different people as opposed to past tournaments, so much so that the atmosphere at games, while always noisy and vibrant, has often lack the hard edge and physicality that big international crunch games ought to have.

While Wilson (2006) acknowledges the diverse demographic attracted to modern football, the reference to 'wives, girlfriends and families with children' emphasises the loss of the 'traditional' experience associated with terrace culture, its kinetic involvement and 'physicality.' This sense of loss operates to preserve the assumption that football's traditional and 'authentic' fan is the working-class man, who attends matches to bond with others of a similar demographic. Wilson's (2006) work seems indicative of the academic literature in which he proficiently identifies the commercial and economic changes that have happened within football culture and the demographics attracted by these changes while using traditional football culture as his starting point.

Walsh and Giulianotti (2001: 62) epitomise this idea, arguing that modern changes to football have given rise to a complex new set of social and cultural relations surrounding the game in which traditional 'community centred ties are endangered.' The academic literature acknowledges the potential impacts of these processes, discussing the scope for social exclusion resulting from these changes, looking to address how traditional fans have been disenfranchised, marginalised and excluded from active spectatorship as a result of football's modernisation (see Fynn & Guest 1994; Bale 1998; Brimson 1998; Giulianotti 2002; King 2002; Ingle 2005: Barr 2009; Pearson 2012), corresponding to the way in which anti-capitalist scholars argue that modern capitalism produces a backdrop of increasing differentiations of wealth between the working classes and the better off (see Mandel 1975; Jameson 1997; Targ 2006; Harvey 2014). Yet as suggested the narrow focus of much of the empirical work ignores the heterogeneity of modern football culture and the new fan experiences engendered by football's modern capitalism.

Here is where the tension lies; the historical literature acknowledges the nuances of football culture, analysing the diverse fandoms associated with each stage of the game's development and different phase of capitalism, exploring fan identity in a wider social context. However, both academic literature and popular texts written by self-identified traditional fans focus on the specific fan identity and fan experiences of the working-classes and how football's assimilation with modern capitalism has disenfranchised their fandom. As suggested, modern consumer fans are 'othered' and treated with contempt for reflecting the processes that have led to the game's contemporary capitalism without considering the legitimacy or nuances of their fandom. The literature does not look to understand their position within the culture or how they negotiate their explicit positioning as consumers both by football's governing bodies and self-identified traditional fans. As Morley (1994) suggests, those that hold a reified nostalgic image of their fandom as something necessarily stable and unchanging are those who are hostile to newcomers who are seen to be both cause and symptom of change.

The central issue with contemporary football culture is that a specific fan identity and fan experience is used as the standard for critique. I argue that this supports the claims of authenticity made by traditional fans keen to maintain their centrality to the culture. As indicated, the literature focusing on football culture has consistently operated with a broad scope making highly perceptive links between changes within football culture and changes within wider society, situating their arguments within wider social contexts. This book looks to continue this tradition, adopting a consumer-oriented cultural studies approach to contribute to wider debates concerning collective identity formation in modern capitalist society, exploring the tensions between autonomy and constraint, while providing consumer fans with an opportunity to conceptualise their own fan identity.

Notes

1 This has been evoked throughout the game's development, most notably in the context of hooliganism and contemporarily in the evocation of melancholia.
2 West Ham United, Arsenal, Manchester United, Stoke City, Millwall, Coventry City, Sheffield United, Crewe Alexandra, Leyton Orient, Reading and West Bromwich Albion; teams with rich histories all originated this way.
3 Ross (2005) notes the popularity of shows such as *Dixon of Dock Green* and *This Is Your Life*, suggesting that they were increasingly given priority over attending live matches.

Bibliography

Adorno, T (2001) *The Culture Industry: Selected Essays on Mass Culture*. London. Routledge.
Armstrong, G & Harris, R (1991) Football Hooligans: Theory and Evidence. *Sociological Review* 39 (3) 427–458.
Austin, S & Slater, M (2008) *English Player Numbers at New Low*. BBC Sport [Website] Available from: http://news.bbc.co.uk/sport1/hi/football/7417746.stm (Accessed 25 January 2012).
Bale, J (1998) 'Virtual Fandoms: Futurescapes of Football' Cited in Brown, A *Fanatics: Power, Identity and Fandom in Football*. London. Routledge.
Barker, C (2004) *The Sage Dictionary of Cultural Studies*. London. Sage.
Barns, S (2007) 'How Pavarotti Changed the Perception of Football' Cited in Mortimer, G *A History of Football in 100 Objects*. London. Serpents Tail.
Barr, W (2009) *Real Football Real Fans: A Journey to the Heart of Football*. London. Morrow & Co.
Baudrillard, J (1993) *The Transparency of Evil: Essays on Extreme Phenomena*. London. Verso.
Brimson, D (1998) *The Geezers Guide to Football: A Lifetime of Lads and Lager*. London. Mainstream Publishing.
Brown, A (1998) *Fanatics: Power, Identity & Fandom in Football*. London. Routledge.
Buford, B (1992) *Among the Thugs*. London. Mandarin.
Burgess, C (2005) What on Earth has Happened to Football? *The Guardian* [Website] Available from: http://www.theguardian.com/football/2005/feb/09/sport.comment (Accessed 16 November 2012).
Carrington, B (1998) "Football's Coming Home,' but Whose Home? And do we Want it?' Nation, Football and the Politics of Exclusion.' Cited in Brown, A *Fanatics: Power, Identity and Fandom in Football*. London. Routledge.

Cohen, S (2011) *Folk Devils and Moral Panics*. London. Routledge.
Conn, D (2005) *The Beautiful Game? Searching for the Soul of Football*. London. Yellow Jersey Press.
Conn, D (2011) Sheik Mansour's Largesse at Manchester City a Sign of the Times. *The Guardian* [Website] Available from: http://www.theguardian.com/football/blog/2011/nov/18/sheikh-mansour-manchester-city (Accessed 12 January 2012).
Crampsey, R (1990) *First 100 Years: Scottish League Football*. Edinburgh. The Scottish Football League Press.
Devine, TM (2012) *The Scottish Nation: A Modern History*. London. Penguin.
Ewen, N (2010) *The Cultural Psychology of Football in England and Scotland: History, Economics, National Identity and Nostalgia*. [PhD Thesis.] University of East Anglia.
Fiske, J (1986) Television, Polysemy and Popularity. *Critical Studies in Mass Communication* 3 (2) 391–408.
Fiske, J (1992) 'The Cultural Economy of Fandom' Cited in Lewis, L *The Adoring Audience*. London. Routledge.
Fynn, A & Guest, L (1994) *Out of Time: Why Football Isn't Working*. London. Simon & Schuster Press.
Gilroy, P (2004) *After Empire: Melancholia or Convivial Culture?* London. Routledge.
Giulianotti, R, Bonney, N & Hepworth, M (1994) *Football, Violence and Social Identity*. London. Routledge.
Giulianotti, R (2002) Supporters, Fans and Flaneurs: Taxonomy of Spectator Identities in Football. *Journal of Sport and Social Issues* 26 (1) 25–46.
Graham, G (2006) *The End of Capitalism (As we Knew it)*. Minnesota. University of Minnesota Press.
Hall, S (1978) 'The Treatment of Football Hooliganism in the Press.' Cited in Ingham, R *Football Hooliganism: The Wider Context*. London. Inter-Action Imprint.
Harvey, D (2014) *Seventeen Contradictions and the End of Capitalism*. London. Profile Publishing.
Hayward, K & Yar, M (2006) The 'Chav' Phenomenon: Consumption, Media and the Construction of a New Underclass. *Journal for Crime, Media and Culture* 2 (9) 10–28.
Holt, R (1989) *Sport and the British: A Modern History*. Oxford. Clarendon.
Hopcraft, A (2006) *The Football Man: People and Passion in Soccer*. London. Aurum Press.
Horrie, C (1992) *Sick as a Parrot*. London. Virgin.
Hussey, A (2005) How Heysel's Lost Lives Saved a Sport. *The Guardian* [Website] Available from: http://www.theguardian.com/football/2005/apr/03/newsstory.sport14 (Accessed 18 December 2011).
Hutchinson, R (1997) *The Toon: A Complete History of Newcastle United*. Edinburgh. Mainstream Publishing.
Imlach, G (2005) *My Father and Other Working-Class Football Heroes*. London. Yellow Jersey Press.
Ingle, S (2005) Football Fans Are Idiots. *The Guardian* [Website] Available from: http://www.theguardian.com/football/2005/sep/02/sport.blueprintforabetterfootball (Accessed 23 October 2011).
Jameson, F (1997) Culture and Finance Capitalism. *Critical Inquiry* 24 (1) 246–265.
Kelso, P (2011) Chelsea Owner Roman Abramovich Counts the Cost of European Failure. *The Telegraph* [Website] Available from: http://www.telegraph.co.uk/sport/football/teams/chelsea/8436348/Chelsea-owner-Roman-Abramovich-counts-the-cost-of-European-failure-740-million-and-rising.html (Accessed 12 January 2012).

King, A (2002) *The End of the Terraces: The Transformation of English Football in the 1990's*. London. Leicester University Press.
Lash, S (2007) 'Power after Hegemony: Cultural Studies in Mutation?' *Theory, Culture and Society* 24 (3) 55–78.
Mandel, E (1975) *Late Capitalism*. London. Humanities Press.
Marcuse, H (1991) *One Dimensional Man: Studies in the Ideology of Advanced Industrial Society*. London. Routledge.
McDowell, L (2011) *Redundant Masculinities: Employment change and White Working Class Youth*. London. Wiley.
Morley, D (1994) 'Active Audience Theory: Pendulums and Pitfalls' Cited in Levy, MR & Gurevitch, M *Defining Media Studies: Reflections on the Future of the Field*. Oxford. Oxford University Press.
Murray, B (1998) *The World's Game: A History of Soccer*. Urbeana. University of Illinois Press.
Pearson, G (1999) Legitimate Targets? The Civil Liberties of Football Fans. *Journal of Civil Liberties* 4 (1) 28–47.
Pearson, G (2012) *An Ethnography of English Football Fans: Cans, Cops and Carnivals*. Manchester. Manchester University Press.
Platts, C & Smith, A (2010) *'Money, Money, Money?' The Development of Financial Inequalities in English Professional Football. Soccer & Society* 11 (5) 643–658.
Rafferty, J (1973) *One Hundred Years of Scottish Football*. London. Pan.
Redhead, S (1991) *Football with Attitude*. Manchester. Wordsmith.
Redhead, S (2007) Those Absent from the Stadium are Always Right: Accelerated Culture, Sport Media and Theory at the Speed of Light. *Journal of Sport and Social Issues* 31 (3) 226–241.
Ross, D (2005) *The Roar of the Crowd: Following Scottish Football Down the Years*. Edinburgh. Argyll.
Sandvoss, C (2003) *A Game of Two Halves: Football Television and Globalisation*. London. Routledge.
Sandvoss, C (2005) *Fans*. Cambridge. Polity.
Scheil, A (2008) *'Abandon All Hope': Consumerism and Loss of Identity in Bret Eaton Ellis's American Psycho*. Santa Cruz. Grin Publishing.
Sennett, R (2006) *The Culture of the New Capitalism*. London. Yale University Press.
Sport on the Box (2012) *Sky Spot and BT Secure Live Premier League Rights*. Sport on the Box [Website] Available from: http://sport-onthebox.com/2012/06/13/football-sky-sports-and-bt-secure-live-premier-league-rights-from-201314/ (Accessed 14 May 2014).
Stott, C & Pearson, G (2007) *Football 'Hooliganism': Policing and the War on the 'English Disease'*. London. Pennant Books.
Syal, R (2013) British Male Identity Crisis 'Spurring Machismo and Heartlessness'. *The Guardian* [Website] Available from: http://www.theguardian.com/politics/2013/may/14/male-identity-crisis-machismo-abbott (Accessed 11 March 2014).
Symanski, S & Zimbalist, A (2006) *National Past Time: How Americans Play Baseball and the Rest of the World Plays Soccer*. New York. Brookings Institution Press.
Targ, H (2006) Late Capitalism, Neoliberal Globalisation and Militarism. *New political Science* 9 (2) 15–26.
Taylor, M (2007) *The Association Game: A History of British Football*. London. Routledge.
Wagg, S (1984) *The Football World: A Contemporary Social History*. London. Longman.

Walsh, A & Giulianotti, R (2001) This Sporting Mammon: A Normative Critique of the Commodification of Sport. *Journal of the Philosophy of Sport* 28 (1) 53–77.
Ward, C (1990) *Steaming In*. London. Sportspages.
Weed, M (2008) Exploring the Sport Spectator Experience: Virtual Football Spectatorship in the Pub. *Soccer and Society* 9 (2) 189–197.
Williams, J (2000) 'The Changing Face of Football: A Case for National Regulation' Cited in Mitchie, J et al. *Football in the Digital Age: Whose Game is it Anyway?* London. Mainstream Publishing.
Wilson, P (2006) It Was the Best of Cups, It Was the Worst of Cups. *The Guardian* [Website] Available from: http://www.theguardian.com/football/worldcup2006blog/2006/jul/09/itwasthebestofcupsitwas (Accessed 25 June 2013).

Chapter 3

Changing formation

Participatory research is traditionally celebrated for its inclusivity, democratic value and moral imperative. The moral and political dimension of participatory research is reflected in the belief that all participants, regardless of age, gender, level of education and in this context different fan identities, have a right to participate in decisions that claim to generate knowledge about them (Heron 1981; Lather 1986; Singer 1993; Van der Riet 2008). It is my argument that contemporary football culture does not operate to this ideal.

Sandvoss (2005: 42) argues that cultural studies have undergone a cultural shift, no longer focusing on the exclusionary relationship between particular demographics and objectively identifiable textual structures but:

> The subjectively constituted readings and appropriations of texts that reflect the contemporary multi-polar distribution of power in the complex connectivity between class, gender and ethnicity.

In other words, he argues that rather than looking to understand the meaning inscribed within texts by their producers, textual meanings need to be considered in the interaction between the text and diverse readerships. Van der Riet (2008) develops this principle, arguing that the ontological assumptions of a static, constant, predictable culture have become outdated, opposed by cultural pluralists that argue that cultural stability is constantly challenged by social developments. It is in this context that my research adopts a consumer-oriented approach.

While wider cultural studies look to deconstruct and challenge the dominant discourses inscribed within texts, analysing the ways in which their meanings are variously interpreted by diverse audiences, football culture revolves around an essential relationship between the text (football culture) and its archetype (the traditional fan).

While Sandvoss (2005) describes the need to understand the way in which texts are interpreted and imparted in acts of fandom by different classes, genders and ethnicities, these readings are restricted within football culture, with different identities within the culture considered to deviate from the traditional identity of the 'traditional' working-class fan, threatening the aura associated with football's traditional culture. I argue that the active agents within football culture, particularly the self-identified traditional fans, operate to control the boundaries of the culture in a way that speaks to their self-interest, denying consumer fans' subjectivity. Indeed, consumer fans through both their positive and negative positioning as consumers within football culture are denied the opportunity to self-identify as fans, something that is considered a perquisite in fan studies (see Jameson 1991; Fiske 1992; Hills 2002; Barker 2004; Sandvoss 2005).

Rosenberg (1988) argues that social science should operate to understand behaviour by rendering it intelligible. To develop a more nuanced understanding of modern football culture, I argue that it is vital to challenge the aura associated with traditional football culture, giving consumer fans an opportunity to articulate their fan identity and engage in negotiation with the discourses operating on them within the culture. Not only is this a more ethically aware approach to research, but also inclusivity is vital to establish a valid insight into the true complexity of a culture. Appropriating the idea of Thornton (1995), cultures need to be considered as a multi-dimensional social space rather than flat folk cultures, with the role of the 'other' more than merely the bottom rung of a linear social ladder.

Thornton (1995) argues that cultures are not stable but are constantly in flux. In collaboration with Gelder (1997), Thornton (1997) writes extensively about hierarchies within cultures yet the pair recognise that power is enacted multi-directionally between different agents. Within football culture power is predominantly exercised 'over' consumer fans to deny them agency. However, Thornton (1995) suggests that power is constantly exercised 'within' cultures, arguing that those perceived to be at the bottom of the cultural hierarchy prescribe their own meanings to their actions, helping them negotiate the powers operating upon them in a way that demonstrates their agency.

With these factors in mind, ethnography was used to conduct my research. The term 'ethnography' has its provenance in Greek, a fusion of the terms 'ethnos' (tribe) and 'graphia' (writing). Literally translated it means 'writing about people.' The central aim of ethnography is to provide rich holistic insight into the participants' views and actions, as well as the locations they inhabit, through the collection of detailed observation and interviews. Hammersley (1992: 18) develops this idea:

> The task of the ethnographer is to document the culture, the perspectives and practises of people in these settings. The aim is to 'get inside' the way in which each group of people see the world.

Rather than pathologising the object of study, ethnographic research places a strong emphasis on exploring social phenomenon rather than looking to prove a predetermined hypothesis. Ethnographers typically gather participant observations, necessitating direct engagement and immersion into the culture they are studying. In the context of football culture, this can be seen as empowering.

Indeed, the ethnographer's objective of 'getting inside' the culture of study corresponds to my aim of exploring the ways in which power is enacted within the culture by consumer fans. As Fay and Moon (1994: 33) suggest:

> Understanding human action requires identifying the rules and structures under which human actions fall, and the role they occupy in the system of *which they are part* (emphasis added).

Fundamentally ethnography acknowledges the role of the participants within the culture of study. As de Garis (1999) notes, it is a kinetic, active process rather than a passive recording of the researcher's beliefs and predispositions. This is significantly different to the way in which football culture is usually studied with ethnography recognising participants as cultural agents. Immersing myself into modern football culture enabled me to present a more objective depiction of the experiences of modern fandom, providing fans themselves with opportunities to articulate their fandom and discuss their representation within football culture as active agents engineering their own cultural space.

Subsequently I argue that the central tenants of ethnography correspond explicitly with my research aims to assess:

- How consumer fans understand the ways in which agents of the game's capitalism and agents of the game's traditional culture position them within football culture.
- The ways consumer fans enact agency and experience constraint within football culture.
- How consumer fans engage with the hegemonic discourses of 'tradition' and 'capitalism' that define football culture.
- The ways consumer fans conceptualise their own identity within football culture.

It is vital to recognise that ethnography has never been a neutral term, or a neutral tool for collecting data. Scott-Jones and Watt (2010) argue that classical ethnographic studies were largely ideological, serving as tools to justify colonisation, imperial ambition and reinforce long-standing discourses of the 'racial other.' This discourse is explicit in Malinowski's (2014: 7) account of his study *Argonauts of the West Pacific*:

> Proper conditions of ethnographic work ... consist mainly in cutting oneself off from the company of other white men and remaining in as close proximity to the natives as possible.

Despite my intentions to maintain the validity and objectivity of my research by adhering to the participant centrism and morality of modern ethnography, it would be disingenuous to suggest that the method was selected without an agenda. As Thornton (1995) suggests, perceptions of culture depend upon the filters that are placed upon the lens of examination and I am striving to widen the lens and sharpen the filters. I believe that the participant centrism of ethnography will enable me to do this, giving consumer fans a platform to frame their own identity. In doing so it is fitting that my research mirrors the 'proper conditions' (Malinowski 2014: 7) of ethnographic work, in which I look to separate my research from the discourses associated with the culture of the 'white man' (the working-class traditional fan) to analyse the culture of football's new 'native' (the consumer fan).

Sands (2002) argues that conducting successful ethnography requires the selection of the right populations. In the context of my research this refers to the selection of the right fan groups and the right clubs that would allow me to address my research questions and make perceptive generalisations about contemporary football culture.

To achieve this, I conducted a range of pilot studies throughout the 2011/2012 football season, attending live matches at different clubs within each echelon of the football league. I became a 'complete participant' of the football event (see Reed-Danahay 1997; Bryman 2008; Scott-Jones & Watt 2010), arriving at matches at least two hours before kick-off to experience the atmosphere outside the stadium and within the catering areas. When matches were in progress I took my position within the stadium, observing the behaviour of the fans and participating in conversations happening around me both within the stadium and catering areas. King (2002: 151) suggests that talking about football is a natural part of fandom, and it was easy to both join and prompt discussion with fans in close proximity.

My pilot studies enabled me to develop an insight into the culture of each club and the demographic of fans that they attract. Pilots were undertaken at Gillingham (League 2), Northampton Town (League 2), Scunthorpe United (League 1), Milton Keynes Dons (League 1), Bolton (Championship), Peterborough United (Championship), Norwich City (Premier League) and Chelsea (Premier League). I rationalised these choices with the notion that clubs from different levels of the football league would enable me to pick up on relevant discussions concerning collective identity particularly in relation to class, commercialisation, gender and ethnicity. The selection was made to reflect different regions of the country, to account for the north-south divide but also different levels of commercialisation and vested interest by subsidiary consumer industries.

Considering the data from my pilot studies, Milton Keynes Dons, Norwich City and Chelsea were selected as case studies. While I am aware that these selections do not reflect the north-south divide or allow me to validly look at fandom throughout the football league system, I maintain that the clubs suitably reflect the diversity of modern football culture with each club promoting a fan experience that corresponds to different characteristics of the game's modern capitalism.

Norwich City has been selected as 'a family club,' a club that actively looks to attract families and young supporters. In the club's recent history (2006, 2007 and 2010), Norwich City has been awarded prizes from the Football League for their creative 'Community and Family' initiatives. In 2008 the club won the title of 'Best Family Club in English Football,' while the fans were deemed the 'Best Behaved' in the Premier League for the 2011/2012 and 2012/2013 seasons. The appeal of the game to families is considered to reflect the civilisation process of the sport with 'family culture,' antithetical to the game's tradition of machismo associated with working-class fans.

Milton Keynes Dons was selected to represent a 'community building' approach to football fandom. The MK Dons are considered to represent the first example of a 'franchise football club,' starting life as Wimbledon before being purchased and relocated by venture capitalist Pete Winkelman, re-branding the club to maximise its commercial potential and appeal to the largely un-serviced population of the city. The departure of the club from its locality and its subsequent re-branding is condemned for threatening the 'blood and soil' relationship between fan, football club and local community. The club purposively assimilates itself with wider leisure industries, looking to attract fandom as repeat patronage and consumer loyalty.

Finally, Chelsea have been selected to represent the 'entertainment' approach to football fandom, where attending live matches is promoted as an 'event.' Foreign ownership and investment in English football is now commonplace, but Roman Abramovich's take over in 2003 and the significant cash injection he has put into the club can be considered a watershed moment. The world class players and subsequent success brought to the club in the decade of Abramovich's ownership have attracted enthusiastic 'football tourists,' with the club making active attempts to position themselves as a London monument to appeal to a cosmopolitan fan base.

Sandvoss (2005: 6) offers caution with participatory research using the metaphor of a map:

> A map that colours in only a small section of territory may be accurate as far as these sections are concerned, yet a lesser value in navigating through the territory at large.

My research focuses on a small section of 'the map,' namely the southeast of England. I am conscious that my work is geographically limited and does not account for the north-south divide or indeed represent the hierarchal structure of the football league, with my research omitting the identity of fans of League 2 or the Conference divisions clubs. I am not suggesting that my research has enabled me to navigate football culture in its totality, however I maintain that the selection of my case studies has permitted me to collect a significant amount of rich, in-depth data, enabling me to interrogate my section of the map with strong validity.

While pilot studies were conducted with clubs throughout the football league system, the case studies were selected in spite of their geographical limitation due to the way in which the culture of each club explicitly represents different characteristics of the game's capitalism. Indeed, my research indicates that the culture of each club is foundational to the way in which the participants negotiate their identity, with their identification with their club producing different expectations for fandom. While I argue that this vindicates their selection for analysis, I do not dispute the fact that further research is required to analyse the true complexity of contemporary football culture and the nuanced identity of consumer fans throughout the football league.

Due to their different marketing strategies and club cultures, my pilot studies indicated that Norwich City attracted a significant number of family groups; MK Dons attracted a sizable number of middle aged, middle-class fans, while Chelsea appealed to a global fan base. Breaking this down into themes for analysis, Norwich City was initially selected to interrogate gender, Milton Keynes was selected to analyse class and Chelsea was selected to analyse ethnicity.

My selections were based on the idea that each case study would enable me to assess different ways that modern fans are positioned as consumers, while similarly contributing to debates concerning gender, class and ethnicity, applying a consumer-oriented cultural studies approach to my research to analyse the ways in which different demographics engage with the culture of their club in the substantiation of their identity. Despite this idea, after an extended period within the field, it became clear that the themes that I identified were not concomitant with the way in which the participants articulated their own identity. While the participants discussed at length their understanding of the game's wider culture, self-identifying as consumer fans, they largely failed to articulate their fandom or sense of identity in relation to my themes of analysis: gender, class and ethnicity.

My research indicated that participants did not engage with the specific attributes of their identity or articulate them in relation to their fandom but instead framed their collective identity as consumers of their club. Appropriating the term from Sands (2002: xxvi), the participants' identity as a fan was articulated as their 'core identity.' Sands (2002) uses the term in his study of college level, American football players, in which he suggests that the 'core identity' of the athletes comes from their shared identification as American football players and the shared behaviours and motivations that inform their identity as athletes. In the context of my research I argue that the shared identification of the participants as 'consumer fans' informs their 'core identity,' with their mutual engagement with the culture of their football club informing their identity to a greater extent than the attributes of identity that I had initially selected.

After this realisation, I abandoned my categorisations and adopted a grounded theory approach concurrent with my desire for the participants to direct the research. With methodological freedom I approached my research with a fresh perspective. Indeed, I argue that this change of focus helped me frame my research in-line with consumer-oriented cultural studies. As suggested, the clubs were selected for analysis for the way in which their culture corresponds to different facets of capitalist football culture. The way that the participants frame their 'core identity' in relation to the culture of their club could be seen to confirm their status as consumers within the culture, however this is not to suggest that they are passive in their consumption or that their consumption was based on a shared sense of need.

My initial research indicated that fans constructed their identity in relation to the unique culture of their club and the way it meets their individual needs as consumers. This prompted me to consider each club as individual 'texts.' As Sandvoss (2005) suggests, cultural studies look to explore the 'exceptional readings' audiences conduct with capitalist texts. Analysing the 'exceptional' and different ways that each fan group negotiates and understands the culture of their club enabled me to develop a more nuanced understanding of contemporary football culture, exploring the different ways in which collective identities are enacted in relation to three distinct case studies.

Operationalising the term ethnography for my research, it was a method in which I:

- Immersed myself into a social setting (the modern stadium) for an extended period of time, attending four live games at each club.
- Made regular observations of the behaviour of members of that setting, both within the stadium and catering/communal areas.
- Developed an understanding of the culture of the group and the individuals' behaviour within the context of each club.
- Complimented my observations with semi-structured interviews (eight for each club), informal chats and auto-ethnographic reflections.

In the stadium, when matches were in progress, I took a covert research position as a matter of practicality as it was virtually impossible to inform everybody in the stadium of my research intentions. My observations focused on the experience of the football event engendered by the culture of each club in conjunction with the participants' understanding and enactment of fandom within the cultural environment. I adopted the role of the 'complete participant' (Reed-Danahay 1997; Bryman 2008; Scott-Jones & Watt 2010) as a member of the crowd, looking to embrace the sensory experience of the stadium. While this enabled me to develop an understanding of the culture of each club, my role as a 'complete participant' similarly helped to reduce the hierarchy between myself and the participants, challenging the dichotomy of the 'objective researcher' and 'subjective researched.' Despite my attempts to identify with the fans, it is important to note that I conducted my research with a level of distanciation, to ensure that I was not distracted by the spectacle or overawed by the atmosphere, to maintain the validity and objectivity of my observations.

While 'the other' is still the central preoccupation of ethnographic research (see Comaroff & Comaroff 1992; Kuper 1999; Scott-Jones & Watt 2010), contemporary ethnographies are mindful of the power dynamic between the researcher and the participants, with researchers careful to ensure that their work is ethically reputable, and bias is accounted for (see Denzin 1997; Klein 1997; Sands 2002; Bolin & Granskog 2003). The use of auto-ethnographic reflection is often part of this (see Ellis 2004), in which the researcher acknowledges their role within the culture of observation. Schrijvers (1991: 169) argues that research cannot be valid if the power differential between the researcher and participants is too large, and my auto-ethnographic reflections are included to further reduce the hierarchy between myself and the participants, yet it would be disingenuous to pretend that I was another fan solely engaging with the sensory spectacle of the match. The inclusion of auto-ethnographic reflection enables me to address this issue, helping me to evaluate my role within the research process. Indeed, I document throughout this book instances when I believe that my status as a researcher may have influenced responses from the participants or prompted them to act in a way that may have been seen as 'what was expected' of them.

My categorisation of each club, Norwich—family club, MK Dons—community club and Chelsea—tourist attraction, prompted my selection of participants to take part in my research. As suggested, my pilot studies indicated that each club operates with a clear business strategy that cultivates a unique fan experience. I was keen to assess the validity of my categorisations and the extent to which the culture of each club influences the fans' sense of identity. Consequently, a purposive sampling method was used in which I approached participants that seemed to correspond to my perception of family, community and tourist fans. For example, I looked to approach fans in family groups at Norwich City, groups of middle aged, middle-class fans at MK Dons (those drinking wine instead of beer, dressed in smart clothes instead of the leisure wear associated with traditional fans) and fans dressed in merchandise and carrying cameras at Chelsea.

The selection of the participants was based solely on my judgement and categorisation. The subjective and non-probable nature of the selection means that I cannot make claims as to the representativeness of my sample to the entire fan community of each club. Unlike the various sampling techniques that can be used under probability sampling, the goal of purposive sampling is not to randomly select participants to create a sample with the intention of making generalisations from that sample to the wider population of interest. Instead the main goal of purposive sampling is to focus on particular characteristics of a population that are of interest which will best enable the researcher to answer their research questions. In the context of my research this refers to fans that correspond to the categories that I have associated with each club. Purposive sampling is used as a method when the research questions that are being addressed are specific to the characteristics of a particular group of interest. In the context of my research this group is consumer fans. Purposive sampling enables the researcher to examine identified groups in detail, so while my research may prevent me from making generalisations about each club's wider fan community, my research does permit me to make generalisations from the sample that is being studied.

Interviews were loosely guided by an inventory, with initial conversation framed around the impending contest in an attempt to demonstrate my identification as a football fan and my understanding of the culture associated with each club. It was vital that I developed a level of rapport with the participants, to ensure that the data that I obtained was as valid as possible. As an outsider to the community, I expected that I would be treated with a level of suspicion, particularly in relation to the way in which much of the literature written by 'outsiders' on contemporary football culture has an agenda of disenfranchising the consumer fan. I was keen to present myself as more than a researcher but as a self-identified 'researcher fan,' who identified with the participants' understanding of capitalist football culture. By positioning myself as a 'researcher fan' looking to share the experiences of the participants, I believe that I was treated with a level of openness that enabled the collection of fascinating, in-depth data.

After an initial level of rapport had been established, participants were given as much autonomy as possible to articulate their fan identity and direct the conversation. Indeed, the initial period of establishing identification with the participants seemed to create a 'cascading effect,' with the participants engaging in dialogue with me based on a rapport and sense of reassurance that had been established previously in the conversation (Lindlof & Taylor 2002: 182). The participants' responses were vital to the research process and subsequently I offered to buy them snacks as a gesture of gratitude. Again, I think it is important to maintain parity and reduce the power imbalance between the researcher and participants and wanted to 'give something' to them in return for their participation (see McNeill 1997), however I was conscious that this process could have been interpreted as 'giving them a reward' for what could be perceived to be the 'correct answers' (see Alderson & Morrow 2004). As a result, I thanked them upon completion and offered them refreshments after the interviews had been concluded to try and ensure that the gesture did not influence their responses.

Talking about football is a natural part of the culture; indeed, fans seemingly unaware of my research often approached me wanting to talk about the game. I argue that these spontaneous conversations are a central part of the football event that helped me establish a valid insight into the culture of each club. Subsequently extracts from these informal conversations are cited throughout my research, as I believe that they provide me with an insight into the fans' identification with the culture of their club. Similarly, some of these conversations helped me to contextualise the ideas articulated by participants that I had previously interviewed.

I did not direct interviews or discussions to explore sensitive themes, yet I occasionally became privy to crude, sexist and racist language both happening around me as part of the football event and used in conversation by participants. I did not stop these conversations or intervene. As suggested my research is participant centric with ethnography employed as a method explicitly for the way in which it attempts to 'look within' culture to provide consumer fans with opportunities to articulate their fandom and engage in negotiation with the discourses surrounding them within the culture. To ensure that I achieved this aim I continued to let the participants direct the agenda of the interviews even when it veered into provocative territory. While the behaviour of the participants was occasionally reprehensible it has to be recognised that the motivations underpinning these expressions relate to the participants' fan identity or, importantly, their *expectations* of how to enact and articulate their fandom identity. While some of these responses were uncomfortable to hear and thus may be uncomfortable to read, I argue that they provide significant insight into the participants' fan identity and their understanding of the discourses surrounding the culture, the game's capitalism and tradition.

Bibliography

Alderson, P & Morrow, V (2004) *Ethics, Social Research and Consulting with Children and Young People*. London. Barnardo's Press.

Barker, C (2004) *The Sage Dictionary of Cultural Studies*. London. Sage.

Bolin, A & Granskog, J (2003) *Athletic Intruders: Ethnographic Research on Women, Culture and Exercise*. New York. State University of New York Press.

Bryman, A (2008) *Social Research Methods*. New York. Oxford University Press.

Comaroff, J & Comaroff, J (1992) *Ethnography and the Historical Imagination*. Colorado. Westview Press.

de Garis, L (1999) Experiments in Pro Wrestling: Towards a Performative and Sensuous Sport Ethnography. *Sociology of Sport Journal* 16 (1) 65–74.

Denzin, N (1997) *Interpretive Ethnography: Ethnographic Practices for the 21st Century*. California. Sage.

Ellis, C (2004) *The Ethnographic I: A Methodological Novel about Autoethnography*. California. Alta Mira Press.

Fay, B & Moon, JD (1994) 'What Would an Adequate Philosophy of Social Science Look Like?' Cited in Martin, M & McIntyre, L *Readings in the Philosophy of Social Science*. Cambridge. MIT Press.

Fiske, J (1992) 'The Cultural Economy of Fandom' Cited in Lewis, L *The Adoring Audience*. London. Routledge.

Gelder, K & Thornton, S (1997) *The Subcultures Reader*. London. Routledge.

Hammersley, M (1992) *What's Wrong with Ethnography*. Oxford. Psychology Press.

Heron, J (1981) 'Experiential Research Methodology' Cited in Reason, P & Rowan, J *Human Inquiry: A Sourcebook of New Paradigm Research*. London. Wiley.

Hills, M (2002) *Fan Cultures*. London. Routledge.

Jameson, F (1991) *Postmodernism or the Cultural Logic of Late Capitalism*. London. Verso.

King, A (2002) *The End of the Terraces: The Transformation of English Football in the 1990's*. London. Leicester University Press.

Klein, A (1997) *Baseball on the Border*. Princeton, NJ. Princeton University Press.

Kuper, A (1999) *Among the Anthropologists: History and Context in Anthropology*. New Brunswick. Athlone Press.

Lather, P (1986) Issues of Validity in Openly Ideological Research: Between a Rock and a Soft Place. *Interchange* 17 (4) 63–84.

Lindlof, T & Taylor, B (2002) *Qualitative Communication Research Methods*. London. Sage.

Malinowski, B (2014) *Argonauts of the West Pacific*. London. Routledge.

McNeill, P (1997) Paying People to Participate in Research: Why Not? *Bioethics* 11 (1) 390–396.

Reed-Danahay, D (1997) *Auto/Ethnography: Rewriting the Self and the Social.* Oxford. Berg.
Rosenberg, A (1988) *Philosophy of Social Science*. Colorado, Westview.
Sands, R (2002) *Sport Ethnography*. Illinois. Human Kinetics.
Sandvoss, C (2005) *Fans*. Cambridge. Polity.
Schrijvers, J (1991) 'Dialectics of a Dialogical Idea: Studying Down, Studying Sideways, Studying Up.' Cited in Nencel, L and Pels, P *Constructing Knowledge: Authority and Critique in Social Science*. London. Sage.
Scott-Jones, J & Watt, S (2010) *Ethnography in Social Science Practice*. London. Routledge.
Singer, P (1993) *Practical Ethics*. Cambridge. Cambridge University Press.
Thornton, S (1995) *Club Cultures: Music, Media and Subcultural Capital.* Cambridge. Polity.
Van der Riet, M (2008) Participatory Research and the Philosophy of Social Science: The Moral Imperative. *Qualitative Inquiry* 14 (1) 546–565.

Chapter 4

Norwich City

'The best pies in the league'

As a longstanding football fan, I have developed relationships with fans throughout the Football League. On 15 September 2012 Norwich City were to host West Ham United at Carrow Road, a match I was planning to attend. Two days preceding the match I received a series of texts from 'Joe,' an away season ticket holder with West Ham.

Norwich City was selected for analysis as 'a family club,' a club that markets itself to attract families, appealing to women and children. While 'Joe' (2012) predicts West Ham's victory on the pitch, the exchange continually refers to the culture of Norwich City, with 'Joe' comparing the family culture of the club with the perceived traditional culture he associates with West Ham. The exchange revolves around this subtext of tradition and legitimacy with the concept of winning associated with the status of each club within the culture as much as the result. The binary 'Joe' creates between the clubs: Norwich—capitalism, West Ham—tradition, draws upon the discourses that I highlight in the previous chapters, emphasising the hierarchy in which traditional football culture is perceived to be more legitimate than modern football culture.

In our exchange, West Ham becomes metonymic of the game's traditional culture while Norwich is presented as the embodiment of the game's capitalism. This seemed significant, vindicating my categorisation of Norwich City as a 'family club,' but also my argument that the perception of football culture and the identity of its fans continue to be shaped by these discourses and, importantly, the fans' understanding and negotiation of these discourses. 'Joe's' (2012) conception of each club epitomises this idea in which he explicitly frames the culture of each club and their associated fan identities in relation to football's traditional culture and its modern capitalism.

'Joe': Can't wait for Saturday; we (West Ham) are going to smash the Canaries. Come on you irons (COYI)!

Oliver: 2–1 Norwich, mate. It will be close, but City will just sneak it.

'Joe': Ha-ha, did you see how they played against Fulham!? We are going to destroy them 6–0.

Oliver: That was away though, a one-off. The crowd will be up for it on Saturday. It's a sell-out and it will be a big atmosphere.

'Joe': Oh, I bet it's a GREAT atmosphere [sarcasm]. Norwich is a club for pussies, mate. I bet all the families and day-trippers there with their kids make it really intimidating!

Oliver: The stadium is sold out every week and the fans are really passionate. I think you will be surprised.

'Joe': Doubt it, mate. I'm West Ham. You want REAL atmosphere, you come to Upton Park again. You know we're a proper football club.

Oliver: What do you mean a 'proper football club?'

'Joe': We've got history, we've got tradition. West Ham are respected. We won the World Cup,[1] we've got the best academy and we've got the best firm. We're a proper football club.

Oliver: So that makes you a proper club?

'Joe': We are a proper football club. We're respected. Talk to fans about West Ham and they will tell you 'West Ham are a proper club.' Ask them about Norwich and they will tell you they're small time, there's no tradition, no atmosphere; it's a 'nice,' little 'family club.'

'Joe' (2012) positions himself in opposition to Norwich's 'day-trippers', perpetuating a carefully considered fan narrative that correlates with the traditional 'ideals' of football culture as described by Imlach (2005). As documented in Chapter 2, Imlach (2005: 213) argues that traditional fan identity is defined by long-standing familial lineage, geographical ties and emotional attachment encouraged by the knowledge of club history and its reflection of the local community. In his attempts to construct his 'traditional' identity 'Joe' describes West Ham as a 'proper' football club, explicitly drawing upon these themes.

'Joe' (2012) focuses on the sporting success of the football club, as referenced by Bobby Moore (history) and the club's academy[2] (history, local community, family lineage and emotional attachment). This idea of local representation seems foundational to 'Joe's' fandom, in which he continually draws on the club's geographical anchorage in the traditionally working-class, East End of London (geographical ties and history) and the club's history of hooliganism with their 'firm,' the Inter City Firm (ICF), infamous within football culture (history and local community).

I argue that 'Joe' (2012) looks to frame his fan identity in relation to the discourse surrounding the club emphasising its traditional culture in opposition to what he perceives to be the less legitimate culture associated with Norwich City. As 'Joe' indicates, the discourse surrounding Norwich City does not hold the same subcultural capital (see Thornton 1995). The club is situated in the middle of an out-of-town retail park, indicative of modern football's symbiotic relationship with wider leisure industries. Similarly, the club's affiliation with consumer industries and the awards that it has obtained for its family initiatives[3] has led to the club developing the reputation of being a 'nice' football club.

While 'Joe' (2012) presents West Ham as a 'proper football club,' Norwich City are defined as a 'club for pussies.' This binary produces certain expectations about the demographic attracted to each club and the identity of the fans. Pearson (2012) suggests that working-class narratives of hooliganism and 'capers' from the terraces act as badges of honour to modern football fans keen to associate themselves with the machismo of the terraces to position themselves in opposition to the game's modern capitalism. In the context of our exchange, the game's capitalism is represented by Norwich City. 'Joe' looks to frame his fan identity in a similar fashion, in which he attempts to associate himself with West Ham's traditional culture. In this context it is poignant that he personifies himself as the embodiment of the club, 'I am West Ham,' constructing a profile for himself indicative of the 'traditional' fan or, as I suggest, his *expectation* of what it means to be a traditional fan.

I suggest in Chapter 2 that consumer fans are trapped in discourses of representation, positioned positively as consumers by agents of the game's capitalism and negatively as consumers by agents of the game's tradition. This complex orientation of the modern fan is reflected in 'Joe's' (2012) fan identity, positioned as a consumer via his status as a home and away season ticket holder with the club while self-identifying as a traditional fan, framing his fan identity in relation to traditional discourses. If, as I argue, consumer fans are 'trapped' in discourses of representation then it is to be expected that fan identities are similarly trapped in the confines of these hegemonic discourses, yet it is significant that while drawing on these discourses 'Joe' *actively* ignores his relationship as a consumer to the club, knowingly framing his identity as that of the working-class fans traditionally associated with West Ham.

While 'Joe' (2012) exercises power over Norwich fans in his dismissal of their identity, I argue that he similarly exercises power in the active creation of his own identity. This provided me with foresight to a pattern that would emerge as I continued my research. Participants that I engaged with continually enacted processes of discursive negotiation, constructing their identities by drawing on the hegemonic discourses that continue to surround the culture: capitalism and tradition, but also their individual understanding of how they *should* identify as fans of their specific clubs.

This chapter analyses the way in which Norwich City fans negotiate their identity, engaging in 'exception readings' (Sandvoss 2005) with the family culture of their club. The chapter argues that Norwich fans constitute their identity in relation to their different consumer needs as fans. I argue that the different needs of the fans correspond to their identification with the club's family culture and, importantly, their desire to frame themselves as a specific *type* of fan.

'You just feel part of something'

While 'Joe' (2012) looked to position himself as a traditional fan, the participants that I interviewed on my first trip to Carrow Road (Norwich City Vs Fulham,

31 December 2011), 'Roy' and 'Pam,' in attendance with son 'Chris,' aged 10, explicitly identify as consumers. The participants frame their fan identity in correlation with the club's marketing strategy, describing the way in which the club caters to their needs as a family.

Oliver: So how are you feeling about the match today … optimistic?

'Roy': Cautiously optimistic. We were outclassed the other night (against Tottenham) but sometimes you have to hold your hands up and say the better team won. She [indicates to 'Pam'] couldn't make it the other night, but we are all back together, so I think we will do the business tonight. They usually do all right when we are all together.

'Pam': Yeah, I was disappointed to miss the game the other day, I really wanted to see Gareth Bale, but I was at the sales (shopping). It's the best bit about Christmas, so many games in a short space of time. It's nice to be back and make up for it today. I think the team will get things going again.

Oliver: That's the best thing about football over the Christmas period: there are so many games in a short space of time so you can move on from a bad result and get it out of your system with a quick win a couple of days later. So you are a good luck omen, are you? [Directed at 'Pam.']

'Pam': [Laughs.] I don't know about that, but when I come with the boys they are usually good games.

Oliver: Are you all season ticket holders?

'Roy': 'Chris' and I are. I used to come a few years ago but had to stop with work and with 'Chris' and everything, but then he started to get into football and started playing it at school, so I took him to a couple of games and it went from there.

'Pam': They would be going off every Saturday without me and I felt like I was missing out. [Laughs.]

'Roy': You really love it, don't you? [Directed at 'Pam.'] She felt like she was missing out, so we managed to get her a ticket for a game one week and now she's hooked. I'm always trying to get her tickets; she's on the season ticket waiting list (for next season).

Oliver: Was there anything in particular that you enjoyed about the matches that made you want to keep coming back or is there anything specific you really enjoy about coming here?

'Pam': Delia's pies (Delia Smith, TV Chef and Norwich's majority shareholder). They are the best pies in the league. I mainly come for the pies. No, it's really good to see the superstars and the big team but I just wanted to spend time with the boys and see what all the excitement was about. Once you come a few times you get a taste for the atmosphere, you get hooked.

'Roy': It is just a really good atmosphere; it's something that's fun to be part of. With the teams doing well, the ground has a good bit of noise about it and you just get caught up in it. It's exciting.

'Pam': But it's not an intimidating atmosphere, is it? It's passionate but it's not threatening. I was a bit nervous about coming to start with, especially bringing 'Chris.' I didn't really know what to expect and just thought it would be drunken men looking for trouble, but once I got here and on the walk up (to the stadium) noticed the number of children and families I knew it was going to be ok.

Oliver: Norwich has that reputation for being a family club.

'Roy': That's right, you only have to look around the place, there are loads of youngsters, women and elderly people. That's one of the nice things about the club: everyone is welcome, and I think that is why the stadium is packed every week.

'Pam': I think the club tries really hard to please everyone; there are the mascots going around the ground for the kids and things like that over there [points to a display board with coloured pictures by young fans] to show you that children are important to the club. I think that's it, when you come it's like you are part of something; everyone is made to feel welcome.

In Chapter 2 the question was posited: how can fans maintain their fandom when clubs are doing everything in the power to transform them into consumers (see Fynn & Guest 1994; Bale 1998; Brimson 1998; Giulianotti 2002; King 2002; Ingle 2005; Barr 2009; Pearson 2012)? 'Pam' and 'Roy's' (2011) responses provide a possible solution. Positioned as consumers by the football club, the participants self-identify as consumers, accepting the club's business strategy and consumer culture. This notion is epitomised by 'Pam's' playful suggestion that she 'mainly' attends football matches for 'Delia's pies,' explicitly aligning her fandom with processes of consumption, with the reference to celebrity chef Delia Smith. This idea is supported by her reference to the January sales, framing herself as a consumer, highlighting the symbiosis between consumerism and modern football culture.

Despite this idea, I argue that the humorous tone of her response subverts the idea that her consumption makes her fandom passive. On the contrary, she is active in her consumption as suggested by the way that she presents her choice, whether to consume the products of the sales or the performance of Gareth Bale. I argue that this understanding of choice emphasises 'Pam's' (2011) active and flexible conception of fandom. Self-identified as a consumer she alludes to the idea that she is free to make decisions within the market, her fandom 'a form of sustained affective consumption' (Sandvoss 2005: 9). Contemporary fan studies argue that fandom is reliant on the products of capitalism (see Jameson 1991; Fiske 1992; Hills 2002; Barker 2004; Sandvoss 2005). I do not dispute this idea, but 'Pam's' acknowledgement of her choice, and awareness of the powers operating on her as she does so, suggests that she enacts fandom with an autonomy rarely afforded to consumer fans by self-identified traditional fans like 'Joe' (2012), that view consumer fans as 'corporate dupes.'

The exchange indicates that the participants are both aware of the culture of the club and the wider capitalism of the sport. 'Roy' (2011) explicitly makes this connection, describing the club's agenda to appeal to a large demographic: 'families, women, elderly people' and their success in 'filling the stadium every week.' It is this rapacious marketisation that is said to lead to the loss of identity, autonomy and community within football culture, concomitant with larger anti-capitalist discourse. On the contrary, I argue that the exchange emphasises the autonomy of the fans in their self-conception of identity. As Bates (1994 cited by King 2002) suggests, rather than disenfranchise the fan, football's modern capitalism addresses their developing needs as consumers. In this context the participant's 'need' relates to their desire to enact rituals of family.

'Pam' (2011) suggests that she started attending matches to spend time with her husband and son: 'They would be going off every Saturday without me and I felt like I was missing out,' suggesting that her fandom originates from the shared family experience afforded to her by the culture of the club. 'Roy' (2011) develops this idea, forming associations between the team's success on the pitch and the cohesion of the family within the stand: 'Pam couldn't make it, but we are all back together tonight, so I think we will do the business' and 'they usually do all right when we are all here.' Like 'Joe' (2012), 'Roy' personifies the family as a reflection of the club, creating a unique, personal fan narrative. 'Roy' assimilates the victory of the team on the pitch with the family's ability to come together and share leisure time, creating a link between the success of the team and 'success' of the family. If 'Joe' (2012) presents himself as an archetypal traditional fan, 'Roy,' presents the family explicitly as modern consumers, 'buying' into the culture of the club and the overall narrative of family that it promotes and helps to stage. It is obvious that the participants have internalised this narrative with the idea of communality evident throughout the exchange. As 'Pam' suggests: 'when you come it's like you are part of something.'

While the culture of the club is largely dictated by the norms of modern consumerism, the club creating an inclusive experience concomitant with the 'catch all' dictates of capitalism, the participants' fandom revolves around the affordance permitted to them by the culture of the club to develop and engineer their own staging of family. This indicates that despite the overall commercialisation of the sport and the explicit marketing of the club to attract family fans, the participants are still able to create their own meaning within the cultural parameters afforded to them by the club. Indeed, the exchange indicates that the participants knowingly 'buy' into the club for the way in which it enables them to enact family. 'Pam's' (2012) decision to consume the products of the sales over the performance of Gareth Bale seems microcosmic of the fan's active consumerism. Her choice was one she exercised knowingly in the market.

Despite my argument that the participant's fandom can be considered as active consumer choice, it is significant that 'Roy' (2011) suggests that the family's fandom was encouraged by the way in which they were made to feel like they were 'missing out.' While I am keen to emphasise the agency of modern fans, I am not ignoring the power of capitalism. The quotation epitomises the imperialism of the system, with its discourse permeating into the products that embody its hegemony, constantly creating need through an anxiety of exclusion or 'alienation' (see Marx 1932). As Gasper (2005) argues, capitalism requires a constantly expanding market to keep selling its products. To do so, it continually creates a need for consumer goods. This is the argument made by both popular and academic text, framing the consumer fans as a profitable market for football clubs to exploit (see Fynn & Guest 1994; Bale 1998; Brimson 1998; Giulianotti 2002; Ingle 2005; Pearson 2012).

In this context the participant's consumer fandom could be considered as a further example of the wider capitalisation of society, with 'Pam's' (2011) assimilation of football and the sales epitomising modern football's attempts to 'turn fans into consumers.' However, I dispute Gasper's (2010) argument that the further capitalisation of society 'robs people of their creative potential.' I argue that the exchange indicates that the participants accept their relationship of consumption with the club for the way in which it enables them to engage in rituals of family.

This link between the culture of the club and the enactment of the family is evident in the way in which 'Pam' (2011) explicitly rejects the norms of traditional football culture, allying her initial fear of attending live matches to the stereotypes of traditional fandom. I argue that this emphasises her motivations for fandom and corresponds to the idea that the participant's fandom can be seen as consumer choice. Indeed she suggests that her fandom was encouraged by the security she feels within the stadium as part of the club's wider 'family.' However, it is significant that the binary that she creates similarly demonstrates her understanding of the discourses surrounding the demographic of fans associated with different eras of football culture, emphasising the way in which the discourse surrounding football culture helps to create impressions and expectations of fan identity.

I was keen to explore the wider identity of Norwich fans, assessing the ways in which they engaged with the family culture of the club. To explore this, I started my larger data collection by positioning myself within the Aviva Community Stand. My research vindicates my argument that the club's family culture has a significant impact on the participants' fan identity and motivations for fandom, however it became apparent that the family culture of the club had not been totally embraced by the club's fan base. Appropriating the label from Pearson (2012), I encountered a large sub-sect of 'carnival fans:' participants that actively looked to substantiate their identity by negotiating the game's capitalism and also the family culture of the club. The latter part of the chapter documents the way in which these supporters use the culture of the club as a base from which to transgress, engaging in carnival to construct their identity in opposition to the club's family culture, to enact identity in keeping with their expectations of what it means to be a traditional fan.

'Bugger off to the Snake Pit'

I identified this alternative fan identity when Norwich hosted Leicester City in the fourth round of the FA Cup (18 February 2012). Cup games usually function as entry-level games for new fans, providing those without season tickets rare opportunities to attend live matches. With this in mind, the match seemed the perfect opportunity to engage with what I presumed to be new enthusiasts. I was keen to determine what attracted them to Carrow Road.

The first group I approach refused to be interviewed, while the second group seemed to take exception to the idea that they might be 'new' to Carrow Road, informing me proudly that they had been season tickets holders for 'longer than they could remember' and were not 'jumping on the bandwagon,' an attitude that I was not expecting having discussed with 'Roy' and 'Pam' (2011) the way in which the club fostered a sense of community. Initially I interpreted this as the group's scepticism towards me as an outsider to their 'family.' As suggested in the previous chapter, I expected that I would be treated with a level of suspicion due to the way in which much of the literature written by 'outsiders' operates with an agenda of disenfranchising modern football fans. On reflection these exchanges typified the day's events, with a distinct sub-set of fans looking to constitute their identity in opposition to the club's 'nice' family culture.

I approached 'Jack' (2012) who had brought his young son 'Ben,' aged five, with him to see his first match. Describing himself as a 'casual' fan, 'Ben' was clearly excited about bringing his son to his first match.

Oliver: Are you looking forward to the game today?

'Jack': Yeah, mate, I'm really looking forward to it. Should be a cracking game; expecting a load of goals and some good entertainment.

Oliver: Me too. We never seem to do well in the Cup, but this should be a great opportunity to get a bit of a run going, get to the next round and keep the confidence up with a win.

'Jack': You're right, it would be nice to have a bit of a Cup run. Got my good luck mascot with me today [indicating to 'Ben'], so we'll be alright.

Oliver: Do you get to many games?

'Jack': Not really. I try and get to a game every now and then. I was here for the Burnley Cup game (7 January 2012) and Sunderland (26 September 2011) at the start of the season but I don't get here as much as I would like. And today, well today is 'Ben's' *first* game.

Oliver: Oh, cool are you excited? [To 'Ben']
['Ben' nods.]

Oliver: So, it's quite a big day for you then. It must be special bringing your son for the first time?

'Jack': Oh, it is, mate. I've wanted to bring him for a while, he's still quite young, he's five, so I haven't known if he's too young really or if he'll enjoy it but yeah, it's a good one for me.

Oliver: Was there a reason that you decided to bring him with you today?

'Jack': Well we could both get tickets for a start. I came to the Burnley game the other week and sat here and there were so many kids I just thought why not, they seemed to be having a good time, and there was no bother or anything. I remember going to football with my Dad when I was young and I want to do that with 'Ben.' I just hope he enjoys it and gets into it.

Like 'Pam' and 'Roy' (2011), 'Jack' (2012) associates his motivations for fandom with the orientation of the club, Norwich's family culture encouraging him to share the experience with his son: 'there were so many kids I just thought why not, they seemed to be having a good time.' 'Jack' similarly describes his motivations for fandom in relation to the affordance permitted by the club to enable him to enact rituals of family, to re-live the experience of attending matches with his father, something he remembers fondly and was keen to replicate with 'Ben.' Despite the similarity in the way in which 'Jack' frames his fandom in relation to the club's family culture, it seems significant that he self-identifies as a 'casual' fan. This emphasises his motivations for fandom, alluding to the idea that he looked to enact fandom not through a sense of emotional attachment or communal representation, but for the way in which the culture of the club corresponded to his consumer need, his desire to engage in a family ritual with his son.

Ironically there is a tension here. In his desire to re-enact an experience he had with his father, 'Jack' (2012) uses modern football culture to re-stage an experience that he presumably experienced in football's 'traditional' period. This serves as an analogy to the complex positioning of modern fans, encouraged by traditional discourses to reject the game's capitalism to enact traditional fan performances as demonstrated by 'Joe' (2012). Conversely it is 'Jack's' acceptance and understanding of the game's capitalism and the culture of the club that he recognises as a 'casual' fan, that encourages him to enact a fandom that he experienced as a product of the game's traditional culture. This compliments my argument made in Chapter 2 that football's modern capitalism should not be considered as separate from its traditional era, while emphasising the ability of the fans to negotiate the discourses surrounding the game's capitalism and traditional culture to construct their own self-narratives within football culture.

This emerging pattern supports my agenda to analyse contemporary football culture with a consumer-oriented cultural studies approach. Sandvoss (2005) argues that modern cultural studies analyse how texts carry meanings that articulate fan identities and their objective and subjective position within society. I argue that this idea is manifested in 'Jack's' (2012) articulation of fandom, with the family culture of the club enabling him to objectively and subjectively enact traditional rituals of family, macrocosmically as part of the community fostered by the club and microcosmically in the re-staging of the family ritual that he experienced with his father.

It is significant that like 'Roy' (2011), 'Jack' (2012) creates a link between the family and the outcome of the match, describing 'Ben' as a 'good luck mascot.' Again 'Jack' assimilates the team's success and his ability to enact family. Like 'Roy,' this indicates that 'Jack' has unique motivations for fandom that extend beyond the football event itself. It is significant that they assimilate themselves with the action occurring on the pitch, perpetuating the idea that like the players they are active in their relationship with the game. In this context, their active involvement with the event supports the idea that their fandom is an informed choice, that they are *active* in their consumption. Like 'Pam' and 'Roy' (2011), 'Jack' (2012) demonstrates his awareness of the game's capitalism; like 'Pam,' he knowingly uses humour to suggest that his fandom was encouraged by the fact that he 'could *actually* get tickets.' This indicates that he recognises his fandom as a transaction, the process, a norm of modern consumer society in which he willingly pays for the service and experience that he associates with the club.

Taking my seat, towards the back of the stand, it was fortuitous, that 'Jack' and 'Ben' were sitting two rows in front of me. As the match started there was a general feeling of optimism with the Barclay, home to Norwich's most vocal fans, starting the chant of 'On the ball, City' and the young fans adjacent to me attempting to join in. As I looked down towards 'Jack' and 'Ben,' both were transfixed on the game, 'Ben' mimicking his father in applauding good periods of play. On the five-minute mark Leicester scored against the run of play, a moment that changed the pattern of the game and the atmosphere around the stadium. Symbiotically the Barclay fell silent and the quality of play on the pitch started to deteriorate. By the ten-minute mark each misplaced pass became punctuated by load groans, most of which seemed to originate from the opposite end of the stadium, however audible sighs could be heard coming from a group of middle-aged men adjacent to me on the other side of the concourse.

Despite their general sloppy play Norwich managed to equalise in the twenty-third minute; 'Jack' (2012) leapt to his feet and had 'Ben' in has arms swaying and bouncing to the music played over the PA system. The jubilance of the celebration belied the quality of the game, the celebration seemingly more to do with the occasion than the goal itself. As 'Jack' suggested, he was keen for 'Ben' to 'get into' the game and 'enjoy it.' The goal was an opportunity for the pair to engage in collective celebration, corresponding with 'Jack's' desire to experience the ritual he enjoyed with his father.

As insinuated by the interview, the quality of the match seemed incidental to 'Jack' (2012). Little time was spent discussing the match or specifics of the team. The day was significant as he had chosen to engage in the ritual of attending the match with his son. My questions were open ended to enable 'Jack' to direct the conversation, yet it is significant that the majority of the exchange focuses on the relationship he has with his son rather than the match itself. In other words, I argue that the conversation revolves around the family ritual that was facilitated *by* their fandom, rather than his fandom *with* the club. This correlates to 'Jack's' identification as a casual fan. 'Jack's' individual identification with the culture of the club is replicated in his celebration, his fan performance, an individual expression that seemed to relate to his experience with his son more than the football event happening on the pitch.

The rest of the stand had taken to their feet and responded to the equaliser with muted applause; the general mood was epitomised by the exasperated group adjacent to me who had audibly become more frustrated throughout the game. 'Tom' (2012) glanced towards his friend and puffed his cheeks, signalling his relief, a gesture I acknowledged with laughter. Hearing this and catching sight of me out of the corner of his eye, 'Tom' turned and mouthed his assessment: 'We're crap.' I found it significant that he only mouthed his judgement, rather than openly verbalise it. I interpreted this as his internalisation of the club's culture. There are numerous signs around the stand warning fans about the club's family ethos, instructing them that as a 'family club' bad language would not be tolerated.

My conception of his fandom was compounded by a brief chat I had with him at half time:

Oliver: We aren't good, are we?
'Tom': No, we're bloody terrible.
Oliver: I don't know how we got back into it to be honest.
'Tom': Me neither, we don't deserve to. I haven't seen us play this bad under Lambert (Paul Lambert, Norwich manager at the time of research).
Oliver: I could hear you getting frustrated; some of the play is so sloppy today.
'Tom': It's bloody awful. I'm doing well to bite my tongue; if it weren't for all the bloody kids around here I would be going mad.

'Tom' (2012) describes his efforts to curtail his behaviour, acknowledging that his natural response would be incongruent with the club's family culture. While the interviews that I had previously conducted indicated that the culture of the club facilitated a sense of community, 'Tom' indicates that the family culture of the club prohibits outbursts of anger or frustration, leading him to censor his natural responses.

There is an interesting tension here: 'Pam' and 'Roy' (2011) suggested that the club's allure relates to the way in which it appeals to a diverse demographic, making 'everyone feel welcome,' whereas my exchange with 'Tom' (2012) contradicts this idea, suggesting that the club values a specific *type* of fan that enacts within a specific type of identity. Sandvoss (2005: 9) argues that contemporary fandom is the process of emotionally engaging with products of capitalism. While I argue that the club undoubtedly values 'Tom's' fandom as patronage, his emotional engagement is not valued by the club, with limits being placed upon his behaviour to ensure that it conforms to the club's family culture. This notion corresponds to discourse that suggests that modern football has become sanitised and panopticised (see Bale 1998; King 2002; Weed 2008).

I argue that 'Tom's' (2012) fandom evokes Fromm's concept of 'authoritarian conformity' (1963); the idea that dominant cultures manage to obtain consent despite their subjects' awareness that their agenda is likely to impinge upon their freedoms. Fromm (1963: 159) describes the knowing consent to culture like the 'protective colouring animals assume,' describing conformity as a defence shield against cultural alienation. 'Tom' faces the prospect of exclusion if he does not conform to the norms of club culture, so to engage in fandom 'Tom' submits to the norms of the market and the culture of the club, enabling both systems to perpetuate.

'Tom's' (2012) choice to manage his fan identity indicates that like the other participants his fandom relates to a sense of need that is addressed by attending live football matches, yet his needs and motivations for fandom do not correspond with those of 'Pam,' 'Roy' (2011) and 'Jack' (2012). While this made me reconsider the way in which I had operationalised the club's 'inclusive' family culture, I believe that this supports my consumer-oriented approach to research with the participants indicating that their fandom relates to their different needs as consumers. While 'Roy,' 'Pam' and 'Jack's' fandom can be considered in terms of a negotiation between the culture of the club and their individual needs as consumers, their fan identities correspond with the family culture of the club. Conversely, 'Tom's' identity seemed to be enacted almost in spite of the culture of the club, offering an indication of that way in which consumers can engage with capitalist texts while still opposing their agenda (see Barker 2004).

The second half started in a similar manner to the first; Norwich were careless in possession with Leicester dictating the play. The atmosphere heralded by 'Pam' and 'Roy' (2011) was flat. With sixty-five minutes on the clock, Norwich had not managed a shot in the second half; 'Jack' (2012) remained glued to the game, and the group adjacent of me were silent. In the seventy-first minute, Leicester inevitably took the lead. The reaction around the stand was minimal. A few fans started to head for the exit while 'Tom' (2012) slammed his fist into his leg. 'Tom's' reaction was poignant; while an aggressive action, it was personal.

As the final twenty minutes were played out, it was clear that much of the stand had lost interest, particularly 'Ben' (2012). By the seventy-fifth minute, he had stopped watching the game and could be seen staring at the floor swinging his feet back and forth under his chair. A couple of minutes later, he turned his back on the game and started climbing around his seat. 'Jack' (2012), noticing this, tried to focus his attention back on the contest, giving him a running commentary. This had been ongoing for five minutes when 'Tom' (2012) finally lost his composure:

'Jack': Oh look its Fox, he has it and he gives it to Adam Drury. He gets it and gives it back to David Fox. Fox tries to pass it to Jackson, but he doesn't get the pass right and gives it to one of the Leicester players. Oh no! I hope they don't score again. The Leicester player, he gives it to his friend on the left. Where are our midfield players? Oh yes, Hoolahan

with a tackle, Hoolahan ... what a funny name! He scored our goal, but he has lost it and its back with Leicester.

'Tom': Jesus, mate, give it a rest. This has been painful enough, I don't want a bloody commentary. If I did, I'd put my radio on or something.

'Jack': Come on, mate, I'm with my son. I'm just trying to...

'Tom': Just keep it down. He has eyes, doesn't he? Let him watch the game and let us watch it without you prattling for the last ten minutes.

With 84 minutes on the clock, 'Jack' (2012) got out of his seat, taking 'Ben' by the hand, and made his way along the row to the concourse. Allowing 'Ben' to lead the way until he was out of direct earshot, he paused for a moment in front of 'Tom' (2012):

> What's your problem, pal? Look around, there are kids everywhere. If you've got such a problem, why are you here? You're a dinosaur, mate. If you're going to be such a prat, why you don't bugger off to the Snake Pit?

'I'm a proper 'Naaarwich' fan boy'

The Snake Pit to which 'Jack' (2012) refers is a nickname given to the stand in the Thorpe corner infill that connects the Barclay to the City Stand. The Snake Pit was colonised by 'hardcore' fans in an attempt to recreate the community described as a facet of terrace culture (Walsh & Giulianotti 2001: 62). The Pit was where songs would emanate, housing the club's traditional fans as the club transitioned from bureaucracy to capitalism. It is this 'traditional' conception of what the Snake Pit represents that 'Jack' evokes in his rebuke of 'Tom' (2012), suggesting that his behaviour is incongruent with the family culture of the club and football's wider civilisation process.

Having witnessed the rebuke, I was keen to develop a further understanding of the way in which the Snake Pit is understood by the club's modern fans and to test my assumption that the culture of the club facilitates the enactment of different identities. After speaking to a contact I made through the Pink Un fan forum, I was put in touch with a family, 'May,' 'Pip' and their teenage sons 'Lee' and 'Nick' (2012), who had season tickets in the stand. In accordance with the literature that documents football's historical development, the group indicated that the modernisation of the sport and the family orientation of the club had seen the traditional fans associated with the Snake Pit deterred from attendance, the stand becoming subsumed into the club's family culture. The boys seemed to find my questions amusing, 'Lee' mockingly suggesting that having a ticket in the 'Snake Pit' meant that he was 'well hard,' using match days as an excuse 'to get pissed.' Getting in on the joke, 'Nick' adopted a stereotypical Norfolk accent,[4] playing the role of a traditional fan typically associated with the stand: 'Oh yeah boy, you h'aint a proper fan coz ya h'aint there in that ol' Snake Pit boy. I'm a proper 'Naaarwich' fan boy.'

While humorous, the exchange mocks the nostalgic idea of what it means to be a traditional fan. The humour is in the idea that traditional fans are out of touch with modern football culture, as implied by the unflattering and dated Norfolk accent. It was this idea that 'Jack' (2012) evoked in his lamentation of 'Tom's' (2012) fan identity; his outburst was incongruent with the culture of the club and subsequently he was perceived to be 'out of touch,' a 'dinosaur.'

After witnessing the incongruity of 'Jack' and 'Tom's' fan identity I sought to experience a match within the Snake Pit. After some negotiation and suitable remuneration had been agreed with 'May' and 'Pip' (2012), I managed to obtain tickets for three matches, Norwich against Wigan (10 March 2012), Wolves (24 March 2012) and Everton (7 April 2012).

While families were present within the Snake Pit the dynamic of the stand was significantly different to the Aviva community stand. The vast majority of the inhabitants were male, aged between twenty and fifty. Approaching a group before the Wigan match, 'Rob,' 'Stu' and 'Paul' (2012), it was clear that they attempted to frame their identity in a way much different to the participants that I had previously engaged with in the Aviva Community stand, giving their fandom different meaning.

Oliver: Looking forward to the game, guys?
'Rob': Alright, mate? Yeah, I'm buzzing.
'Stu': Yeah, mate, feeling good; 6–0 City.
[Group laugh.]
'Paul': F*** off will it be 6–0!
Oliver: I'd be happy with 6–0, but whatever the score, we should win today.
'Paul': We should win every week. I'm not one of these types that turn up for a nice day out. I come here wanting a win *every* week.
Oliver: I know what you mean. I just meant if you look at Wigan's form we should be well in this week.
'Rob': Yeah, Wigan are shite. You were right 'Stu,' it is going to be 6–0.
[Group laugh again.]
'Stu': The funny thing is they know it as well. We went to the away game at the start of the season and they were singing 'we are Wigan, we live in mud huts.'
[Group laughs.]
Oliver: I went to that game too; I thought we were pretty lucky to get a point. Moses could have scored a couple and we did well to hang on that day.
'Rob': We've come a long way since then though, it was first day of the season and you could see the players were nervous. Wigan have got worse too, it's not like they will have that start of the season optimism now.
'Paul': Piss off 'Rob,' don't act like you're a football expert, you're pissed.
Oliver: Is that your normal pre-match routine, a few drinks?
'Stu': I like a few. Just walked up from Weatherspoons and we'll have a couple here before half time.

'Paul':	That's football ... a few drinks with your mates.
'Stu':	It's how it is, right? A day when you don't think about anything else: work or kids or whatever.
Oliver:	Can I ask you what you guys do?
'Stu':	'Rob' and I are teachers, 'Paul' is a business consultant.

While the participants suggest that match days provide them with a shared experience as indicated by the participants within the Aviva Community stand, their collectivity is not described as their motivation for fandom. Contrarily, their fandom challenges the family culture endorsed by the club. The group swear throughout the interview, constantly make jokes, emphasise their drinking rituals and recall stories from away days, explicitly constructing their fandom in correlation with the norms of traditional football culture, evoking the themes Pearson (2012: 38) identifies in his ethnography of 'traditional' Manchester United fans: swearing, 'bantering,' singing and drinking.

Like the fans that I previously interviewed, I argue that the group are highly aware of the discourses surrounding both traditional and capitalist football culture. Like 'Joe' (2012), I argue that their fandom reflects the dual way in which modern fans are encouraged to both positively and negatively identify as consumers. While the group present their identity in opposition to the club's family culture, it is significant that as attendees to both home and away matches, the group still have a relationship of consumption with the club.

While the group appear to have different motivations for fandom than the participants that I had previously engaged with, they similarly draw upon the culture of the club and the wider capitalism of the game to substantiate their identity. McKinley (1997) argues that resistance in fan cultures can only arise if there is a discontinuity between the hegemonic culture and its producers. Significantly the group's fandom draws on both hegemonic discourses surrounding the culture, tradition and capitalism, suggesting that it would be problematic to make a case that their fan identity is resistive in the wider sense. However, as Jenkins (1992) suggests, while there may not be anything empowering about the texts fans draw upon, empowerment can be found in the things that fans do with these texts. Indeed, like the self-identified consumer fans that I had previously engaged with, the group construct their identity, negotiating the way in which the family culture of the club corresponds to their consumer needs. In this context I argue that ironically their *consumer* needs relate to their desire to enact *traditional* identities.

While the previous participants frame their fan identity in correlation with the club's family culture, I argue that the group construct their identity in opposition to the club's family culture providing them with a base culture from which their transgression can be measured and comprehended. Correspondingly, the way in which the group draw upon both dominant discourses within the culture, the game's tradition and its capitalism, in the construction of their fan identity challenges the complex positioning of the modern fan, with the group both positively and negatively presenting *themselves* as consumers. The group acknowledge that they have a consumptive relationship with the club (negative consumption), yet they do so knowingly, in a way that enables them to construct their fan identity against the dominant conception of the consumer fan within the culture and the 'family' fan synonymous with the club.

Throughout the exchange the fans self-identify as traditional fans in opposition to the club's family culture; this indicates that the group construct their identity in relation to their understanding of the discourse surrounding traditional football culture and importantly their perception of what constitutes 'traditional' fan identity. As Sandvoss (2005: 44) argues, fan performances are always constituted between text and context. Taking Norwich City as the text I argue that the group construct their identity in negotiation of Norwich's 'nice, family club' reputation. The concept of carnival can be used as a tool to assess the complex negotiation of the group's identity. Like modern football culture, carnival allows a level of autonomy while regulated by wider constraints. As Foust (2010: 12) argues:

> While raucous, carnival is nonetheless sanctioned by the social order. Transgressions ultimately uphold the dominant regime, even though carnival temporarily violates this.

Bakhtin (1965: 147) can be used to expand upon this ambiguous idea, arguing that the carnival is the place for working out 'in a concretely sensuous, half-real and half-play-acted form, a new mode of interrelationship.' While I argue that their identity draws on the norms of both traditional and capitalist football culture, their identity is formed in negotiation at the juncture of these discourses, creating a 'new mode of interrelationship' with their club in a manner that demonstrates their agency within the culture.

Bakhtin (1965: 147) describes carnival as the people's 'second life;' a highly distorted mirror image of their 'official' life, fashioned from their desire and need for change. I argue that this corresponds to the desire of the group to change the perception of the club but also their intention to enact an identity incongruent to their professional identity. Bakhtin (1965: 148) suggests that carnival is the world 'turned upside down,' where rank is suspended and roles are redistributed. This notion of carnival relates to the discontinuity between the participants' fan identity and their social and economic identity. It is their enactment of traditional fan identities that I consider as the participants' 'second life,' a carnival role they have adopted that belies their everyday position within society with its associated responsibilities as 'teachers' and as 'business consultants' ('Rob' 2012). 'Stu' (2012) develops this notion by indicating that football is a time 'when you don't think about anything else: work or kids or whatever,' enabling the group to leave behind their roles within society to engage in a carnival transgression that belies the culture of the club and their wider social identity.

Parallels can be established between the embodied acts of carnival and the practices of traditional fandom associated with the terraces. Bakhtin (1965: 72) describes the carnival not as a spectacle but as a lived experience evoking the arguments about the legitimacy of the kinetic terrace experience in opposition to the panopticisation of the modern stadium.

Burke (2009: 255) suggests that the two main components of carnival celebration are singing and excessive drinking; 'Todd' and 'Mike' (2012), participants that I interviewed before the Wolves match (24 March 2012), helped me to develop this association. 'Todd' had a bottle of Carling in his hand and it was clear from their expressions and smell that both men had been drinking prior to the interview.

Oliver: So how many are we going to win by today?

'Todd': Two, I reckon. Wolves are fighting for their life at the moment, but we should do 'em.

'Mike': It might be tougher than you think though; the team are going to need us today.

Oliver: Yeah, we should get a good atmosphere going today; we are playing well so I imagine it will be noisy.

'Mike': There's good noise coming from us (Snake Pit) and the Barclay but you never hear anything from the Jarrolds or the N and P (Norwich and Peterborough) stands. They join in with 'On the ball, City' at the start then you don't hear a thing. It annoys me that the whole grounds don't get behind the team.

Oliver: Why is it, do you think, that certain areas of the ground are much quieter? Is there a reason, or is it just the fans want to be inspired by what is on the pitch?

'Mike': Probably that people turn up and want to be entertained; they come and expect a show, but it doesn't work like that. The team do their best to perform and win for you, but you have to perform for them, you know what I mean?

Once again, I initiated conversation by asking the participants about the game, yet 'Mike' (2012) reoriented the conversation to talk about the wider experience of the football event, supporting my argument that fandom serves as a conduit for the participants to address their individual needs. It is the idea of need fulfilment that demonstrates the agency of the modern fan, indicating that their relationship to modern football is negotiated rather than exploitative. Like 'Rob,' 'Stu' and 'Paul' (2012), 'Mike' constructs his fandom in opposition to the club's family fans that merely 'turn up and want to be entertained,' evoking the idea that modern fans are passive consumers.

'Mike's' (2012) suggestion corresponded with my observations that the Aviva Community stand and the Norwich and Peterborough stand are quiet areas of the grounds, not areas from which songs emanate. As he suggests, fans from all around the grounds join in with the customary chorus of 'On the ball, City,' the club's official anthem, yet they largely remain quiet until they become enthused by the performance of the team. My interviews indicate that the family fans are far from passive, yet 'Mike' positions them as consumers that sit back and wait to be entertained. In creating the binary between (his) active traditional fandom and their passive consumer fandom, 'Mike' correlates his fandom with the action of the players on the pitch, describing them symbiotically: 'The team do their best to perform and win for you, but you have to perform for them.'

A common theme throughout the chapter has been the way in which the participants create a link between their fandom and the activity of the players on the pitch. 'Mike' (2012) articulates this idea, indicating that the football event requires both a successful performance by the players and the fans. I argue that this relates to the agency of the modern fan, and, significantly, the idea that they construct their identity knowingly. As Lancaster (2001) indicates, fans articulate their status and autonomy by turning texts of consumption into an activity. In other words, Lancaster suggests that while fans engage in consumptive relationships with texts, they are not passive consumers. He argues that fans have interactive, personal relationships with fan texts in which they actively shape their meanings. The link established by the participants epitomises this concept, in which the association made by the participants demonstrates their ability to construct their own identity within the culture. By associating themselves with the players on the pitch they suggest that they are responsible for the active creation of the football event rather than its consumption. This corresponds to my argument that fans engage in active processes of negotiation in which the football event and the significance attached to it by the fans corresponds to their individual need and sense of self-identity.

At this point we can return to Hutchinson's (1997) historical work surrounding Newcastle United that I document in Chapter 2. Hutchinson (1997: 39) acknowledges the way fans established their sense of identity in the game's bureaucratic era, not just through their sense of affinity to their club but through their active fandom:

> During the late 1890s the Newcastle crowd had turned ... into fans. It was a transformation that was taking place all over Britain... The customers began to recognise and enjoy their own power to affect a match and create atmosphere. They had begun to use their voice.

The correlation between the ways in which both sets of fans constitute their identity in the active association with the players on the pitch again supports my argument that contemporary football culture should not be treated as a separate entity to traditional football culture.

'We are the Snake Pit, we do what we want'

With the significance the participants placed on the 'lived experience' of fandom and their active relationship with the club, I was surprised that a significant minority of the fans within the Snake Pit did not join in with 'On the ball, City' before the start of the Wigan match. I had not noticed this the previous week and it seemed significant. I was keen to explore this to see if it related to the identity of the fans in the Snake Pit. Before the kick off at the Wolves match (24 March 2012) I attempted to quiz fans about it. Even in the Aviva community stand, everyone around me had taken to their feet and had joined in with the anthem. I had taken it for granted that this would be replicated throughout the stadium.

Oliver: You know at the start of the match when the PA signals the start of 'On the ball, City,' it always makes me really excited for the game. Everyone is on their feet and singing, but I noticed last week that a few people in the Snake Pit don't join in. Do you join in and do you know why that is?

'Gaz': Well I join in. I can't speak for anyone else but that is the only song that a lot of the fans know: 'On The Ball, City' and some of the songs about the players. I don't know if it's a thing not to sing the song [in the Snake Pit] but, yeah, most of the crowd do.

While 'Gaz' (2012) admits to singing the song, he provides a possible answer to my question. As he suggests, 'it is the only song that a lot of the fans know.' The chant is recognised by the Football League as the oldest football song on record, dating the song to 1902 (see Eastwood & Davage 1986: 24); subsequently, the chant is well known throughout football culture. The club are very proud of this and seem to have incorporated it into their family culture, using the song as a way to unify the fans through a shared sense of history. I recalled on a previous visit I made to Carrow Road that there were placards tucked into seats throughout the stadium providing the words to the song for new season ticket holders, giving them the 'tools' to join in, presumably, as 'Pam' (2011) suggests, making new fans 'feel part of something' and share in the wider feeling of family that the club endorses.

Once again, before kick-off at the Everton match (7 April 2012), the opening lines of 'On the ball, City' were played over the PA system. While the majority of the stand were on their feet, there was a minority not joining in. I propose that the rejection of the song relates to 'Gaz's' (2012) suggestion that 'it is the song that everyone knows,' endorsed by the club and recognised by the Football League as the club's 'official anthem.' In his study of Manchester United fans, Pearson (2012: 41) suggests that carnival is found in the rejection of club initiatives as their incorporation and perpetuation by the club prohibits their powers of transgression. Following this argument, the rejection of the ritual can be interpreted as a metaphorical rejection of the club's family culture and the club's attempts to promote the culture throughout the stadium. I suggested previously that 'Tom's' (2012) fan identity could be considered in terms of 'authoritarian conformity' (Fromm 1963), with his knowledge of the culture of the club encouraging him to censor his natural expression. The fans' rejection of the club's official anthem can be seen as the inverse of this, with their abstinence marking their rejection of the club's family culture. Indeed, the longer I spent within the stand the more it became apparent the many of the inhabitants actively enacted fandom that was incongruent to the club's family culture, framing their identity in opposition.

The Snake Pit had their own anthems but, unlike 'On the ball, City,' these anthems were not created with the intention of them being incorporated throughout the stadium. I argue that the fans created these songs knowingly in an attempt to emphasise their transgression, juxtaposing their identity to the family fans largely attracted to the club. Parallels can be established with 'Joe' (2012), who knowingly framed his fan identity by drawing on the traditional discourses associated with West Ham. As previously suggested Norwich City does not have the same traditional discourses associated with them, so to position themselves as traditional fans participants within the Snake Pit had to engage in rituals that not only emphasise their opposition to the culture of the club but also show their engagement with the discourses surrounding traditional football culture. While the fans that I engaged with in the Aviva Community stand looked to engage in traditional rituals of family, facilitated by the culture of the club, the fans that I encountered in the Snake Pit looked to engage in traditional rituals associated with the terraces, like 'Joe' (2012), constructing an identity for themselves in negotiation of the club's family culture.

The majority of the songs featured swearing and threats of violence. One such example was the song dedicated to Norwich striker Grant Holt. As indicated by 'Gaz' (2012), songs referring to specific players are generally popular and well known by fans and refer to the player's skill. When a particular player impressed the crowd, it was customary that their song reverberated around the stadium. When Holt scored a late equaliser to earn Norwich a point against Everton, his song could be heard emanating from the Barclay:

> He scored three goals against the scum, Grant Holt. Grant Holt.
> He scored three goals against the scum, Grant Holt. Grant Holt.
> He scored three goals against the scum and Wesley scored the other one.
> Super Grant Holt, Norwich number nine.

While playfully referring to Norwich's rivalry with Ipswich the song is largely inoffensive. After a couple of minutes the song had died down, and at this point the Snake Pit voiced their appreciation:

> Grant Holt. We f***ing love Grant Holt.
> We f***ing love Grant Holt.

This song ignores the signage around the stadium with its crudeness challenging both the family culture and the 'nice' impression of the club upheld within football culture. There were other more extreme examples of this in which aggressive songs were adopted to abuse rival players and officials. When Wigan striker Victor Moses was awarded a cheap free kick for what looks like an elaborate dive, his actions were greeted with boos from the Barclay and City stand, while those close enough to witness the action in the Snake Pit ferociously lambasted him with song: 'Moses, you're a c*nt. Moses, Moses, you're a c*nt.'

I was surprised to hear a chant this crude considering the stand still housed a number of children, however this collective abuse was common throughout my research within the Snake Pit, notably directed at a lineman at the Wolves match (24 March 2012) when his inability to spot an offside decision resulted in a goal for the opposition. Evidently the chanting represents a total rejection of the club's family culture and I was keen to engage with the fans to develop an understanding of their motivations for their performance. At half time at the Wigan (10 March 2012) match I approached 'Dom,' 'Tony' and 'Aaron' (2012). After a brief chat about the events of the half I progressed to the subject of Moses, his dive and the subsequent chant.

Oliver: How bad was that dive by Moses?
'Dom': Shocking.
'Tony': Cheating c*nt.
Oliver: The fans let him know it too.
'Tony': Too right, that was well funny. He looked well upset.
Oliver: There are quite a lot of kids around the stand. The chant was hardly 'family friendly.'
'Aaron': Mate, it's the Snake Pit; they shouldn't be there if they can't handle a bit of swearing. What do they expect?

'Aaron' (2012) seemed surprised by my question, with the retort 'what do they expect' seemingly directed at me. The intonation in his voice put emphasis on the fact that it was 'the Snake Pit,' drawing on the stereotypes associated with the stand to accentuate the 'natural' association between his fan identity and traditional football culture. I argue that this relates to 'Aaron's' intention to construct his identity as a traditional fan. The question was posed almost knowingly, leading me to believe that his response was influenced by my presence as a researcher. I argue that his knowledge of my research and his desire to construct his identity as a traditional fan influenced his response, encouraging him to frame his identity in correlation with his understanding of traditional football culture and the recognition that as a self-identified traditional fan he would be expected to oppose the club's family culture. The way in which 'Aaron' frames his identity supports my argument that modern fans establish their identity in negotiation, with his identity influenced by both his knowledge of the game's tradition and capitalism but also his personal understanding of how he should enact fandom as a self-identified traditional fan.

It is evident from my observations within the Snake Pit that creating an impression and having their identity recognised was a fundamental part of the participants' fandom. As previously suggested, while carnival fans may oppose the family culture of the club, I argue that they fundamentally rely on its order and stability from which their identity can be seen to transgress. Like the carnival itself, I argue that participants rely on the stability of the outside world to experience the excitement of transgression.

While 'Aaron' (2012) seemed particularly keen to emphasis the culture of the Snake Pit in our exchange, it was evident that many of the songs emanating from the stand were sung with the intention of creating an impression of the Snake Pit. When Norwich opened the scoring against Wolves (24 March 2012), the Barclay started a chorus of 'On the ball, City.' Rather than join in with this chant, a significant number of the Snake Pit took to their feet to chant their own anthem: 'We're the Snake Pit, we're the Snake Pit, we're the Snake Pit over here.' I argue that the Snake Pit rejects the club's official anthems to promote their own collective identity. It is significant that the Snake Pit seemed desperate for their transgressions to be acknowledged by the club's family fan groups. Indeed, throughout my time within the Snake Pit, I encountered numerous examples of fans attempting to emphasise their transgression. When Norwich took the lead against Wigan (10 March 2012) a large group of fans remained on their feet. Noticing this, a group of stewards made their way up the concourse to ask them to sit down; their requests were ignored, and the stewards were lambasted with a chorus of defiant song: 'We are the Snake Pit, we do what we want,' signing in protest against modern football's all seating policy, directed against the official custodians of the club's family culture.

Pearson (2012) suggests that 'banter,' 'piss taking' and 'wind ups' define carnival football culture, with fans constantly coming up with new ways to insult others and make football a place where societal norms of politeness are suspended. This seems particularly relevant in relation to the chants emanating from the Snake Pit, with the fans enacting their identity knowingly in transgression. The more time I spent in the Snake Pit, the more it became evident that the fans were keen to create an impression of their fan identity, their songs directly corresponding to the key themes of traditional terrace culture and, significantly, the key themes of carnival.

Other songs of significance related to sex and violence: 'There's only one Tony Martin, one Tony Martin. We shoot burglars, say, we shoot burglars,'[5] and 'Snake Pit boys, we are here, f*** your women and drink your beer.' The songs evoke the stereotypical machismo associated with the terraces, with the fans mobilising this discourse associated with violence and virility to frame their identity in opposition to the club's family culture. Despite efforts to transgress the culture of the club, fundamentally I argue that like the consumer fans that I engaged with in the Aviva Community stand, the identity of those within the Snake Pit is still enacted in negotiation with the club's family culture. As indicated by my exchange with 'Aaron' (2012), I argue that Snake Pit fans seek recognition from the family fans of the club, keen that they acknowledge their behaviour to recognise its incongruity. As suggested, for this to be achieved, the Snake Pit fans engage in a consumptive relationship with the club, becoming part of the club's 'family' to construct their identity in opposition. Again, I argue that this emphasises the way in which Snake Pit fans both positively and negatively identify as consumers.

While the idea of carnival serves as an effective epistemological concept to interpret the motivations of the fans within the Snake Pit perhaps its relevance here is best articulated by Stallybrass and White (1986: 44), who suggest complexly that the carnivalesque both humiliates and mortifies, but also rewards, a duality that Bakhtin (1965: 119) encapsulates in 'the primary carnavalistic act, the mock crowning and subsequent decrowning of the carnival king.' For the fans in the Snake Pit, their transgression gives them the feeling that they are active within the culture, with the enactment of traditional fan identities enabling them to negotiate the 'nice' family culture of the club and their social responsibilities (see 'Rob' and 'Stu' 2012). The carnival image presented by Bakhtin (1965: 119) is highly ambivalent, capturing the complex way in which the fans construct their identity. While their identity revolves around the transgression of the club's family culture, their patronage ensures that it is fundamentally a sanctioned transgression.

While I argue that the Snake Pit can be considered as a carnival space within the stadium, it is significant that these fans are corralled into a specific area of the stadium, indicating that the club are happy to sanction this transgression as long as the fans maintain their relationship of consumption. Similarly, while the fans are active in the construction of their identity, this is not to suggest the family fans necessary interpret their identity in the way that the Snake Pit fans may have intended. Indeed, rather than being feared, recognised or respected for their deviant behaviour, 'Lee' and 'Nick' (2012), the teenagers I shared a joke with, and 'Jack' (2012) in his lamentation of 'Tom's' (2012) identity, indicate that they consider the Snake Pit to be a joke, indicative of an era incongruent with modern football culture and the community fostered by the club.

Negotiated identity

It is significant that both the family fans and carnival fans that I engaged with enact their identity in negotiation with the culture of the club and the discourses surrounding the game's traditional culture. While this may not challenge the hegemony of the game's modern capitalism or help to shatter the aura surrounding the game's traditional culture, I argue that the way in which the fans negotiate their identity emphasises their agency.

This chapter emphasises the significance of analysing contemporary football culture with a consumer-oriented cultural studies approach, treating Norwich City as a 'text' to analyse the different ways in which fans substantiate their identity in patronage of the club. The fans demonstrate that they are active in their consumption, using the culture of the club as a conduit to address their individual consumer needs. While the family fans and the Snake Pit fans indicate that they have palpably different motivations for fandom, the chapter argues that the fans engage in a similar process of identity formation in which they substantiate their identity by negotiating the hegemonic discourses surrounding the culture, capitalism and tradition, with the unique identity of the fans similarly influenced by their different levels of identification with the club's family culture and their individual needs as consumers.

My argument is that the different ways in which the fans negotiate their identity corresponds to their desire to enact a specific type of fan identity; the family fans identifying with the culture of the club for the way in which it enables them to engage in rituals of family, while the Snake Pit fans recognise that to substantiate their identity as 'legitimate' fans they need to emphasise their transgression, 'buying into' the club's 'wider family' to emphasise their incongruity.

Notes

1 Reference to Bobby Moore, England's World Cup winning captain.
2 This reference to the club's academy alludes to the continued relationship between the club and the community. Notable players from the local community to come through the West Ham academy include Frank Lampard, Joe Cole, Rio Ferdinand and Mark Noble.
3 In 2006, 2007 and 2010 Norwich City have been awarded prizes from the Football League for their creative 'Community and Family' initiatives. In 2008 the club won the prestigious title of 'Best Family Club in English Football.' The fans were deemed the 'Best Behaved' in the Premier League for the 2011/2012 and 2012/2013 season.
4 Words pronounced with a twang similar to the traditional Somerset accent.
5 A song in reference to Norfolk farmer Tony Martin, who shot and killed a young burglar that he caught trying to break into his house.

Bibliography

Bakhtin, M (1965) *Rabelais and His World*. Bloomington. Indiana University Press.

Bale, J (1998) 'Virtual Fandoms: Futurescapes of Football' Cited in Brown, A *Fanatics: Power, Identity and Fandom in Football*. London. Routledge.

Barker, C (2004) *The Sage Dictionary of Cultural Studies*. London. Sage.

Barr, W (2009) *Real Football Real Fans: A Journey to the Heart of Football*. London. Morrow & Co.

Brimson, D (1998) *The Geezers Guide to Football: A Lifetime of Lads and Lager*. London. Mainstream Publishing.

Burke, P (2009) *Popular Culture in Early Modern Europe*. Farnham. Ashgate Press.

Eastwood, J & Davage, M (1986) *Canary Citizens*. Cambridge. Almeida.

Fiske, J (1992) 'The Cultural Economy of Fandom' Cited in Lewis, L *The Adoring Audience*. London. Routledge.

Foust, C (2010) *Transgression as a Mode of Resistance*. California. Lexington.

Fromm, E (1963) *Fear of Freedom*. London. Routledge.

Fynn, A & Guest, L (1994) *Out of Time: Why Football isn't Working*. London. Simon & Schuster Press.

Gasper, P (2005) *The Communist Manifesto: A Road Map to History's Most Important Document*. Illinois. Haymarket Books.

Gasper, P (2010) *Capitalism and Alienation*. Socialist Solidarity [Website] Available from: http://socialistsolidarity.ca/alienation.html (Accessed 20 November 2014).

Giulianotti, R (2002) Supporters, Fans and Flaneurs: Taxonomy of Spectator Identities in Football. *Journal of Sport and Social Issues* 26 (1) 25–46.
Hills, M (2002) *Fan Cultures*. London. Routledge.
Hutchinson, R (1997) *The Toon: A Complete History of Newcastle United.* Edinburgh. Mainstream Publishing.
Imlach, G (2005) *My Father and Other Working-Class Football Heroes*. London. Yellow Jersey Press.
Ingle, S (2005) Football Fans Are Idiots. *The Guardian* [Website] Available from: http://www.theguardian.com/football/2005/sep/02/sport.blueprintforabetterfootball (Accessed 23 October 2011).
Jameson, F (1991) *Postmodernism or the Cultural Logic of Late Capitalism.* London. Verso.
Jenkins, H (1992) *Textual Poachers: Television Fans and Participatory Culture*. New York. Routledge.
King, A (2002) *The End of the Terraces: The Transformation of English Football in the 1990's*. London. Leicester University Press.
Lancaster, K (2001) *Interacting with Babylon 5*. Austin. University of Texas Press.
Marx, K (1932) *Economic and Philosophic Manuscripts of 1844*. Moscow. Progress.
McKinley, EG (1997) *Beverly Hills 90210: Television, Gender and Identity*. Philadelphia. University of Pennsylvania Press.
Pearson, G (2012) *An Ethnography of English Football Fans: Cans, Cops and Carnivals.* Manchester. Manchester University Press.
Sandvoss, C (2005) *Fans*. Cambridge. Polity.
Stallybrass, P & White, A (1986) *The Politics and Poetics of Transgression*. New York. Cornell University Press.
Thornton, S (1995) *Club Cultures: Music, Media and Subcultural Capital.* Cambridge. Polity.
Walsh, A & Giulianotti, R (2001) This Sporting Mammon: A Normative Critique of the Commodification of Sport. *Journal of the Philosophy of Sport* 28 (1) 53–77.
Weed, M (2008) Exploring the Sport Spectator Experience: Virtual Football Spectatorship in the Pub. *Soccer and Society* 9 (2) 189–197.

Chapter 5

MK Dons

Fear and loathing in Milton Keynes

> As if you're looking at 'Franchise United.' If you are researching football fans why are you looking at them? They aren't even a real football club, they don't have *real fans*. No one takes them, seriously do they?
>
> ('Craig' 24 November 2011)

Milton Keynes Dons have been selected for analysis as they are said to represent the first example of a 'franchise football club,' starting life as Wimbledon before being purchased and relocated by venture capitalist Pete Winkelman, re-branding the club to maximise its commercial potential and appeal to the under serviced population of the city. Wimbledon were without a stadium base in South-West London and had very few active fans, but the departure of the club from its locality and its subsequent re-branding is condemned by sport's scholars and rival fans for threatening the 'blood and soil' heritage of football culture and the deep historical traditions of the game as outlined in Chapter 2 (see Crampsey 1990; Imlach 2005; Devine 2012). The commercial imperative informing the relocation and re-branding of the club has seen the club continually cited as a metaphor for the cultural reorientation of English football and the game's assimilation with capitalism.

The club has become the target of much animosity, with the criticism directed towards the Dons following the imperative of the nostalgic literature that Winkelman actively looked to replace the 'fans' associated with Wimbledon with affluent new 'consumers' in Milton Keynes (see Fynn & Guest 1994; Bale 1998; Brimson 1998; Burgess 2005; Conn 2005; Ingle 2005; Pearson 2012).

The epigraph, a quotation from 'Craig,' a Chelsea fan that participated in my research (see Chapter 6) epitomises the general way in which the club and their fans are presented. It is my argument that Dons' fans can be considered as the most marginalised group within football culture. In correlation with the social justice element of my research and my aim to assimilate football scholarship with cultural studies, this chapter looks to provide Dons' fans with a platform to articulate how, as fans of a 'franchise football club,' they comprehend their *own* fandom in a culture that largely rejects their existence.

This chapter analyses the complex fandom of the participants in response to their unique position within the culture. First, I explore the ways in which the fans have developed a strong sense of togetherness, embracing the club's attempts to 'build community.' The fans internalise the idea of community perpetuated by the club, developing strong internal bonds with fellow fans to create support networks in the face of the constant adversity they face from the game's wider culture. The fans are aware of the business decisions that led to the club's inception, accepting the club's commercial origins, expressing their appreciation of Winkelman's (2012a) vision to provide the city with a 'world-class stadium,' a 'focus of the community for sport and music.' I argue that the football club acts as a totem for the city, serving the function that Winkelman had envisioned by becoming a monument around which community is enacted and formed.

It is significant that the fans accept the commercial origins of the club but largely refuse to acknowledge it's associated with Wimbledon, emphasising its status as a 'new football club.' I argue that this tension corresponds to the complex ways in which modern fans are both positively and negative positioned as consumers, with the fans positively self-identifying as consumers in support of Winkelman's community building project, while denying the club's association with Wimbledon as a defence against the way in which they are negatively positioned as consumers by wider football culture.

The second part of the chapter focuses on the explosive derby between the Dons and AFC Wimbledon, the team established by the Wimbledon Supporters Association, considered to represent the rebirth of Wimbledon. The teams met for the first time in the second round of the FA Cup (2 December 2012). The contest created a frenzy within the game's wider culture in which the match was presented as a moral contest between the game's tradition (AFC Wimbledon) and the game's consumerism (MK Dons). While the Dons' fans that I initially engaged with tried to downplay their association with Wimbledon, the derby match saw the fans actively drawing on the association of the clubs, again mobilising the idea of 'community,' to demonstrate their support of Winkelman and the commercial decisions that lead to the club's inception while also goading AFC Wimbledon about the processes that resulted in the dissolution of *their* club and *their* community.

There is fascinating tension here that involves the fans both engaging with and ignoring the history of their club and its relationship to Wimbledon that revolves around the conflicting ways that the fans draw upon the idea of community, evoking the nostalgic idea that football clubs 'belong to' and reflect the character of the local community. In doing so the fans both emphasise their legitimacy as a 'new football club' and status as a franchise. I argue that the Dons' fans have a flexible fandom, effortlessly slipping between the roles of both victim and aggressor within the culture, at one moment making passionate arguments for the club to be viewed in its own right, about the unique community fostered by Winkelman, the next making jokes about the collapse of the community surrounding Wimbledon, drawing on the processes that led to their club's creation.

This chapter explores the complex relationship between Dons' fans as agents and the structural confines of the game's capitalism and tradition, the first discourse leading to their club's creation, the second influencing their constant marginalisation and exclusion from the game's wider culture. Lash (2007: 59) argues regarding the concept of hegemony that 'the preponderant influence or domination of one nation over another' was the concept that crystallised cultural studies as a discipline. Indeed, part of the rationale for selecting MK Dons for analysis is the way in which the club is marginalised within the culture. I argue that the discourses of capitalism and tradition still exert 'power over' the modern fan, however as indicated with Norwich fans in the previous chapter, fans are able to negotiate these discourses and impart them in the construction of their own identity, an idea I explore in relation to the Dons' fans and their different engagement with the 'community' culture of their club.

'You dirty franchise bastards'

In the 1990s, the FA made a concerted effort to encourage the middle-classes, families and young women to watch live football. In the wake of the Hillsborough disaster and the terrible reputation of the game developed throughout the 1980s (see Baudrillard 1993; Hussey 2005; Symanski & Zimbalist 2006; Barnes 2007). The FA were aware of the financial and cultural gains clubs could make by attracting families and women to the sport, recognising their improved social stake, financial independence and decision-making role within the family (Williams 2000: 99). King (2002: 91) associates these developments with the commercial logic of wider leisure industries, suggesting that attracting new fans significantly improved attendance figures, generating more revenue for clubs in terms of merchandising and the sale of ancillary branded products, while also helping to implement middle-class club cultures. It is against this backdrop of football's modern capitalism that the relocation and the re-branding of Wimbledon was posed and subsequently sanctioned. The club was sold to Pete Winkelman in 2002, who for many years harboured the vision of introducing league football to Milton Keynes.[1] Winkelman's proposal to make the club the focus of the community for world-class sport and music events corresponded perfectly with the FA's commercial logic and desire to position football in line with wider leisure industries. The newly built Stadium MK has notably hosted Olympic Football as part of London 2012, was selected as a venue to host the Rugby World Cup 2015, was selected as the host venue for England's 2018 failed World Cup bid, while annually chosen as the site of *Collectormania*, an internationally renowned sci-fi convention.

Fundamentally, Wimbledon was unprofitable as a football club. With the team well established in the Premier League attendances peaked at 18,235 in the 1998/1999 season, however paying attendance declined dramatically, falling by two thirds over the next two seasons, the club attracting an average crowd of 6,961 the season of their relegation in 2000/2001. Before the club's relocation in 2003, Wimbledon was averaging only 1,145 fans. The fate of the club can be considered a 'phantom menace' (Sandvoss 2005: 150), the breakdown of the projective relationship between fan and fan object. The move was sanctioned on cultural grounds with the belief that the creation of the club would enrich the city of Milton Keynes, providing the inhabitants with more leisure opportunities and create jobs, while also generating more revenue for the FA and local businesses.

While the origins of the Dons are commercial, this is not to say that the relationship between the club and its fans becomes a purely market-based relationship without complexity. A key feature of football's new capitalism, and its targeting of a middle-class fan base, has been the widespread adoption of 'community initiatives,' which involves clubs seeking to promote themselves as a positive feature of the local community. A year after the club's inception, Winkelman created the MK Dons Sport and Education Trust with the aim of substantiating the club within the community, developing 'quality, innovative and inclusive sporting, educational, social and healthy lifestyle opportunities' (MK Dons Sport and Educational Trust 2014), something that has garnered the club and Winkelman much recognition. In 2012 the club was awarded the accolade of 'Community Club of the Year,' while Winkelman was awarded an honorary doctorate in 2013 for his commitment to 'education and community building through football' (The Open University 2013).

Falcous and Rose (2005: 12) are highly sceptical about these initiatives, describing them as ideological projects to 'mask and legitimise the reformulation of the community-sport relationship,' generalising and naturalising the interests of private capital to appear in the public good. Indeed, it is this argument that was posited against the club by the Wimbledon Supporters Association; they argue that the communal 'benefits' of the club's relocation to the people of Milton Keynes comes at the expense of the community already established around the club, causing its community in Wimbledon to disband. The association evokes the nostalgic principle that a football club centres around a natural sense of community and collective meaning and that fandom is formed around a shared geographical rootedness rather than shared consumer demand (see Crampsey 1990; Imlach 2005; Devine 2012).

Current chairman of the Scottish FA, Neil Doncaster (cited by Williams 2000), develops this principle and has often been openly critical about the creation of the Dons. Doncaster suggests that the vitriol directed towards the club stems from the fear they inspire in wider football fans, that after decades of clubs establishing community and 'proud histories' it could all be eradicated in the pursuit of greater financial gains and commercial opportunity. Evoking Imlach's (2005) binary between sports culture in England and America documented in Chapter 2, Doncaster (cited by Williams 2000: 119) suggests that:

> (English Football) is in a dangerous and frightening time when as in the USA rich men like Winkelman can easily buy and sell clubs and use them

> as investments and their playthings... What happened with Wimbledon and the dispersal of their community should never be forgotten.

Doncaster (cited by Williams 2000) encapsulates the feeling of powerlessness associated with the collapse of Wimbledon. While his argument focuses on the club, he speaks nostalgically about the wider de-territorialisation of contemporary football, with the relocation of the club becoming analogous for the reorientation of the game and how power has been stripped from the fans. The Wimbledon fans were powerless to stop the demise of their club, akin to the argument that 'traditional' fans are powerless to stop the commercialisation of wider football culture.

It is significant that Doncaster (cited by Williams 2000) suggests that 'What happened with Wimbledon and the dispersal of their community should never be forgotten.' If, as I argue, Wimbledon is analogous for traditional football culture, then his rebuke of the processes that resulted in the creation of the Dons can also be considered as a celebration of traditional football culture when power was said to reside with the fans. Following this argument, I maintain that fans within the culture look to enact power by opposing the existence of the Dons, engaging in traditional fan performances such as sustained protests that I have witnessed on each of my visits to the Stadium MK. Fans look to enact a level of autonomy rarely afforded to them in modern football culture by mobilising themselves against the Dons.

Cherry (2002) argues that being a fan in contemporary consumer society requires commitment in the face of dominant opposition; in football culture this can be seen as both the dominance of capitalism and the discourse of 'traditional' football culture that is mobilised by those that oppose the club's existence. 'Steve' (2012), a participant in my research, outlines his concerns about bringing his young son to matches due to fears of recrimination from away fans there 'just to have a pop' at them, suggesting that the atmosphere outside the ground could at times seem hostile and intimidating. By engaging in such protest, I argue that the fans send a constant reminder to the ruling bodies of English football that they still have an active role within the culture and as Doncaster (cited by Williams 2000: 119) suggests, the history of Wimbledon and the dispersal of their community will 'never be forgotten.'

While fans mobilise in opposition to the Dons, as suggested, Wimbledon was failing as a business, incurring huge debts and continually operating with losses. In the two seasons preceding Winkelman's take over, Wimbledon had incurred losses of over £8 million (MK Dons Supporters Association 2014). While the relocation of the club is used to exemplifying the de-territorialisation of modern football and the powerlessness of traditional fans, it could be argued that in their falling attendance, the fans symbolically relinquished their stake within the club, handing both the incentive of relocation and power to the club's owners, a principle that is developed later within the chapter. The independent commission ordered by the FA to assess the sale and relocation of the club vindicate this argument, suggesting that there was no longer a stable sense of community associated with the club. Accordingly, relocation was deemed the only viable option for the club's continuation:

> We do not believe, with all due respect, that the club's links with the community around the Plough Lane site or in Merton are so profound, or the roots go so deep, that they will not survive a necessary transplant to ensure Wimbledon's survival. What is unusual about Wimbledon fans is that they do not seem to come from a single geographical area. Indeed, the vast majority of Wimbledon fans do not live in Merton or Wimbledon. 20% of current season ticket holders live in Merton and 10% in Wimbledon. We do not accept that Wimbledon will die if the club relocates. The club has been in Croydon for 11 years (almost half its Football League history). There is no stadium which is a focus for the community in Merton and has not been for 11 years.
>
> (Walmsley 2010)

The Dons are a unique case. While Falcous and Rose (2005) consider community building initiatives as negative attempts to 'reformulate' the community–sport relationship, it is equally possible to interpret the inception of the Dons as an attempt to create, re-establish and save the community associated with the club. The Dons' fans that I interviewed were adamant that the club should be considered unique in its own right; the Dons a separate club with a separate history to Wimbledon. In this context it would be wrong to suggest that the establishment of the Dons 'reformulated' or disbanded the community–sport relationship established between Wimbledon and its locality but alternatively the creation of the club can be considered to mark the onset of a sporting culture within Milton Keynes.

Second, Falcous and Rose (2005: 12) suggest that these projects 'mask ... and naturalise the interests of private capital,' however my research suggests that the fans accept and understand the processes that led to the club's creation and appreciate football's capitalism for enabling league football to be established in the city. The fans have a 'particular commitment' (Cherry 2002) to the club and its community-building project in which their understanding of the processes that led to the club's creation are foundational to their fandom.

The community project

Rather than being oblivious to the processes Falcous and Rose outline (2005), my research suggests that the Dons' fans identify with the club's attempts to build community, recognising the club's need to establish communality, figured in patronage to secure its long-term financial future and vindicate the decisions that lead to the club's creation. 'Matt' (2012) articulates these ideas, demonstrating both an appreciation of the business strategy of the club, tapping into the largely un-serviced local community, but also the unique sense of community that the club have fostered as a 'franchise.' Having initially been attracted to the club as a consumer and lured in by cheap ticket prices, 'Matt' suggests that he has subsequently become a season ticket holder, regularly taking his son to matches.

Oliver: What attracted you to the Dons? Was there something that made you want to come to live matches?

'Matt': Well, I've always been a big fan of football, but around here there is only Luton and I was never that bothered with them. I just watch the games on TV. Most of my friends have other teams and go into London to see West Ham and Arsenal, but I've never had a team really.

Oliver: So, the creation of the club gave you a team to support?

'Matt': Well, sort of. I was interested when the idea of the club was first talked about, it caused a bit of excitement around the city, but to be honest it wasn't as if I got caught up in it or really thought about being a fan or getting involved at that point.

Oliver: Why was that?

'Matt': Well, I hadn't really gone to many games before and you know how it is; I was comfortable watching on telly. Then with all the controversy and that surrounding it, I didn't really know how I felt about it.

Oliver: Do you mean the processes that led to the club's creation?

'Matt': Well, there is still a lot of anger directed towards the club, and I didn't really know how I felt about it … I didn't want to get caught up in it.

Oliver: In that case, what happened? I have been speaking to some fans who were saying that you get a lot of away fans here looking to cause trouble and at times there can be a bit of an aggressive atmosphere around the place. What changed your mind to make you want to come here?

'Matt': It was curiosity really. I was coming to IKEA (on the retail part adjacent to the stadium) and saw a billboard advertising tickets for a fiver or something, and thought why not? For the price, it was a good opportunity to watch football.

Oliver: Did the game ease your concerns? Or was it more a case of just enjoying the experience.

'Matt': It was both really. The game was really poor; I think we lost 3–1, but, yeah, it was good to be there. It wasn't the atmosphere I was expecting … the club works hard to get the community behind the team and you get a lot of young children and families. I think it gives the place a good feel to it. There is so much negativity surrounding the club but when you come here it's the opposite really and people just seem happy to be here and watch football.

Oliver: Walking around the stadium I saw posters offering 'kids for a quid' (ticket deals) and I have noticed a lot more women and children than at other clubs I have been to.

'Matt': The club does deals like that all the time. If it's a mid-week game or one of the smaller teams in the division, they usually do the cheap tickets

and it definitely helps to boost the attendance. A couple of months ago they did a ladies' day, and did a deal for a ticket, a champagne party with a meal and karaoke after the match … I've never seen anything like it at a football match.

Oliver: Do you think the club actively looks to attract more young families and women? Is there a strategy behind it?

'Matt': At the end of the day I think it is about getting people into the stadium. If you think about it, it was a business decision to bring the club here. If you think about it, this is a new club; people are just really keen for it to work out and to get behind it … Especially by trying to get the kids into the club, it's like the club are trying to secure their long-term future. Get them in at an early age and get them passionate about the club. As I said, it worked with me. I brought my boy to one of these cheap nights and he loved it; he comes to games with me now, and has the kit and all the merchandise.

'Matt' (2012) astutely identifies the commercial orientation of the club, referring to the processes that led to the club's inception, recognising the need for the club to justify its creation and appeal to the large catchment area unserved by league football. Throughout the conversation he assimilates the club with wider capitalism, demonstrating how he understand and identifies with the club's commercial initiatives: 'I saw on the billboard tickets being advertised for a fiver,' 'the club works hard to get the community behind the team and attract a lot of young children and families with cheap deals,' 'at the end of the day I think it is about getting people into the stadium' and 'if you think about it, it was a business decision to bring the club here.'

'Matt' (2012) self-identifies as a 'consumer fan,' outlining how he was attracted to the club, not by an 'indescribable sense of emotional attachment' or 'family lineage,' the traditional ways in which fandom is conceived (see Imlach 2005), but by an advertisement on a billboard in a retail park. However, far from being a 'corporate dupe' (see Brimson 1998; Lee 1998; Conn 2005; Ingle 2005), 'Matt' recognises that his patronage, and particularly that of families and young supporters, are vital to the club's existence and future prosperity. 'Matt' (2012) punctuates this with the example of his son, recognising that it is in the club's interest to cater to younger fans, both to secure the long-term future of the club to 'get them (children) in at an early age' but also to increase their revenue by appealing to the lucrative family market, with potential for greater expenditure: 'he ('Matt's' son) comes to games with me now, and has the kit and all the merchandise.'

Sandvoss (2005: 13) argues that while fan texts may be commodities fundamentally generating revenue for capitalist industries, they are appropriated by fans for their use value. Rather than feel exploited by the ways in which the club look to generate revenue, I argue that 'Matt' (2012) accepts the business strategy of the club and the capitalism of the game as part of the process in which the community have been afforded the chance to watch live football. The Dons' fans' acceptance of the game's capitalism is something that I have not encountered before and seems unique to them as a club, something that I believe relates to their status as a 'new' football club, conceived as a product of the game's capitalism. Gasper (2005) argues that capitalism has become an all-encompassing framework for modern life. 'Matt's' responses show an appreciation of this, indicating that he accepts the capitalism of modern football, internalising the club's agenda and imparting it in his understanding of fandom.

'Matt' (2012) describes his fandom as fulfilling a function, figuring the relationship between the club and the community as mutually beneficial. He indicates that the creation of the club provided him with *his own* club to support, providing him with the incentive to leave the house ('I just use to watch it on TV') and experience live matches. Bale (1998) and Weed (2008) explicitly assimilate the modern stadium experience to the 'passive' process of watching football on television, yet 'Matt' describes his fandom as an active process, both in support of the team, physically engaging with the live experience, and in patronage to the club, presenting his fandom as a form of financial support. In this sense 'Matt' evokes the discourses surrounding the disbanding of Wimbledon, creating a juxtaposition between his active, consumptive fandom and the passive, 'traditional' fandom that resulted in the club's dissolution. However, it is poignant that 'Matt' creates this distinction without making a direct reference to the club itself.

Following this argument, it is significant that the terms used by 'Matt' (2012) throughout the exchange draw upon the sense of community engendered by the club's creation: 'The club works hard to get the community behind the team,' 'you get a lot of young children and families here,' 'it is about getting people into the stadium,' 'it's like the club are trying to secure their long-term future,' 'it caused … excitement around the city' and 'I think people are just really keen for it to work out and to get behind it.' These expressions accentuate the active attempts of the club to 'work hard' and foster community around the club, while 'Matt' indicates that the community are similarly active in their coalescence around the project. This idea is encapsulated by 'Matt's' (2012) description of the atmosphere within the stadium:

> There is a lot of negativity surrounding the club but when you actually get inside the ground it's the opposite really and people seem excited to be here and watch football.

Seen as the 'bastard franchise' of Wimbledon, the club is scorned as the antithesis of the game's tradition yet, as suggested, the Dons' fans' self-identify as consumers, recognising their fandom as a product of the commercial processes that led to the club's inception. 'Matt's' (2012) enthusiastic description of the club's 'ladies' day' can be used to explore this binary. The nostalgic literature openly criticises the influx of women in contemporary football culture for 'feminising' and 'sanitising' the game (Brimson 1998; Hopcraft 2006; Wilson 2006). As Thornton (1995: 135) argues, in fan culture there is always a double articulation of the low and the feminine, in which 'other' cultures are continuously characterised as feminine, and feminine cultures are devalued as imitative and passive. Yet 'Matt' recognises the commercial intent informing the event, as an opportunity for the club to build community, describing it as an opportunity to 'get more people to the football club.' 'Matt' (2012) describes the event like nothing he had 'seen at a football match before.' In doing so I argue that he acknowledges the unique position of the club.

The club, like the event, operates with a capitalist agenda; without an established fan community to draw upon, the club look to implement commercial strategies that help to garner support from the local catchment area, directly marketing themselves as a leisure resource, evoking the way in which fans are positively positioned as consumers. Correspondingly the ways in which the club look to create community are central to the participants' understanding of their fandom, in which their awareness of the processes that led to the club's creation gives them a sense of responsibility with community formed in support of the project and figured in sustained patronage. I argue that this exemplifies the complex relationship between the fans and the club in which their fandom, while active and informed, operates within the structural confines of capitalism and the processes that led to the club's creation (see Jenkins 1992; Hills 2002; Sandvoss 2005). While the capitalist orientation of the club may require a 'particular commitment' (Cherry 2002) from the fans, Fiske (1991) questions: are pleasures of fandom necessarily constructed in opposition to the dominant power system?

'Kate' (2012) helps to develop this point; she is aware of the commercial agenda of the club, assimilating it with the retail park on which the ground is situated, acknowledging the way in which the fans are targeted as consumers yet stating that she is happy to support the club for providing the community with enrichment. Her response suggests that like the participants in Ang (1985) and Radway's (1984) studies, her pleasure as a fan comes as a result of the capitalist orientation of the text, in this case, the football club. This vindicates my argument that 'support' of the club relates to the players on the pitch but also the processes that led to the club's creation:

> The club is trying to build something. It's a new club and it is trying to create its own history. As a new club it has nothing to fall back on, so it is really important that the club creates that feeling of togetherness with the supporters, it's always trying to bring new people in and establish ties with the surrounding communities ... The club has always been honest with us. We know how the club came to the city and Pete (Winkelman) is an entrepreneur at the end of the day. The club is part of his empire and fits with the retail park surrounding the ground, but you have to remember that it was a risk to bring football here. You know all the controversy it has caused, and Pete stuck his neck out to do this ... Just look at the crowd. You can see that it gets good support from the fans ... we get around 13,000 every week. I think people are just really happy to have something like this in the city ...

> there's nowhere I'd rather be every other Saturday and despite all the stick we get, the fans rally round the club and show our support.
>
> ('Kate' 2012)

Like 'Matt' (2012), 'Kate' (2012) possesses an astute understanding of the commercial processes that led to the club's creation. She demonstrates her comprehension of the nostalgic arguments posed within contemporary football culture, acknowledging modern football's association with wider commercial and leisure industries by reference to the retail park in which the club is situated and 'fits perfectly,' and entrepreneurial ownership, accentuating the idea that the club is merely a part of 'Pete's empire.' While framing the commercial origins of the club she similar indicates that the club receives wide support from the local community, '13,000 every week,' indicating that the fan community of the Dons accept and appreciate the commercial origins of the club for providing the city with a valuable leisure resource and somewhere to be 'every other Saturday.'

It is significant that like 'Matt' (2012), 'Kate' (2012) speaks openly about the club striving to *create* community. This compliments my argument that the fans knowingly define themselves as consumers with their fandom directly inspired by the corporate orientation of the club. As I have previously argued, the fact that the fans find pleasure from capitalist texts does not mean that they are corporate dupes. Indeed, de Certeau (1984) describes life under capitalism as the constant struggle to make meaning from that which is imposed upon us. Taking this into account I argue that Dons' fans can be assimilated with Radway's (1984) participants who immersed themselves in romance novels to create an 'autonomous temporal space,' to achieve a form of emancipation and escape from their everyday routine. Similarly, Dons' fans can be considered to engage with the club to help develop a space of communality, a focus for the community in which they can coalesce while largely 'autonomous,' both ideologically as a franchise and temporally as a 'new club' from wider football culture.

'Kate' (2012) emphasises the idea that 'the club has always been very honest' with the fans. I argue that the fans in their articulations of fandom reflect this honesty. By being transparent about the business decisions that led to the creation of the club and the complete re-branding and relocation of Wimbledon, the club perpetuates the idea constantly promoted by Winkelman in his media appearances that the Dons are a *new* club looking to create their own history (see Hayes 2013). The club took the sensible measure of handing all memorabilia associated with Wimbledon back to the Supporters Association, symbolically severing all ties with their history, a particularly astute part of the club's business strategy. First, by severing all ties with Wimbledon and emphasising the infancy of the project, as something *unique* to Milton Keynes, the club effectively helped to ease any sense of guilt from the fans who are constantly told by the wider culture that they are ersatz with disingenuous claims to fandom. As 'Matt' (2012) suggests, he was initially deterred from engaging with the club due to the controversy surrounding it and the fear of recrimination. Second, by accentuating the infancy of the Dons, the club perpetuates its connection with the community. The club is no longer associated with Wimbledon or the borough of Merton but perceived to be a unique club to cater *specifically to* Milton Keynes and the surrounding community, something that they can take ownership of to build and develop.

I believe that this accounts for the way in which the fans explicitly ignore the existence of Wimbledon in our exchanges, with the narrative of struggle helping them to establish a sense of solidarity with the club; as 'Kate' (2012) suggests, 'Pete stuck his neck on the line to get the club here' and subsequently 'the community get behind it.'

Sandvoss (2005) argue that fans develop strategies and tactics, enabling them to construct their own meanings from the objects of their fandom. In this context, accepting the commercial origins of the club enables the fans to psychologically take ownership of the Dons. The way in which the fans recognise the need of the club to 'build community' suggests that they are aware that the failure of Wimbledon's fan community to support the team resulted in the club's dissolution, yet it is key that the supports do not directly reference this. In the statement issued by the Wimbledon Supporters Association outlining their opposition to the disbanding and relocation of the club, they use the arguments perpetuated by those that oppose football's modern capitalism, that the identity of a football club is bound to its community:

> The basis on which British football was founded is the affinity between the club and the locality in which it plays. A club … is the property of its community and its fans.
>
> (White 2003)

I argue that the fans astutely draw upon this idea, playfully drawing on the game's traditional culture while similarly emphasising their status as a capitalist football club. By engaging with the commercial origins of the Dons, internalising it as a 'new club,' the fans are able to accept it as something intrinsic to Milton Keynes. By accepting the idea that the club is 'new,' the fans internalise the idea that there is an affinity between the club and the community, a point that is reinforced by the narrative of struggle that underpins the creation of the club.

Fiske (1991) argues that fans engage in polysemic readings with the texts of their fandom enabling them to distinguish themselves from 'normal audiences.' I argue that the fans that I interviewed engage in 'strategies and tactics' (Sandvoss 2005) that enable them to accept the commercial origins of the club, despite the opposition they face from the game's 'normal audience,' forming community based on a sense of togetherness between the club and the service it provides. I argue that it is this mutual understanding of the processes that led to the creation of the club and the fans' willingness to support the project that has encouraged the fans to accept the community-building project of the club. In his study of Bruce Springsteen fans, Cavicchi (1998) argues that fans create community not through shared experiences but through a mutual shared expectation of experience, that leads to fans engaging in a shared appropriation of their object of fandom. In the context of the Dons, I believe that fans share an expectation of the opportunity afforded to the community resulting from the club's creation, with the inception of the club providing the city with a world-class leisure venue. Similarly, the Dons' fans are unified in the animosity that they face from wider football culture in which they are seen as 'Nazis' within the culture (see Gilroy 2004). It is this shared sense of expectation and positioning by the wider culture that has encouraged the formation of the tight-knit community around the club. As Cavicchi (1998: 38) suggests, the shared expectation and positioning of the fans 'shapes the tenor and quality of interactions not only with each other but with other non-fans.'

The 'W' word

It is refreshing that the fans possess a pragmatic view of commercial football culture, yet I am cautious not to overstate the representativeness of their response and the validity of my interpretation. As Falcous and Rose (2005: 12) stipulate, criticism of traditional fandoms and resistance to more rational approaches to capital accumulation as reactionary and anachronistic is often the retort used by those seeking to justify transformations within sport cultures. Equally the responses I received could have been measures to defend the integrity of the club and the legitimacy of the participants' fandom to an outsider, someone that does not share the same 'expectations' and positioning within the culture (see Cavicchi 1998). While 'Matt' (2012) and 'Kate' (2012) engage with the commercial origins of the club to substantiate the idea that the Dons are a 'new' football club, it is problematic that they rely on the past narrative of how the club was formed to substantiate these claims. While they do not make references to Wimbledon specifically, I argue that any reference to the club's origins and the 'efforts' made to bring the club to Milton Keynes implicitly evokes the history and demise of Wimbledon. Consequently, while I have highlighted the strategy implemented by the club to promote the infancy of the Dons, encouraging certain expectations from the fans, it is significant that the participants seem to go out of their way to ignore the existence of Wimbledon. Indeed, many of the fans I approached, particularly preceding the derby match with AFC Wimbledon, were very uncomfortable talking about the club. At the more accommodating end of the scale I was playfully reprimanded for using the '"W" word' ('Kane' 2012), while a significant number of fans refused to talk to me if I made reference to the club. It became clear that this was an uncomfortable topic with a few groups particularly aggrieved that I formed the association. I was told to 'f*** off' on several occasions. To an extent I expected this. As suggested, the fans constantly face criticism from wider football culture and as an outsider I understand why I was treated with a level of suspicion. Again, this alludes to their strong sense of insular community, to which my attempts to engage with the fans about a 'grey area' ('Steve' 2012) in their history were seen as a challenge to their community, an example of the way in which Cavicchi (1998) suggests that a sense of community affects the way in which fans engage with outsiders.

'Steve's' (2012) use of the term 'grey area' is very fitting, encapsulating the tension in the way in which the Dons' fans seem to both simultaneously engage with and ignore the history and community of Wimbledon. The more I immersed myself into the field the more I started to pick up on a fascinating tension. It became increasingly apparent that the fans seemed to have an interactive, flexible relationship with their club's history, or lack of, choosing to identify with it and distance themselves from it interchangeably. This notion is exemplified by a conversation I had with 'Fran' and 'Greg' (2012):

Oliver: So, what do you think about the argument that football clubs are about community? You know, like the argument the Wimbledon Supporters Association made was that the club was the property of the community and it was wrong to take that away from them?

'Fran': That's rubbish. Fans need to understand that with the big investment in football now, like Abramovich at Chelsea, they, or 'the community,' don't own anything. It's Abramovich that buys the players and success, not the fans. Abramovich owns Chelsea, he owns the club, he buys the players, he's the man with all the power there. They love him when they do well, they won loads when they got (Jose) Mourinho, didn't they; he's the man that made the decisions and brought him to the club.

Oliver: That's interesting. A lot of the fans that I have been speaking to have been saying that the Dons are a 'community club,' that Winkelman has gone out of his way to bring it to the city and make it something for the community to get behind and be proud of. Do you think this is the case, or are you suggesting that, like Abramovich, it's really his club and the idea of community isn't important?

'Greg': Well, we have a community, the club has worked really hard to attract fans and develop a strong sense of community … but the club is not *reliant* on it or *owned* by the community. When a club depends for its finances on its gate receipts, its merchandising, then the fans are in charge and, in a way, own the club. But when a club accepts massive financial investment from outside it can no longer be considered the same as a club which relies on its community.

Oliver: Like Chelsea, you mean? They get loads of money in from shirt sales and ticket prices, merchandise, but at the end of the day Abramovich is still the owner and he is so rich he doesn't need the money?

'Fran': He's talking about Wimbledon. You're right about Chelsea, but it's the same as what happened with them. They used to get really good attendance, around 9,000 fans even when they were a non-league club, and even when they went to Crystal Palace they had good attendance, I think it was around 20,000 fans for the first few years of them being there, but then the club started to slip down the league and the numbers

kept dropping. I think they went from 20,000 average crowds one season down to 6,000 in the space of a year.

'Greg': That's right. There's no doubt about it, without the fans there was no money coming in. They said it was about community and it's wrong to move the club, but they already moved it across London, it wasn't in its original borough the time they were in the Premiership, and 'the community' weren't exactly coming out to support the club. Clubs these days have to make money and by not turning up, in my mind, the fans basically gave control to the owners. They stopped putting money into the club, so they have no right to decide on its future. Pete (Winkelman) came in with the money and he saved the club from bankruptcy, so he's entitled to do what he wants in my book.

Like 'Matt' (2012) and 'Kate' (2012), 'Fran' and 'Greg' (2012) address football commercial culture in a highly astute manner relating to their position as fans of a franchise football club, but what is fascinating about the conversation is the way in which the pair initially approach the origins of the club in a manner that both demonstrates their understanding of Wimbledon's history and similarly their reluctance to engage with it, using Chelsea as an analogy to demonstrate their knowledge of the culture without having to step into the provocative territory of discussing Wimbledon. Significantly, this was the second time that I had chatted with the participants and subsequently we had started to develop a rapport. This seems to come through in the conversation, with the exchange marking the point in which they lowered their guard and started to open up about the unavoidable link between the clubs.

I was surprised that the themes of 'guilt' and 'blame' became prominent features of conversation with the pair attributing blame for Wimbledon's dissolution upon their fan base. As they suggest, in most cases commercial arguments would deter clubs from relocating and re-branding themselves. It would not make economic sense to relocate a team from its established community, without even considering the moral argument, but the alarming decline of attendance figures that punctuated Wimbledon's temporary residency at Selhurst Park[2] are interpreted by 'Fran' and 'Greg' (2012) as a symbolic transfer of power away from the fans and into the hands of Wimbledon's investors.

It is poignant that while the Dons' fans are scorned for their supposedly disingenuous relationship with their club, 'Fran' and 'Greg' (2012) explicitly question the integrity and passion of the Wimbledon fans, echoing the argument made by Winkelman (cited by Conn 2012), who has described his amazement that Wimbledon fans did not fight harder or coalesce to buy the club and prevent its relocation. The exchange is multidimensional, in which they convincingly challenge the moral argument upheld by those that resent the creation of the Dons, shrewdly emphasising the significance of capitalism to contemporary football culture in a manner than aims to legitimise the origins of their club and their fandom, situating it within the norms of modern consumer society. In doing so the fans constitute their self-identity as consumers in relation to their understanding of the culture of the club, supporting my interpretation of the way in which community is formed around the club.

It is telling that towards the end of the conversation 'Greg' (2012) had a wry smile on his face. I left the pair with the impression that they were almost disappointed that I did not react to their provocations. While there is a lot of reason in their argument, it was almost as if they were purposefully trying to get a reaction from me. Fiske (1991) famously analysed the negotiation of jeans in everyday American consumer society, approaching the clothing as a polysemic text. While a standardised mass commodity, he argued that they allow for a variety of different uses by different audiences. Similarly, I argue that the Dons can be considered as a standard commodity, used by traditional fans to embody the capitalisation of football culture (see Gilroy 2004). Like Fiske's (1991) study of jeans, I argue that the club has different meanings and use values to the fans. While I argue that 'Matt' (2012) and 'Kate' (2012) use the 'transparency' surrounding the creation of the club to present the Dons as a 'new club,' resisting the moral arguments against them by accepting their role as consumers, 'Fran' and 'Greg' (2012) fully engage with the Dons 'secret history,' evoking the cultural shift from a period of tradition and bureaucracy to capitalism.

I argue that the two different articulations of the club's history relate to different ways in which fans draw upon the idea of community in their fandom. 'Matt' (2012) and 'Kate' (2012) deny the link with Wimbledon, internalising the idea that the Dons are a new club as a staple of the local community. As a club born from capitalism, the fans support the club's 'community building project' through sustained patronage. Conversely 'Fran' and 'Greg' (2012) focus on the disintegration of Wimbledon's fan community, questioning their commitment and ability to move with the times and embrace how football's consumerism fosters new modes of fandom. The fans have a sophisticated way of mobilising traditional ideas of community, both emphasising their knowledge of traditional football culture and the ties between football clubs and the local community, while seemingly revelling in their role as 'pantomime villains' within the culture, knowingly engaging in self-fulfilling prophecies and playing the role of capitalist fans of a franchise football club that have been the beneficiaries of the game's cultural shift, enabling them to appropriate the identity of Wimbledon.

'No one likes us and we don't care'

The knowing fan performance enacted by 'Fran' and 'Greg' (2012) was something that became prevalent at the explosive derby match between the Dons and AFC Wimbledon (2 December 2012), with the fans evoking the 'traditional' association between football club and community to emphasise the ways in which the creation of the Dons both came as a result of and led to the disbanding of the community formed with Wimbledon.

In the weeks preceding the match, both the mainstream media and football blogs were helping to create frenzy within the culture with a barrage of hyperbolic headlines;[3] in the context of this frenzy Pete Winkelman appeared as a guest on Talk Sport Radio (2 December 2012) three hours before kick-off, appealing for calm from the fans. With the controversy surrounding the club Winkelman has made numerous media appearances defending the Dons; this interview followed suit, with Winkelman emphasising the significance of the club to the local community, indicative of the responses that I received from 'Matt' and 'Kate' (2012):

> What I've learnt in this whole process is how important the supporters are. The community is at the heart of everything we do here at Milton Keynes Dons … The most important thing we've created over the last eight years is our home. We have brought the community together and at the end of the day that is what the whole debate is about.
>
> (Winkelman 2012a)

To this statement, the presenter, Paul Hawksbee, asks Winkelman that while this may be the case, how would he respond to the claim that the creation of the community in Milton Keynes has come at the expense of the community formed around Wimbledon? I have heard Winkelman respond to this type of question before, with his response drawing on the report made by the independent commission that ruled in favour of the relocation, the idea that there was not an established community associated with the club, with relocation the only viable option to ensure the club's symbolic continuation (see Walmsley 2010). This time, seemingly cautious of the frenzy surrounding the contest, Winkelman (2012a) made a remarkable backtrack, admitting to feelings of guilt and regret in relation to processes that led to the club's creation:

> I've learnt a hell of a lot from the process and I'm sorry. I can't say I'm particularly proud of my intent at the beginning … What happened should never happen to a club … they should never have become homeless.

I found this admission both fascinating and highly astute. Like the fans that I interviewed, Winkelman seems to both ignore and engage with the club's association with Wimbledon, emphasising the benefits the Dons as a 'new' club have brought to the local community but also a sense of guilt about the processes that led to the club's inception and the pain that it caused. Winkelman centres the conversation around the fans of both teams, seemingly trying to deflect animosity away from the two sets of fans and direct it upon himself. He continues suggesting that both clubs have 'fantastic supporters,' who will create a 'fantastic atmosphere' and ensure that they 'get behind their teams in the right way' (Winkelman 2012a).

In conclusion to the interview, Winkelman (2012a) is asked about his hopes for the match:

> I just want to see a good game of football played in the right spirit. The two teams have great supporters and I know they will get behind their respective teams and make the match a great occasion. At three o'clock I hope that we are in the next round .... I just want to put this behind us; I'm sure Erik (Samuelson, AFC Wimbledon Chairman) is the same. I suppose it was inevitable that the teams would meet at some point but I'm looking forward to getting it over with and concentrating on securing promotion to the Championship.

At this point Hawksbee interjects once again, asking that if he is so keen to 'put it behind him,' and has 'learnt from the process,' then why not make a gesture of good faith and drop 'the Dons' moniker from their name, giving it over to AFC Wimbledon. 'The Dons' nickname was famously associated with Wimbledon, the 'Don' coming from the suffix of Wimbledon, and is considered to be the last remaining connection between the two clubs. Again, I have heard Winkelman (2012b) respond to this question before on BBC Look East (15 November 2012), with his previous response a bullish denial:

> We are the MK Dons but we can't change the history of what it was (Wimbledon). It's my gift to the community (the club) while recognising the history of the club that came before us.

His response seems problematic; in the same interview Winkelman emphasises the idea that the Dons are a new club striving to make 'their *own* history,' yet he suggests that the club have incorporated the name to pay tribute to the history of Wimbledon and how the Dons came to fruition. In this context I can see why the name could be seen as antagonistic to AFC Wimbledon fans, and, as a 'new' club, see little benefit in keeping the title. Once again Winkelman backtracks on his previous statements, again responding to the question with caution, in a manner that shows his engagement with the issue while simultaneously distancing himself from any decision. Winkelman again refers to the role of the community in the operation of the club, suggesting for the first time that he would be open to the name change 'but only if it was something the supporters wanted' (Winkelman 2012a).

After my conversations with 'Matt' (2012) and 'Kate' (2012), in which they were keen to emphasise the affinity between the club and the local community, I presumed that the move to 'drop the Dons' would be welcomed by the fans. 'The Dons' tag is an uncomfortable reminder of the processes that led to the club's creation and the fans, along with Winkelman, seemed particularly keen to emphasise the legitimacy of the Dons as a 'new club' with a 'new history.' Having listened to the interview, I was encouraged that Winkelman seemed to express a level of sympathy for the AFC Wimbledon fans. Subsequently, I presumed that after the match had been played Milton Keynes would likely drop the Dons from their title, a symbolic gesture that would help to ease relations between the clubs and aid in the club being accepted within the culture as a new club reflecting the conditions of modern consumer society. With this in mind I set out before the derby match to canvas the opinions of the fans. I was not expecting the responses I received.

Approaching the stadium, it was apparent that there was a larger police presence than usual, with a blockade formed around the away stand, prohibiting fans from tracing the circumference of the stadium. Similarly, there was a significantly higher media presence than I had previously encountered at Stadium MK. The match was being televised live on the BBC and broadcast on Radio 5 Live and, as the standout fixture of the second round, seemed to have captured the attention of the wider culture. As 'Steve' (2012) had suggested, the atmosphere around the ground could be at times hostile, but this was not a particularly intimidating atmosphere, largely due to the large police presence, but rather an unnerving atmosphere in which I felt the sensation of constantly being watched. It was the first time that I had experienced this sensation, with police and television cameras seemingly tracking your every move and watchful eyes of suspicious fans tracking you from beneath black jackets. I believe that this intense atmosphere contributed to the reluctance of some of the fans to engage with me and accounts for some of the aggressive responses I received in relation to the fans' willingness, or lack thereof, to 'drop the Dons' from their name.

Oliver: I was listening to Pete this morning saying about 'dropping the Dons' from the name, so it would just be Milton Keynes FC.

'Ralph': Did he? He can f*** off with that idea, no way.

Oliver: Yeah, he was saying that he wouldn't be against it but he would leave the decision up to the fans.

'Ralph': I'm against it, there's no way I'd back that idea. The fans won't go for that. Not a chance.

Oliver: Why do you think that would be the case?

'Ralph': Why the f*** would we? It's our name. That would just be letting those hypocrites (AFC) win.

I was taken aback at the strength of 'Ralph's' (2012) opposition to the idea; his response was aggressive, and he seemed to be agitated at the mere suggestion. What was interesting about the response was the idea that dropping the Dons would be like 'letting AFC Wimbledon win.' Initially I almost discarded the response, interpreting it as an emotional reaction to the conditions of the day, the tribalistic 'them and us' perpetuated and encouraged by the media and enacted by the fans in response to the way in which the club have been disenfranchised within football culture. However, the more people I engaged with, the more 'Ralph's' response seemed representative of the larger fan base.

'Kim' (2012) indicated that the name change would be like 'them getting one over on us,' while 'Levi' (2012) suggested that a name change would be 'like admitting to the world that we are ashamed.' The most revealing response came from 'Sam' (2012):

Oliver: I was listening to Pete this morning saying about 'dropping the Dons' from the name, so the club would just be Milton Keynes FC.

'Sam': Yeah, I heard that. He's changed his tune a bit, hasn't he?

Oliver: Yeah, just a bit. It seemed like quite a smart move though, to try and ease a bit of the tension.

'Sam': Oh yeah, I think he knew what he was doing. He's a very smart man, Pete. He knows the fans will never support the idea, but it gives the impression that he's making an effort and extending a bit of an olive branch.

Oliver: You seem to be right. I thought that the fans would support the idea, but everyone I have spoken to today has been completely against the idea.

'Sam': Why would we ever support the idea? It doesn't make sense to me.

Oliver: Well, the club seems to go out of its way to emphasise the fact that it is a 'new' club, trying to make 'new history.' But the Dons tag is the last remaining link to Wimbledon. I understand how important the club is to the community, so why keep the tag when it just reminds people of the past and is used as a stick to beat the club with by other fans?

'Sam': It *is* a new club, we gave all the trophies and memorabilia back to them (AFC) and the Football League saw that as us breaking all ties with the past. So to me we *are* a new club; the name isn't going to change that. The club started out as MK Dons and it is going to stay as MK Dons.

Oliver: But having given everything else back and getting recognition as a new club, why is the name so important?

'Sam': I suppose it's not *that* important, but I just don't see why we should. They (AFC) have a problem with it not because it reminds them of the way we supposedly took over their club, but it reminds them that they *let* us take over the club. They knew the owners were looking to sell and it nearly got moved to Dublin, didn't it, but they failed to get behind the team and they lost it. They see what we are building here, and they are jealous that we are successful. That's the best bit about the name. It winds them up so much. We should keep it to piss them off if nothing else. You've read the stories (surrounding the game) and everyone keeps hammering us, so why should we bow down and do what they what us to do?

As his final remarks suggest, 'Sam's' (2012) response seems emotionally influenced by the occasion, directly referencing the adverse publicity surrounding the club with the build up to the derby, so I am cautious not to overstate its significance, however I argue that there is validity to his statement. Like 'Fran' and

'Greg' (2012), he is keen to emphasise the moral failing of the Wimbledon fans, looking to legitimate his own fandom and the community's support of the club by creating distinction between the active mobilisation of community by the Dons' fans and the passivity of the Wimbledon fans.

The key idea that I have taken from the conversation is that he is not overly concerned about the name and does not provide much of a justification for keeping it apart from the pleasure it provides him in the way in which it antagonises the opposition, suggesting that the club should keep the name to 'piss them off if nothing else' ('Sam' 2012). It is significant that he refers to the way in which the club faces constant criticism from the sport's wider culture, describing the use of the name almost as a form of retaliation and in which he plays upon the way in which the Dons' fans are continually presented as ersatz. Sandvoss (2005: 44) argues that fandom is constituted between text and context; in this instance the Dons' fans explicitly draw upon the processes that led to their club's creation, positioning themselves as consumer fans while creatively demonstrating their autonomy within the culture in opposition to Wimbledon's dispersal.

'Sam' (2012) suggests that AFC fans have a problem with the name because it reminds them that their lack of support enabled Wimbledon to be taken over. Subsequently he believes that they see the way that the community in Milton Keynes are supporting the project and have become jealous of the Dons' success. In doing so he perpetuates both the idea that the club have become successful as a 'new club' and that the club was able to experience this success due to the inability of the community to support the club as Wimbledon. Taking this into account I argue that while the name may be an uncomfortable reminder of how the club originated, the title is important to the Dons' fans as it constantly reminds them of their need to support the project and the significance of community both to the club's history and its future prosperity. I argue that this shared knowledge helps fans form a community around the club, encouraging their patronage.

Evidently the fans were aware of the debates surrounding the campaign to 'drop the Dons,' making their feelings known inside the stadium. In correlation with Lancaster's (2001) work the stadium had become a 'site of performance,' with the fans becoming active participants in the football event. Before kick-off, a huge banner was unveiled with the slogan 'We are keeping the Dons, get over it,' which was met by loud boos from the away fans.

The fans continued their antagonism with sustained choruses of 'MK Dons, MK Dons, MK Dons,' and 'We will always be the Dons, always be the Dons,' emphasising the suffix much to their rivals irritation. The standard of play was poor, but there was a palpable sense of excitement with the bar of the East Wing stand full of loud voices, antithetical to the tense feeling of panopticisation I experienced before kick-off. Keen to develop an understanding of the atmosphere I approached a group for their half-time assessment.

Oliver: The atmosphere is electric today; I haven't experience anything like this here before.

'Zack': It's top, isn't it? That was a great half. The football's not that special but the atmosphere is something else today.

Oliver: The response that banner ('We are keeping the Dons, get over it') provoked at the start was unbelievable.

'Hugo': That was magic! I can't believe how loud the boos were. [Laughs.]

'Zack': They (AFC) are so uptight about it. Every time we would chant MK Dons they were getting furious; it's like they didn't expect us to sing or anything.

Oliver: I'm surprised how wound up they are getting; they surely didn't expect us to just take the abuse and sit in silence.

'Zack': That's it! We get it every week. The away fans come and slaughter us with all that 'franchise crap'... the whole of the country seems to be watching today hoping we get turned over, but we aren't taking it, we're fighting back. I'm loving it, mate.

Fiske (1991: 47) argues that fandom is subversive by design, with pleasure rooted in its ability to enable fans to produce their own meanings with their texts to avoid social disciplining. I argue that this relates to the fandom of 'Sam' (2012), who, like 'Zack' and 'Hugo' (2012), describes the sense of excitement that they experience antagonising the opposition. I argue that parallels can be established between their fandom and that of the fans in the Snake Pit at Norwich City. Similarly, I argue that the Dons fan community draw upon the club's tradition and 'secret history' ('Steve' 2012), developing unique customs relating to their status as a franchise football club to transgress the norms of the game's wider culture. In the context of the derby, the wider football culture, and specifically AFC Wimbledon, represent the dominant culture. As suggested, the Dons in their very existence are seen to challenge and threaten their order and traditions, and 'Sam' (2012), 'Zack' and 'Hugo' (2012) seem fully aware of this notion, revelling in the liminal position of the club and their fan community.

Cavicchi (1998) argues that the symbolic and ideological core of communities imagined by fans is structured via their appropriation of texts. I argue that this is figured in the ways in which the fans look to appropriate the customs and identity of Wimbledon. This is initially encapsulated in the fan performance related to the 'drop the Dons' campaign. It is fascinating that the fans seem to embrace the tag for the way in which it perpetuates the club's own lack of history and artificiality, inspiring hatred from the wider culture for the history that it evokes. The way in which the fans goad the opposition with the name demonstrates their ability to engage with the moral arguments of the culture from which they are largely excluded, demonstrating an understanding of its traditions. I argue that this grounding and understanding of the culture from which they look to transgress is foundational to their fan performance and can be considered as another example of the ways in which Dons' fans seem to both engage and distance themselves from their history.

In their celebration of their name 'the Dons', I argue that the fans actively embrace their role as villains within the culture, actively engaging in self-fulfilling prophecies as consumers of football, who revel in the fact that they have 'consumed' the identity and community of Wimbledon. If, as I suggest, the fans emphasise the significance of the name to accentuate the ways in which they oppose the traditions of football culture for their own amusement and, as suggested, as 'retaliation' ('Sam' 2012) against a culture from which they have largely been rejected, then it is possible to interpret their performances as self-aware celebrations of the community's liminal status within football culture.

Another example of this is the fans' appropriation of the song 'No one likes us and we don't care,' a song made famous by Millwall in the 1970s but appropriated in the 1990s by Wimbledon fans in relation to the team's aggressive, direct tactics. The fact that the fans have appropriated one of Wimbledon's most famous songs alludes to the awareness that the fans have of their club's history and their wider understanding of football's commercial culture. The fans seemed to take pleasure re-appropriating one of the most famous songs associated with Wimbledon, to shock and antagonise their rivals. This not only suggests that the fans experience pleasure from embracing their role as villains within the culture, but also that their wider knowledge of football culture belies their position as disingenuous ersatz. Like the Dons title itself, I argue that the song is used as a tool of communal resistance; what once was indicative of Wimbledon's unique status as football's great amateur underdogs is transformed into a reminder of the commercial process that led to the club's non-existence, and to the creation of the Dons, the 'new' club that attracts admirable loyalty from the local community, who support it both financially and passionately within the stands. In doing so I argue that the fans actively position themselves both positively and negatively as consumers, literally 'buying into' the commercial community-building project of the club while appropriating the traditional culture and identity associated with Wimbledon, demonstrating their awareness of traditional football culture to emphasise their incongruity as fans of a franchise football club.

Notes

1 The nearest league clubs to the city's catchment area, with 18 million people living within ninety minutes of Central Milton Keynes, are Luton Town and Northampton FC. The city's population is constantly increasing and has grown from 225,000 at the time of the club's purchase in 2002 to 260,000 ten years later at the point of my research, a population growth of roughly 18%, highlighting the lucrative and expanding market for the club to serve.

2 The average crowd for the 1998/1999 season was 18,235. This decreased to a mere 7,900 for the 2000/2001 season and 6,900 for 2001/2002 season.

3 'The Bitterest of Grudge Matches' (The Independent 1 December 2012), 'More Than Just a Game' (The Telegraph 30 November 2012), 'The Game That Should Never Happen' (Life's a Pitch 30 November 2012).

Bibliography

Ang, I (1985) *Watching Dallas: Soap Opera and the Melodramatic Imagination*. London. Methuen.

Bale, J (1998) 'Virtual Fandoms: Futurescapes of Football' Cited in Brown, A *Fanatics: Power, Identity and Fandom in Football*. London. Routledge.

Barnes, S (2007) 'How Pavarotti changed the perception of football' Cited in Mortimer, G *A History of Football in 100 Objects*. London. Serpents Tail.

Baudrillard, J (1993) *The Transparency of Evil: Essays on Extreme Phenomena*. London. Verso.

Brimson, D (1998) *The Geezers Guide to Football: A Lifetime of Lads and Lager*. London. Mainstream Publishing.

Burgess, C (2005) What on Earth has Happened to Football? *The Guardian* [Website] Available from: http://www.theguardian.com/football/2005/feb/09/sport.comment (Accessed 16 November 2012).

Cavicchi, D (1998) *Tramps Like Us: Music and Meaning among Springsteen Fans*. Oxford. Oxford University Press.

Cherry, B (2002) 'Screaming for Release: Feminity and Horror Film Fandom in Britian' Cited in Chibnall, S & Petley, J *British Horror Cinema*. London. Routledge.

Conn, D (2005) *The Beautiful Game: Searching for the Soul of Football*. London. Yellow Jersey Press.

Conn, D (2012) Pete Winkelman: 'I'm not Proud of how Football Came to Milton Keynes' *The Guardian* [Website] Available from: http://www.theguardian.com/football/blog/2012/nov/27/peter-winkelman-mk-dons-afc-wimbledon (Accessed 25 June 2013).

Crampsey, R (1990) *First 100 Years: Scottish League Football*. Edinburgh. The Scottish Football League Press.

de Certeau, M (1984) *The Practice of Everyday Life*. Berkley. University of California Press.

Devine, TM (2012) *The Scottish Nation: A Modern History*. London. Penguin.

Falcous, M & Rose, C (2005) Cultural Identities in Transition: Hypercommodification and Fandom in English Rugby League. *Football Studies* 8 (2) 5–26.

Fiske, J (1991) *Understanding Popular Culture*. London. Routledge.

Fynn, A & Guest, L (1994) *Out of Time: Why Football Isn't Working*. London. Simon & Schuster Press.

Gasper, P (2005) *The Communist Manifesto: A Road Map to History's Most Important Document*. Illinois. Haymarket Books.

Gilroy, P (2004) *After Empire: Melancholia or Convivial Culture?* London. Routledge.

Hayes, P (2013) MK Dons Chairman Pete Winkelman Looks Back at the Wimbledon Move Ten Years On. *The Daily Mail* [Website] Available from: http://www.dailymail.co.uk/sport/football/article-2433622/MK-Dons-chairman-Pete-Winkelman-looks-Wimbledon-years-on.html?ITO=1490&ns_mchannel=rss&ns_campaign=1490 (Accessed 16 February 2014).

Hills, M (2002) *Fan Cultures*. London. Routledge.

Hopcraft, A (2006) *The Football Man: People and Passion in Soccer*. London. Aurum Press.

Hussey, A (2005) How Heysel's Lost Lives Saved a Sport. *The Guardian* [Website] Available from: http://www.theguardian.com/football/2005/apr/03/newsstory.sport14 (Accessed 18 November 2011).

Imlach, G (2005) My *Father and Other Working-Class Football Heroes*. London. Yellow Jersey Press.

Ingle, S (2005) Football Fans Are Idiots. *The Guardian* [Website] Available from: http://www.theguardian.com/football/2005/sep/02/sport.blueprintforabetterfootball (Accessed 23 October 2011).

Jenkins, H (1992) *Textual Poachers: Television Fans and Participatory Culture*. New York. Routledge.

King, A (2002) *The End of the Terraces: The Transformation of English Football in the 1990's*. London. Leicester University Press.

Lancaster, K (2001) *Interacting with Babylon 5*. Austin. University of Texas Press.

Lash, S (2007) Power after Hegemony: Cultural Studies in Mutation? *Theory, Culture and Society* 24 (3) 55–78.

Lee, S (1998) 'Grey Shirts to Grey Suits: The Political Economy of English Football in the 1990's' Cited in Brown, A *Fanatics: Power, Identity and Fandom in Football*. London. Routledge.

MK Dons Sport & Education Trust (2014) *MK Dons Sport & Education Trust*. MK Dons SET [Website] Available from: http://www.mkdons.com/club/mkdonsset/ (Accessed 14 May 2014).

MK Dons Supporters Association (2014) *Facts of the Move*. MK Dons Supporters Association [Website] Available from: http://www.mkdsa.co.uk/index.php/dons-history/facts-of-the-move (Accessed 8 October 2014).

Pearson, G (2012) *An Ethnography of English Football Fans: Cans, Cops and Carnivals*. Manchester. Manchester University Press.

Radway, J (1984) *Reading the Romance: Women, Patriarchy and Popular Literature*. North Carolina. University of North Carolina Press.

Sandvoss, C (2005) *Fans*. Cambridge. Polity.

Symanski, S & Zimbalist, A (2006) *National Pass Time: How Americans Play Baseball and the Rest of the World Plays Soccer*. New York. Brookings Institution Press.

The Open University (2013) *MK Dons Chairmen Rewarded Honorary Doctorate from The Open University*. The Open University [Website] Available from: http://www3.open.ac.uk/media/fullstory.aspx?id=25661 (Accessed 1 May 2014).

Thornton, S (1995) *Club Cultures: Music, Media and Subcultural Capital*. Cambridge. Polity.

Walmsley, D (2010) *Story of the Dons 2004–2010*. MK Dons Supporters Association [Website] Available from: http://www.mkdsa.co.uk/index.php/dons-history/2013-11-09-11-06-00/the-story-of-the-dons-2000-2010 (Accessed 29 December 2011).

Weed, M (2008) Exploring the Sport Spectator Experience: Virtual Football Spectatorship in the Pub. *Soccer and Society* 9 (2) 189–197.

White, J (2003) Pitch Battle. *The Guardian* [Website] Available from: http://www.theguardian.com/football/2003/jan/11/clubsincrisis.sport (Accessed 29 December 2011).

Williams, J (2000) 'The Changing Face of Football: A Case for National Regulation' Cited in Mitchie, J et al. *Football in the Digital Age: Whose Game Is It Anyway?* London. Mainstream Publishing.

Wilson, P (2006) It Was the Best of Cups, It Was the Worst of Cups. *The Guardian* [Website] Available from: http://www.theguardian.com/football/worldcup2006blog/2006/jul/09/itwasthebestofcupsitwas (Accessed 25 June 2013).

Winkelman, P (2012a) *The Hawksbee and Jacobs Show*. Talk Sport [Radio] (2 December 2012).

Winkelman, P (2012b) *Interview with Stuart White*. BBC Look East [TV Show] (15 November 2012).

Chapter 6

Chelsea

'Champions of Europe'

On 19 May 2012, Chelsea beat Bayern Munich on penalties in their own stadium, the Allianz Arena, to win the Champions League for the first time in the club's history. I started my research with Chelsea six months prior to the final, taking in the tumultuous events leading to the team's success. In the aftermath of the match, Gary Neville wrote in his article for the Daily Mail (19 May 2012) that the club was 'destined' to win the Champions League as it had been 'written in the stars.' While the quotations can be discarded as dramatic responses to victory, the Chelsea fans that I engaged with throughout the research process harboured similar beliefs about the 'destiny' of the club, with the fans accustomed to success, expecting victory. Indeed, it is my argument that self-identifying as winners within the culture is central to the participants' fan identity.

Like the Dons, Chelsea are said to epitomise football's modern capitalism, the club having severed its ties with its traditional fan base. It is claimed that the club's traditional fans have been priced out of attendance, usurped by football tourists drawn to the club by the prospect of seeing entertaining football played by the world's best players, bankrolled by Chelsea owner, Roman Abramovich. The club positions itself as a 'tourist attraction,' a 'London monument' (see Rolls 2014). With the club explicit in its market orientation as '*Champions* of Europe,' the '*Pride* of London,' drawing on its location in the salubrious borough of Fulham, associations are formed between the club and the wider opulence of the area, emphasising the idea that Chelsea is a successful team for 'winners.' I argue that this relates to the way in which the fans are positively positioned as consumers by the club, attracted by the prospect of sharing the club's success in which their patronage enables them to associate themselves with the players on the pitch and the wider opulence of the borough. In patronage, fans are given the opportunity to identify with the success of the club, evoking the ideas of wider fan studies that need fulfilment and group affiliation can be obtained and signified with acts of consumption (see Jameson 1991; Fiske 1992; Hills 2002; Barker 2004; Sandvoss 2005).

This conception of fandom relates to Vass' (2003) concept of 'cheering for self,' a premise that he developed through his ethnographic study of American college basketball fans. Vass (2003) suggests that when basketball fans 'cheer for self,' they financially and emotionally invest in their team, imparting them into their everyday life, so the team becomes an extension of the self. In the context of Chelsea, I argue that fans similarly invest in the club for the opportunity that it provides them to experience the feeling of victory. By forming a link with the club, the fans internalise the success of the team as their own, enabling them to identify as winners.

As discussed in Chapter 2, modern fans are said to lack identity, depicted as indiscriminate consumers (see Bale 1998; Brimson 1998; Ingle 2005; Pearson 2012). Chelsea fans are considered by rival fans as the epitome of this, desperate to emphasise their status within football culture but lacking the 'cultural capital' (Thornton 1995) or knowledge of 'traditional' football culture to do so in authentic ways. The way in which Chelsea fans identify as consumers is seen to reinforce the negative discourses surrounding the club. Dyer (1999: 28) argues that the consequences of representation are significant to the way that individuals are treated, and I am keen to establish how Chelsea fans perceive themselves in relation to others within football culture.

While Chelsea fans are positioned as consumers within football culture, it is significant that the fans seem to embrace this position, as their 'othering' within football culture as a result of their knowing consumerism helps reflect their status as 'winners.' Indeed, I argue that fans knowingly 'buy into' the culture of the club for the opportunity the club provides them to 'cheer for self' as part of a winning club. The fans largely rely on this sense of hierarchy and 'othering' to substantiate their identity in opposition to rival fans. This is a communality shared between the participants throughout my research, with fan identity constructed and enacted in relation to the participant's desire to be perceived a certain way, as a certain type of fan. As such, expressions of identity are largely informed by the concept of an opposite or an imagined 'other.'

The Chelsea fans that I engaged with at the start of my research, like the Dons' fans in the previous chapter, describe their fandom as active consumption, suggesting that their relationship with the club is mutually beneficial, with the club remunerated for the opportunities that it affords the fans to 'cheer for self' and establish a hierarchal relationship with rival fans. However, as my research progressed I was privy to numerous disconnects between producer (club) and consumer (fans) with the club failing to achieve success, preventing the fans from identifying as winners. I argue that this had a tangible impact on the way in which the participants enacted their identity.

This chapter analyses the way in which Chelsea fans articulate their identity in relation to a shifting conception of the 'other.' My research indicates that when the club are successful the fans identify as consumers to position themselves in opposition to wider football culture, 'buying into' the successful status that Chelsea markets itself on. However, when the club fails to provide fans with opportunities to identify as 'winners,' the fans become mindful of the way in which they are perceived within football culture (see Dyer 1999: 28) and negotiate their relationship with the club. I argue that this negotiation is figured in the different ways in which the fans construct concepts of 'us and them.' As suggested, when the club provides fans with opportunities to 'cheer for self,' and establish hierarchy, the fans identify with the culture of the club. Conversely, when the club fails to figure the relationship that the fans expect, I argue that the Chelsea fans frame their fandom in opposition to the culture of the club, particularly its capitalist business strategy, with the fans drawing on the discourses surrounding traditional football culture that they had hitherto ignored.

This chapter explores how the concept of 'us and them' is constructed and mobilised by the fans. I argue that the concepts of opposition are continually shifting based on the fans' perception of the club's success and subsequently the fans' self-perception within football culture. This chapter subsequently analyses the different ways in which the fans construct their identity in negotiation with the manager, the players, the owner and rival fans.

Andre Villas Boas (AVB): 'He's turned us into a laughing stock'

Since Abramovich's takeover in 2003, Chelsea had amassed an impressive array of silverware, winning the Premier League five times (2004/2005, 2005/2006, 2009/2010, 2014/2015, 2016/2017), the League Cup three times (2004/2005, 2006/2007, 2014/2015), the FA Cup four times (2006/2007, 2008/2009, 2009/2010, 2017/2018), the Europa League once (2012/2013) and the Champions League (2012/2013) once. With the club's continued success key to its business strategy, the club is active in the management of its image as 'winners' within the culture. Correspondingly Abramovich is ruthless in his pursuit of success with mangers rapidly fired if they fail to achieve his objectives. Since his purchase of the club in 2003 the club has experience 13 managerial changes.[1] Prior to the commencement of my research in September 2011, Chelsea sacked Carlo Ancelotti after two seasons in charge of the club. In his first season he had led the team to a League and Cup double, but after failing to deliver success in his second season he was replaced by the young and dynamic AVB, who had risen to prominence in the previous season by winning both the League title and UEFA Cup with FC Porto. The firing of Ancelotti and hiring of AVB was ridiculed within football culture. Doyle (2011) epitomises this sentiment, deriding the appointment as 'short-termist,' a brash attempt to form association between the club and AVB's personal success as a 'winning' manager. The managerial change was said to epitomise the club's modern capitalism and short-term business strategy, with Abramovich's 'hiring and firing policy' depicted in correlation with the wider instability, volatility and lack of identity of modern football culture (see Fynn & Davidson 1996; Williams 2000; Imlach 2005).

I started my research gaging the fans' reactions to AVB's appointment. With the negativity surrounding the sacking of Ancelotti, I was expecting the fans to react with caution to my questions, yet I was surprised by the overwhelming support for AVB. I argue that this support comes from his status at the time of my research as a 'winner' within football culture, enabling fans to confer his success upon the club and by extension themselves. My exchange with 'Bruce' (2011) emphasises this idea:

Oliver: So, what did you think about the appointment of AVB then?
'Bruce': I think it's another quality appointment. He looks like a proper Chelsea manager; he's one of us.
Oliver: A proper Chelsea manager? You mean that he fits the role well.
'Bruce': Yeah, you know, just that he fits the role. He is the real deal. He has a big reputation, he's exciting, he's sharp and he's a winner.
Oliver: He did have a very successful season with Porto. Do you think he will be able to replicate that success here?
'Bruce': Absolutely. He's proved what he can do; he's a winner already. What is he now; 34? Look at what he's achieved already; people can't question his record.
Oliver: I'm not questioning his record, but Ancelotti had a great record too and he's now out of a job.
'Bruce': Carlo (Ancelotti) was great for us but what did he achieve last year? Yes, he won the League and Cup the year before, but we have to keep moving forward. There's no room for sentiment at the top level.
Oliver: I know what you mean but isn't there a danger that hiring and firing managers all the time could be a step backwards?
'Bruce': No, we are not hiring and firing managers all the time; we fire managers when they fail to deliver the goods, simple as that. It's not like we just go and give the job to anyone, we always appoint the best coaches in the world that will get us back to the top.

Throughout the exchange, 'Bruce' (2011) constantly aligns himself with the club as indicated by the constant use of 'we' and 'us.' In doing so it is poignant that he constantly evokes the club's successful reputation within the culture, vindicating my argument that the perceived success of the club is foundational to the fans' sense of identity. This notion is evoked in the opening exchange, with 'Bruce' describing AVB as a 'proper Chelsea manager … one of *us*.' In doing so it is poignant that he lists his characteristics: 'he has a big reputation, he's exciting, he's sharp and he's a winner,' facets of his personality that seem to correspond to the ways in which Chelsea associates itself with success and, correspondingly, how the fans perceive the club.

Fundamentally, 'Bruce' (2011) indicates that a 'proper Chelsea manager' is successful, accentuating the idea that AVB is a winner: 'he's a winner,' 'he's proved what he can do; he's a winner already,' 'people can't question his record,' presenting him as one of the 'best coaches in the word,' that will 'bring the team success.' This highlights the significance that 'Bruce' places upon the status of the club. Correspondingly, the exchange suggests that he has internalised the business strategy of the club, rationalising the sacking of Ancelotti for his inability to deliver success in his second year in charge. As indicated, wider football culture strongly criticised his dismissal, yet 'Bruce' (2011) recognises the need for the club to 'keep moving forward,' and that there is 'no room for sentiment at the top level.' His use of capitalist rhetoric indicates that he has accepted the club's business strategy, complimenting my argument that he self-identifies as a consumer of the club.

'Bruce's' (2011) responses allude to his status as a consumer fan. He has an astute understanding of the sport as a business, evoking the language of rapacious capitalism in the idea that the club needs to 'keep moving forward.' Similarly, the idea that there is 'no room for sentiment at the top level' can be considered as a direct challenge to the discourses of traditional football culture, that harbour a nostalgic image of the past without moving with the times. In Chapter 2, I document how a 'rationalised time' approach to business is presented as a cultural ideal, encouraging fans to establish emotional connections with clubs cultivated over a period of time (see Sennett 2006). It was in the context of 'rationalised time' that the club were criticised for firing Ancelotti, challenging the stability valued within traditional football culture.

Poignantly 'Bruce' (2011) prioritises the success of the club over its stability as indicated by his defence of Abramovich's 'hiring and firing policy,' suggesting that managers are replaced when they 'fail to deliver the goods.' This epitomises the way in which the promise of success is foundational to the fans' identity, with 'Bruce' (2011) speaking proudly of the way in which the club 'always appoint the best coaches' to get the club 'back to the top.' Rather than the emotional connection said to develop over time between club and fans (see Crampsey 1990; Hutchinson 1997), 'Bruce' describes the draw of success, knowing that the club will constantly appoint the best coaches to complement their squad of world-class players, described by 'Bruce' as part of the club's allure, helping Chelsea to cement their status as a global brand and London attraction. I argue that this identification with the club corresponds to Lancaster's (2001) notion of the 'fantasy frame,' the idea that fans immerse themselves into the fantasy of their fan texts to the extent that they 'become part of the frame,' encouraging them to become part of the fantasy. The fantasy offered to the fans by Chelsea is the idea that they can identify as winners, something that 'Bruce' directly looks to 'buy into' in his endorsement of the club's business strategy.

My exchange with 'Bruce' (2011) encapsulated the excitement of AVB's appointment, his 'big reputation,' 'sharp' looks and successful record, encouraging him to accept the club's business strategy and identify as a winner after the club's lack of success the previous season. Despite this optimism, AVB was struggling to fulfil the club's promise and by November, as my research intensified, Chelsea were languishing outside the coveted top four positions. Reports started to emerge in the media about a 'player revolt,' and 'anarchy' within the dressing room. With just two months of the season gone, the fans that I engaged with had lost faith in him.

As I took my position within the 'Shed' end, to watch the team lose 2–1 to a spirited Liverpool side (20 November 2011), I was privy to fans questioning his tactics: 'Why the f*** is he playing Ramirez on the left, he's right-footed for f*** sake,' his squad selection: 'How can he keep playing Torres when we've got Drogba on the bench, he's f***ing clueless,' and man management skills: 'Look at him just standing there, he needs to tear into them, he needs to f***ing change it.' Audible boos punctuated the full-time whistle with the team unable to break down Liverpool's resolute defence. This was my first experience of an emerging disconnect between club and fans. Without achieving success on the pitch, the fans were unable to self-identify as winners, becoming unsatisfied consumers.

Chelsea narrowly qualified out of the Champions League group stage. For qualifying they were rewarded with a daunting double-legged knockout tie against Napoli. While Chelsea were struggling in the league, Napoli were enjoying a successful season, placed second in Series A. I visited the club three days before the away leg of the tie to watch Chelsea host Birmingham City in the fifth round of the FA Cup (18 December 2012). Despite Birmingham's lower league status, they outplayed Chelsea, controlling possession. Birmingham took the lead on the twentieth minute and hung on for much of the game before Sturridge was called off the bench to earn Chelsea a replay. Once again, the fans were furious with audible boos punctuating the final whistle. Talking with the fans after the game it was clear that they had lost faith in AVB.

While the conversation I had with 'Bruce' (2011) at the start of the season encapsulated the optimism of the appointment and the idea that AVB was a 'proper Chelsea manager' who would 'get (Cheslea) back to the top,' 'Harry' and 'Ali' (2012) looked to disassociate themselves from him, presenting him as an outsider to the club and harmful to their identity as 'winners' within the culture.

Oliver: They got away with that today, didn't they?

'Harry': Too right they did, what a load of crap that was.

'Ali': Bloody awful! I swear he hasn't got a clue what he's doing, that manager.

Oliver: At least they are still in the Cup; surely they won't play that badly against them (Birmingham) again.

'Harry': Well, they're not going to be in the Europe after Wednesday.

'Ali': [Laughs.] It'll be a mauling. I wouldn't be too sure they will beat them (Birmingham) either, they were the better team today. The defending was shocking, and they should have had a couple more goals, before AVB *finally* woke up and made some changes.

While 'Bruce' (2011) actively looked to associate himself with the previous success of AVB, using collective terms 'we' and 'us' to emphasise AVB's affiliation with the club, it is significant that 'Harry' and 'Ali' (2012) constantly use the term 'they,' creating distance between themselves and the club under AVB's management. As suggested, at the time of his appointment AVB had status as a winner within the culture, something that 'Bruce' looked to identify with. Since the appointment, his status had declined dramatically to the point that 'Ali' and 'Harry' consider him detrimental to the success of the club and, significantly, their identity as 'winners.' This is epitomised by the contrasting ways in which the participants present him. In September 'Bruce' (2011) described him as a 'proper Chelsea manager,' looking to assimilate his success with the club as a resource upon which he could substantiate his own identity. Two months later 'Ali' (2012) disparagingly de-personalises him, referring to him simply as 'that manager.' While I argue that 'Bruce' (2011) actively attempts to capitalise on his 'winning' attributes, his 'big reputation,' 'sharp' looks and successful record, 'Ali' purposefully attempts to downplay his association with the club. AVB becomes 'othered,' incongruent to the club's success and 'Ali's' identity as a fan. The idea that AVB 'hasn't got a clue what he's doing' seems significant, encapsulating the fans' scepticism of his ability to deliver the club success, at a club that promises the fan opportunities to 'cheer for self.'

The change in the way that AVB is presented corresponds to the change in optimism surrounding the club, influenced both by the team's performances on the pitch and the wider perception of the club within the culture. The excitement generated by the appointment of AVB encouraged 'Bruce' (2011) to suggest that he would get Chelsea 'back to the top,' yet two months into the season the expectations dropped to the extent that 'Ali' (2012) questions whether the club will even beat Birmingham and indicating that the club would face a 'mauling' against Napoli. There was an inevitability about the result: Chelsea were 'mauled,' losing 3–1 (21 February 2012.) Fans and pundits wrote off the team's chance of progression, and AVB's chance of keeping his job. I watched the match with a group of Chelsea fans in a popular sports bar. While harbouring little hope of a positive result, the fans were exasperated by the team's level of performance and manner of defeat, attributing blame to the naivety and inadequacy of AVB. 'Fred' (2012) encapsulates this idea:

> Disappointed doesn't cover it mate, I'm disgusted … No, honestly disgusted. I didn't really think that we would get anything out of it, but they embarrassed us. Everyone can see that defending has been our problem. Everyone has been moaning about the highline, but what do we do? Play a highline, and they were catching us every time. It must be true about all the fighting at training because they can't be doing much work. They aren't playing like a team, are they? The job's just too big for AVB and for the sake of the club he's got to go. We're a laughing stock at the moment. The papers are going to be full of it again tomorrow and I'm sick of the club being a laughing stock, you know.

While passionately demonstrating his disappointment, 'Fred's' (2012) comments epitomise my argument that the fans' identification with the club relies on its 'winning' status. I argue that the club's inability to achieve success has a tangible impact on the way in which the fans present their identity. Like 'Ali' and 'Harry' (2012), 'Fred' attributes blame for the failure with AVB, looking to distance him and his 'failure' from the club. 'Fred' (2012) achieves this by emphasising his 'disgust' and 'embarrassment:' 'Everyone can see that defending has been our problem,' and 'everyone has been moaning about the highline, but what do we do? Play a highline, and they were catching us every time.' Similarly, the exchange emphasises the significance the fans place on the perception of the club within football culture, 'Fred' (2012) suggesting that the club had become 'a laughing stock,' fearing further recrimination from the press.

In the introduction to this chapter I introduced Vass' (2003) concept of 'cheering for self' to illustrate my argument that Chelsea fans invest in the team to the extent that the club becomes a natural part of their everyday life, as a key means through which they construct their self-identity. I argue that in patronage, fans buy in to the business strategy of the club to associate with its 'winning culture.' This corresponds to Sandvoss' (2005) idea that fans seek texts that allow for particular creations of meaning, based on its ability to correspond to fans' wishes, desires and sense of self. Taking this into account, if fans invest in the club to 'cheer for self,' presumably, when the club is failing in their objectives, fans in their protests are effectively decrying themselves.

Sandvoss (2005) suggests fandom is based on the capacity of a text to carry meanings that articulate fans' identities as well as their objective position within society. This would account for the level of anger and embarrassment the fans seemed to express towards AVB, in which his failure is seen as a negative reflection of the club and themselves. Not only were the performances unsatisfactory, but the consistent ridicule the team were receiving from the wider culture seemed to be internalised by fans as personal attacks on their own identity. It was like the Chelsea fans were stuck in an abusive relationship.

In his rebuke, 'Fred's' (2012) repetition of 'everyone' seems poignant, encapsulating the feeling of wider unrest among the fans but, significantly, their collective opposition to AVB. I argue that his use of collective rhetoric works to isolate the manager, in which he, and his personal failure, is presented as incongruent to the collective identity of the club. Throughout the exchange 'Fred' (2012) looks to change the perception of the club, isolating AVB in an attempt to transfer the failure on to him rather than the club. By highlighting AVB's unsuitability for the job, 'Fred' (2012) insinuates that his sacking would improve the team's quality of football, 'for the sake of the club he's got to go,' enabling the team to establish themselves again as winners within the culture. While the quotation emphasises AVB's position as the 'other' in relation to the collective image of the club, it similarly alludes to the idea that his sacking would again enable the club to fulfil the expectation of their consumer fans, helping them re-substantiate their identity as 'winners.'

This interpretation of 'Fred's' (2012) exchange relates to my argument that the way in which the club is perceived within football culture affects the way that Chelsea fans present their fan identity. Noticing a pattern in the way that 'Ali,' 'Harry' (2012) and 'Fred' (2012) looked to distance themselves from the recent 'failure' of AVB, I looked to gauge the wider reaction of the team's defeat to Napoli by analysing a popular Chelsea online forum, 'The Shed End,' recommended to me by one of the participants. Of the 76 posts published in the 'Post-Game' thread twelve hours after kick off (22 February 2012), 33 posts either featured the term 'embarrassed,' 'embarrassing' or strongly insinuated a feeling of shame, as epitomised by poster 'ChechMeOut86' (22 February 2012): 'I'm dreading going to work, I'm just going to keep my head down,' a post that highlights the significance that the fans' place on the status of the club in the wider culture and their sense of shame at AVB's perceived failure. As my interaction with 'Fred' suggests, the idea of embarrassment seemed to encapsulate the wider feeling of the fans. Unable to identify as winners, the fans were desperate to confer the failure of the club onto the manger, positioning him as an outsider to Chelsea's collective culture of success.

An interesting comparison can be made between the articulations of fan identity for Chelsea and MK Dons fans. In the previous chapter I argued that, like Chelsea fans, the Dons fans' sense of identity stems from their perception of the club within the wider culture. While I argued that Dons fans seemed to revel in the negative reputation of their club, engaging in fandom that emphasised their liminality within football culture, my research with Chelsea fans indicates that they felt shame at the way in which the club was perceived. While I argue that Dons fans revel in their position and engage in humorous behaviour to combat their liminality, I argue that Chelsea fans engage in an astute negotiation of their identity in which they look to absolve themselves from ridicule, redefining the collective idea of the 'club' to preserve their winning identity and create a dichotomy of 'them and us,' to emphasise their opposition to their own manager.

Di Matteo: 'It's like I have my club back'

After a comfortable victory against Bolton (25 February 2012), Chelsea lost 1–0 at home against West Brom (3 March 2012), the first time the club had beaten Chelsea since 1979. AVB was sacked the following day, only eight months into his three-and-a-half-year contract. At the same time, it was announced that former Chelsea midfielder Roberto Di Matteo would replace him as the club's new manager. As soon as the news broke I called two participants I had developed a rapport with. While I expected 'Jim' and 'Tim' (2012) to express their pleasure at the departure of AVB, the majority of the conversation revolved around the appointment of Di Matteo, with both participants indicating that the appointment would unite supporters and restore a sense of pride:

Oliver: What do you think about the appointment of Di Matteo then? I wasn't expecting them to give him the job if I'm honest, the team are obviously struggling and he doesn't have much managerial experience.

'Tim': I wasn't expecting it either, but I tell you what, it's a smart move. He's a legend, isn't he, and will get the full backing of the fans. Think about it, the football can't get much worse but with him in charge it will get the fans pulling in the right direction and improve the atmosphere around the place.

'Jim': I think it's a great shout, to be honest. There has been such a strange atmosphere around the place the whole season .... Di Matteo is such a legend here and him in charge will just unite the fans, you know? Robbie is *Chels'* through and through and will be breaking his neck to get things back on track ... it just feels like I have my club back, you know.

In the weeks preceding AVB's sacking, several of the national papers described the job as a 'poison chalice,' speculating as to which high profile coach would be next to take the hot seat. McNulty's (2012) article for BBC Sport (5 March 2012) encapsulates the sentiment, deriding the approach, citing it as an example of the club's lack of identity. I was expecting the participants to be disappointed with the appointment. Under Abramovich, Chelsea have been managed by a succession of world-famous managers. As 'Bruce' (2011) suggests, this is considered part of the attraction. While Di Matteo is rightfully considered 'a legend' of the club, he had left Chelsea the year before Abramovich had taken over. While famed for scoring the winning goal in the 1997 FA Cup final, he was not considered a global superstar like the team's current squad of players. Taking this into account, along with his lack of managerial experience, I was sceptical if the fans would approve of the appointment, another example of the club's failure to maintain its status as 'winners' within the culture. Significantly, the participants supported Di Matteo's appointment.

At the start of my research 'Bruce' (2011) endorsed Abramovich's 'hiring and firing policy,' citing the need for the club to 'keep moving forward,' yet 'Jim' and 'Tim' (2012) explicitly chose to look back at the club's history evoking Di Matteo's status as a 'club legend,' recalling an era before Abramovich's take over. In doing so I argue that the participants could be seen to position themselves in opposition to the club's 'hiring and firing policy,' evoking the stability of the club before his takeover and 'win at all costs' business strategy. By endorsing the appointment of Di Matteo, rationalising it as a way to 'unite the fans' and 'get everyone pulling in the same direction,' I argue that the fans evoke traditional ideas of community, insinuating that Di Matteo's appointment represents a more sustainable business strategy.

Throughout the conversation the participants evoke the traditional, nostalgic ways in which fans are said to identify with their club, through the representation of community: '(he) will get the full backing of the fans' ('Tim' 2012), 'it will get the fans pulling in the right direction' ('Tim' 2012) and '(he) will just unite the fans, you know?' ('Jim' 2012); historical rootedness: 'He's a legend, isn't he' ('Tim' 2012) and 'Di Matteo is such a legend here' ('Jim' 2012); and emotional attachment: 'Robbie is Chels' through and through' ('Jim' 2012) and 'it just feels like I have my club back, you know' ('Jim' 2012) (see Crampsey 1990; Imlach 2005; Devine 2012).

This encapsulates a significant tension in the fans' identity. The participants happily identified with the club's business strategy when the club were experiencing success, indeed as 'Bruce' (2011) indicates the constant appointment of 'world class managers' was considered a part of the club's allure. However, when AVB had failed to achieve the success his appointment promised, 'Harry,' 'Ali' (2012) and 'Fred' (2012) construct their identity in opposition to AVB, while 'Jim' and 'Tim' (2012) look to position themselves against Abramovich's unsustainable 'hiring and firing policy.' I argue that this relates to the self-awareness of the fans, constructing their identity in constant negotiation of the club and its status within football culture. The participants again constructing their identity by negotiating the discourses surrounding both capitalist and traditional football culture.

With the club not supplying them with reasons to substantiate their identity as 'winners,' I argue that 'Tim' and 'Jim' (2012) seek validation from the wider culture, again looking for opportunities to 'cheer for self' (Vass 2003). In this context I interpret 'Jim' and 'Tim's' endorsement of Di Matteo as an attempt to demonstrate their cultural capital, demonstrating their knowledge of the club and its traditional culture before Abramovich's take over. In a period of instability when the fans are unable to identify as winners in the culture, I argue that 'Jim' and 'Tim' look to position themselves against Abramovich and his capitalist business strategy by demonstrating their understanding of the game's traditional culture.

The participants' comments emphasise the reflexivity of their fan identity and complements Sandvoss' (2005: 112) argument that heavily invested fans are prepared to adjust their identification with texts of fandom to suit their individual need. I argue that the culture of the club adds an important level of context to the participants' comments. 'Jim's' (2012) suggestion that he has his 'club back' seems poignant and can be used to explore the dual ways that the participants look to construct their identity. 'Jim' (2012) evokes the traditional idea of community, indicating that the appointment of Di Matteo and his long association with the club would help restore a sense of communality: 'Di Matteo is such a legend here and him in charge will just unite the fans, you know' and 'Robbie is Chels' through and through.' Conversely, I argue that his comments also relate to the club's contemporary status and correspondingly his expectation that the club is successful. As previously indicated, a significant number of the participants that I engaged with suggested that they started identifying as fans after Abramovich's take over, 'buying into' the status of the club within the culture. Taking this into account, the idea of 'Jim' (2012) having his 'club back' can be interpreted as his excitement at the prospect of engaging with a winning team again. The animosity was so strong towards AVB that I argue that simply sacking him would have been enough to appease the fans, however the appointment of Di Matteo was fortuitous for the opportunity that it provided the fans to demonstrate their cultural capital, recalling his status as a 'club legend' in a manner that allowed them to legitimate their 'traditional' identity, providing them with the opportunity to re-construct their identity within the culture when their status as winners was under threat.

The way in which the fans negotiate their identity in relation to the status of the club is clear when considering the opposing ways in which 'Bruce' (2011) and 'Jim' (2012) describe a 'proper Chelsea manager.' 'Bruce' focuses on AVB's 'winning' characteristics, with his status conferred upon the club, something that the fans share in patronage. 'Jim' (2012) similarly evokes the suitability of Di Matteo for the job by the suggestion that 'Robbie is Chels' through and through,' indicating that 'he will be breaking his neck to get things back on track.' The idea that Di Matteo is 'Chels' through and through' alludes to his association with the club before Abramovich's take over, enabling 'Jim' to evoke the ideals of traditional football culture, particularly a strong sense of community, while helping to demonstrate his knowledge of the club's history.

While 'Bruce' (2012) suggests that there 'is no place for sentiment at the top level,' 'Jim' and 'Tim's' (2012) responses directly challenge this idea, exemplifying the way in which the fans both engage and distance themselves from the club's history in relation to the way that the team is playing on the pitch, reflecting the complex ways in which the fans both identify and reject their positions as consumers but also the significance the participants place on the perception of the club, with the fans constructing their identity in a manner that continues to provide them with opportunities to 'cheer for self' (Vass 2003).

Mourinho, Ferguson, Wenger; 'he's Chels' mate, better than all of them'

While 'Jim' and 'Tim' (2012) look to associate the appointment of Di Matteo with the club's move to a more traditional business strategy, significantly Di Matteo made the team win again. I was in attendance for his third home game in charge against Wigan (7 April 2012) and the change in atmosphere around the ground was palpable. Di Matteo's name was chanted throughout the match, something I had not witnessed with AVB even at the start of the season when his reputation as a 'winner' was intact. At the beginning of the season, the fans did not vocalise their support for AVB as they were *expecting* him to be successful. Contrarily with the appointment of Di Matteo the fans seemed keen to emphasise the idea that the appointment represented a change in Abramovich's business strategy. By generating an impressive atmosphere, the fans were able to subvert the idea that as modern consumers they merely turn up and expect to be entertained (see Hutchinson 1997).

Despite the change in atmosphere, I struggled to notice improvements on the pitch. As suggested, both fans and pundits had become exasperated with the team's defending and while Chelsea emerged victorious, beating Wigan 2–1, the team struggled to play with fluency, conceding possession cheaply while leaving space at the back for the opposition to exploit. Walking back to the tube after the game I engaged in conversation with a group of fans about the game. I was surprised at their satisfaction with the performance. It is poignant that the fans were agitated with the way that I questioned the performance, as if my perceived negativity was impinging on their opportunity to 'cheer for self.'

Oliver: Well, they got the job done in the end, didn't they?
'Kat': Yeah, that was a great performance! It was so good to see Didier (Drogba) and Frank (Lampard) back out there.
'Dan': You can see the difference they make, they are always looking forward, always trying to create chances or shoot ... we had a real bit of danger about us today.
Oliver: Yeah, I know what you mean; Drogba is so direct and powerful. But the defending still doesn't convince me.
'Dan': We won the game, what more do you want? I thought we were great today, it was like the shackles had been taken off and the players could just express themselves.
Oliver: Yeah, we looked good going forward, but against better strikers I think we would have lost today. Wigan could have easily won it playing on the break.
'Kat': [Laughs.] What are you moaning about? We won today, and I thought it was a really entertaining game; we were passing it around better than we have in weeks.

If, as I suggest, the participants internalise the status of the club as part of their fan identity, 'Dan's' (2012) suggestion that 'the shackles had been taken off' seems to apply to the performance of the fans as well as the players; the appointment of Di Matteo provided them with new opportunities to substantiate their identity in opposition to Abramovich's 'hiring and firing policy,' but significantly, once again, the victory provided them with the opportunity to identity as winners.

Initially I was surprised that 'Kat' and 'Dan' (2012) refused to acknowledge the team's poor defending. As suggested, the team's inability to defend was considered to be AVB's main tactical failing and with little over a week to implement his football philosophy Di Matteo had to rely on the same tactics. Despite this, the participants passionately defended the team: 'they are always looking forward, always trying to create chances or shoot ... we had a real bit of danger about us today' and 'we won the game, what more do you want?' ('Dan' 2012). I believe that this corresponds to their support of Di Matteo rather than the quality of the football itself. The participants' agitation at my lack of enthusiasm exemplifies the significance of the club's success and, significantly, the perception of success to their fan identity, with the participants keen that I appreciate and recognise the victory. In this context 'Dan's' (2012) question 'what more you want?' seems significant, encapsulating both the primary motivation of the Chelsea fans, the need to engage with a winning team, but also the desperation that their success is acknowledged within football culture.

With the team trailing so heavily after the first leg with Napoli, the participants, like the pundits, gave the team very little chance of qualifying to the next round. Once again, I watched the match in a local sports bar (14 March 2012). Despite the optimism engendered by Di Matteo's appointment, Chelsea were given very little chance of progression. Subsequently the fans seemed to have a strategy in place for viewing the match that would alleviate blame or criticism from Di Matteo:

Oliver: How are you feeling about tonight?
'Scott': I'm not nervous really, I'm just not expecting anything. [Laughs.]
'Dean': I'm expecting us to get beat.
Oliver: So, after the weekend you don't think the team can turn it around?
'Dean': I was encouraged by the way we played Saturday and I think we will go get into the top four now, but he's not a miracle worker, you can't really expect us to win tonight after that first leg.
'Scott': Yeah, like I expect us to pick up in the league and turn that around, but after the way we played in the first leg, you could have Mourinho, Ferguson, Wenger, all of them on the touch line and they wouldn't get us out of the mess he (AVB) left us in.

It is significant that the participants make a distinction between the team's chances of success in the Premier League and the Champions League. With eleven games remaining in the Premier League, the fans present Di Matteo as the retuning hero, coming back to the club to 'salvage their season' and propel them towards the coveted top four positions. On the contrary, the possibility of him guiding the club to a second leg victory over Napoli and overturning a three-goal deficit was regarded as next to impossible, but, significantly, not due to Di Matteo but the defeat the team experienced under the guidance of AVB. 'Scott' and 'Dean' (2012), like 'Ali' and 'Harry' (2012), look to isolate AVB from the collective image of the club in an attempt to confer blame onto him for what they perceived to be an impending defeat.

Once again, I argue that this relates to the fans' desire to manage the perception of the club and self-identify as winners. While the participants are keen to promote Di Matteo as the returning hero: 'I was encouraged by the way we played Saturday' ('Dean' 2012) and 'I expect us to pick up in the league and turn that around' ('Scott' 2012), I argue that their responses similarly highlight their expectations that the club once again establish themselves as 'winners,' that Di Matteo will 'go get (Chelsea) into the top four now' ('Dean' 2012) to provide them again with opportunities to 'cheer for self.' In doing so the emphasis of his credentials as a 'winning' manager contradicts the idea that his appointment represents a more sustainable 'traditional' business model, in which the club are not looking for instant success. This notion is vindicated by the way in which the participants continually emphasise the failings of AVB, alleviating Di Matteo from blame for what was seen to be an impending defeat in an attempt to maintain his status as a winner: 'You could have Mourinho, Ferguson, Wenger, all of them on the touch line and they wouldn't get us out of the mess he (AVB) left us in' ('Scott' 2012) and 'he's not a miracle worker, you can't really expect us to win tonight after that first leg' ('Dean' 2012).

While this helps to maintain Di Matteo's status, the juxtaposition between the 'successful' Di Matteo and the 'failure' AVB serves as a reminder of the ruthless action the club is willing to take to maintain their success. The simplistic opposition between the 'good' (Di Matteo) and the 'bad' (ABV) is problematic. While 'Tim' and 'Jim' (2012) heralded the appointment of Di Matteo as a return to the ideas of community and stability associated with traditional football culture, 'Scott' and 'Dean' (2012) provide a reminder of the ways in which AVB was ruthlessly hounded out of the club for his inability to deliver success, accentuating the significance of success to their fans' identity.

The perceived failings of AVB were so great that the club was left requiring a 'miracle' ('Dean' 2012) to progress. On the night Chelsea were exceptional, beating Napoli 4–1 to win the tie 5–4 on aggregate. The defensive highline the team had struggled to implement had been abolished with the team sitting deeper in their own half, allowing Napoli to keep possession in front of them but prohibiting them space to run in behind. The team were set up to frustrate Napoli, with all eleven players behind the ball when the team were not in possession, only for them to counter attack, catching them on the break when they had committed players forward.

'Scott' and 'Dean' (2012) were ecstatic at the final whistle.

Oliver: I'll be honest; I have to admit that I was unconvinced by the appointment of Di Matteo, but tactically tonight he got it spot on. That is the best I have seen Chelsea all season.

'Scott': How could you not be happy with the appointment? We played like *that* tonight and he's a Chelsea legend.

Oliver: I can't say anything about tonight, the performance was fantastic. He's a club legend but it's dangerous to presume that someone is going to be a great manager just because they had a good career as a player.

'Dean': After what I've seen tonight, he is a great manager. There was all that talk at the start of the season that AVB was the next Mourinho, the next big thing, but that performance was better than anything he gave us. I think that's the problem with Chelsea fans these days, they want the big names all the time, but Drogba continues to show that he is better than Torres and Di Matteo has already done a better job than AVB ... the grass isn't always greener.

Oliver: You said before that he's not a miracle worker and, let's be honest, you were saying before kick-off that you thought the team had no chance tonight, so you can't have been totally convinced by him?

'Scott': Having seen that tonight, he is a miracle worker. To turn the team around like that in the little time that he's been here and get us out of the mess AVB left us in—it's nothing short of amazing. Honestly, he is class. We could go all the way now. There is no one we couldn't beat if we play like we did tonight.

Oliver: Well, you did say it could be Mourinho, Ferguson and Wenger all together in the dugout and we still couldn't win tonight, so I guess Di Matteo must be good?
'Dean': He's Chels' mate, better than all of them.

The conversation epitomises the tension in which the fans both use the appointment of Di Matteo to oppose Abramovich's business strategy, evoking his 'traditional' association with the club, while dually revelling in their status as 'winners' that his appointment has helped to re-establish. I argue that this is highly significant, representing the participants' unique fan identity as consumer fans attracted to the club by its culture of success, while being highly aware of the perception of the club in wider football culture. While I argue that the successful perception of the club largely contributes to the identity of the fans, the dual way in which the participants use the appointment of Di Matteo to establish opposition indicates that the fans are similarly aware of the way in which their consumer identity is perceived within football culture. This notion is epitomised by the way in which 'Dean' (2012) looks to distance his fan identity from the club's 'consumer fans,' attributing blame on them for accepting Abramovich's 'hiring and firing policy.' As he suggests: 'Chelsea fans these days … want the big names … the grass isn't always greener.'

While keen to demonstrate his legitimacy as a fan, challenging the consumer stereotype, it is significant that 'Dean's' (2012) rebuke again came as a response to my perceived lack of enthusiasm towards Di Matteo. Consequently, I interpreted his remark as a derision of my fan identity, in which he attempts to position me with consumer fans that 'demand instant success.' I argue that 'Dean' engages in complex negotiation, placing me in a position of the 'other' to his identity that he constructs in opposition to Abramovich's capitalist business strategy and the club's consumer fans. However, it is 'Dean's' insistence that I recognise the ability of the manager and the magnitude of the victory that compromises his attempts to position himself against the club's consumer fans. Having outlined AVB's failure to alleviate Di Matteo from blame for what was expected to be an impeding defeat, the conversation revolves around the juxtaposition between the success of Di Matteo and the failure of AVB: 'he is a great manager' ('Dean' 2012), 'having seen that tonight, he is a miracle worker' ('Scott' 2012) and 'there is no one we couldn't beat' ('Scott' 2012).

It is ironic that having made a plea for consistency, lamenting consumer fans for constantly yearning for 'greener grass,' 'Dean' (2012) contradicts his statement emphasising how the club's fortunes dramatically improved by sacking AVB, with Di Matteo rescuing the club from the 'mess' he left behind. Significantly, like Di Matteo, AVB had also won his first two games in charge, a point I tried to raise with the participants before being rebuked. Despite their criticism of the frivolity of Chelsea's consumer fans with which I was associated, it was evident that the participants placed a premium on victory that belied the identity that they had fashioned for themselves. While it is understandable that the fans would be elated after such an impressive victory once again, like 'Kat' and 'Dan' (2012) I engaged with after the Wigan game, there was almost a desperation to emphasise the significance of victory in an attempt to convince me of the team's quality, as if my accordance validated their identity as winners. Again, I argue that this demonstrates the significance the participants place on the way in which the club is regarded within football culture, with the participants keen for me to recognise and validate the success of the club to enable them to 'cheer for self.'

'Dean's' (2012) final remark 'He's Chels' mate, better than all of them' seems significant and encapsulates the overall tension of the conversation. The appointment of Di Matteo was used by the fans that I engaged with to reflect the club's 'tradition' and 'history,' indicative of a move to embrace a more stable business strategy, in opposition to Abramovich at a time when his appointment of AVB failed to bring the fans the success they expected, tarnishing the successful perception of the club within the culture. Significantly, Di Matteo had made the team win again and at that moment of my research, represented the fans' ideal image of the club, as victorious and highly successful, achieving a result that would garner them respect from wider football culture. It is poignant that like 'Bruce's' (2011) description of AVB in the opening exchange, Di Matteo is personified by 'Dean' (2012) as a reflection of the club: 'He's Chels'.' While Abramovich's 'hiring and firing policy' and AVB are presented as incongruent to the successful culture of the club, 'Dean' (2012) looks to assimilate Di Matteo with the club's culture of success, an association he looks to establish by emphasising Di Matteo's evocation of the club's history and his ability to win big matches.

'There's only one England captain'

When AVB had stopped achieving the necessary victories he was hounded out of the club, with the participants deriding his appointment as another 'quick fix.' Accordingly, Abramovich's 'hiring and firing policy' was criticised by the fans for 'making the club a laughing stock' ('Fred' 2012). With the club failing to provide fans with opportunities to 'cheer for self' (Vass 2003), the fans constructed concepts of 'us and them' to isolate AVB and Abramovich from the club's culture of success. With the appointment of Di Matteo and the team's return to winning ways, again I noticed a shift in the way in which the fans negotiated their identity, assimilating Di Matteo with the club's culture of success to mobilise a sense of hierarchy upon which the club markets itself. The way in which the fans enacted collective identity in opposition to wider football culture was explicit in the way in which the fans rallied around Chelsea captain John Terry and fellow player Ashley Cole after the pair become embroiled in a controversial racism scandal.

On 24 October 2011, the football world was thrown into chaos as footage emerged of John Terry, Chelsea and England captain, racially abusing Queens Park Rangers' (QPR) defender Anton Ferdinand. While Terry was given a four-game ban and fined £90,000, he escaped punishment in the court of law largely due to the testimony of black defender Ashley Cole. Terry was severely lambasted within football culture, criticised by fellow black professionals and stripped of the England captaincy, while Cole faced similar criticism for 'defending the indefensible,' supporting Terry and preventing the service of justice. Both players were seen to bring the game into serious disrepute. Already unpopular for various misdemeanours in their private lives,[2] the pair became hate figures within football culture, jeered by rival fans whenever they touched the ball. I witnessed this first hand when Newcastle visited Stamford Bridge (2 May 2012). The notoriously vocal Newcastle fans chanted more songs directed at the pair than in support of their own team. Highlights of the repertoire included choruses of 'Scum, scum, scum', 'You know what you are, you know what you are, oh John Terry, you know what you are' and 'John Terry hates you', directed at the team's black players Didier Drogba, Ramirez, Jon Obi Mikel and Ryan Bertrand.

While football culture was quick to vilify the pair, significantly the Chelsea fans that I engaged with refused to admonish their behaviour and even cited Cole's defence of his captain as a way in which the club had developed a great team spirit and sense of cohesion under Di Matteo. 'Craig' and 'Sheena' (2012) encapsulate these sentiments. I approached the couple as 'Craig' was wearing a 'Terry is innocent' shirt being sold by bootleggers outside the stadium.

Oliver: I saw them selling your shirt up the road; you must have wound a few people up with that?

'Craig': I'm not trying to wind anyone up, it's about supporting him (Terry) when he's getting so much stick at the moment.

Oliver: I know he's such a big player for the club but come on, do you *really* think he's innocent?

'Sheena': He swore at him, but it was in the heat of the moment; everyone knows how passionate he is and to say he is racist is just stupid. Ash (Cole) came out and said he's not a racist and if he was as bad as what everyone's saying then the black players would refuse to play with him, wouldn't they? It's just been made into such a big deal by the media and everything because he's one of us.

'Craig': Players abuse each other on the pitch all the time but because its JT (John Terry), because it's one of ours, it's easy for people to try and make an example out of him. It's just another part of the media always having a go against our club. Everyone knows JT is vital to the success of this club and they are trying to bring him down.

Oliver: But he was caught on camera. It's a bit different from the normal banter you get on the pitch.

'Sheena': He's our captain for f***'s sake. He's been at the club his whole life, and put his body on the line week in, week out for us and you can't get over it and support him? I don't care what he's like as a person but when he's wearing the shirt and giving his all he'll get our support and that's how it should be. You protect your own, don't you?

The participants engage in a passionate defence of the players, and while I did not feel threatened, it became clear as the encounter progressed that the pair were becoming increasingly annoyed that I continued to question Terry's morality. Significantly, neither of the participants argued Terry's innocence; indeed, apart from wearing the t-shirt, they carefully avoid answering the question. I argue that Terry's 'innocence' is of little importance to the participants, with the final exchange indicating that they accept his guilt and applaud Cole for 'protecting (his) own' ('Sheena' 2012). Fundamentally the pair's defence of Terry relates to his importance to the team as 'Craig' (2012) suggests 'JT is vital to the team's success.' This indicates that the participants prioritise the success of the team over Terry's racism, and the way in which his action damages the perception of the club within football culture.

Again, a tension is apparent; the participants that I had previously engaged with looked to 'other' AVB and Abramovich, distancing them from the wider image of the club when their individual failings were seen to negatively affect the reputation of the club within football culture. While the team were struggling on the pitch, fans that I engaged with described their sense of embarrassment, keen to ingratiate themselves to the wider culture by demonstrating their engagement with the club's tradition. Ironically, at a time when they should feel a sense of embarrassment at the actions of their captain, the figurehead of the club, the participants defiantly recognise his centrality to the team's sporting success. This seems to be the fans' motivation behind their support of Terry and Cole. With the appointment of Di Matteo the team had been achieving good results, particularly in Europe, beating Benfica (4 April 2012) and tournament favourites Barcelona (18 April 2012) on route to the Champions League final, helping to restore a sense of pride and communality around the club. Problematically, the partisanship created by the appointment and the way in which Di Matteo has been able to galvanise the crowd with good results seemed to have pacified the participants into tolerating racism.

There are numerous indications throughout the conversation that the participants' defence of the players relates to the team's success. As 'Sheena' (2012) indicates, she has little interest in Terry's misdemeanours as long as he gives his all for the team. Similarly, 'Craig' (2012) forms associations between supporting the players and the success of the club as he suggests 'everyone knows JT is vital to the success of this club and they are trying to bring him down,' evoking the idea that the animosity directed towards Terry by wider football culture relates to the team's success and their subsequent jealousy.

A song adopted by the Chelsea fans' after winning the Champions League final encapsulates this notion, emphasising the way in which the fans' support of the players during the scandal relates to their recognition of their importance to the club's success. After the Champions League final as the players paraded round the pitch there were audible chants of 'We know what we are, we know what we are, Champions of Europe, we know what we are,' the fans appropriating the song adopted by away fans in protest of Terry's actions. The song vindicates my argument that Terry and Cole were considered as vital elements to the team's success, the song both evoking the scandal and goading the wider culture to re-substantiate the idea that Chelsea are 'champions.' Similarly, important is the use of the term 'we;' while the song evokes the incident and importantly the reaction of wider football culture in response to the incident, the use of collective rhetoric recalls the way in which 'Bruce' (2011) used collective rhetoric to construct his identity in association with the culture of the club. The song works in a similar way, with the fans accentuating their constitutive relationship with the club to self-identify as champions. As I have previously suggested, in cheering for the self, fans invest in players to the extent that they become part of their identity. By refusing to condemn Terry, but instead recognising his ability as a player concomitant with his figurehead role as captain of the club, the fans were able to cheer for him, maintaining their total investment in the collective image of the club. This would allow them to feel at one with the celebration as part of the collective while absolved of guilt for his personal misdemeanours.

There are indications throughout the conversation that the participants are aware of their status as consumers within football culture, with 'Sheena' and 'Craig' (2012) drawing upon the way in which they are perceived due to their self-identification as winners within the culture. They suggest Terry was an easy target due to his association with the club and his status as a winner: 'It's just been made into such a big deal … because he's *one of us*,' and 'because it's JT (John Terry), because it's one of ours, it's easy for people to try and make an example out of him.' Rather than Terry or Cole, it is significant that I became the 'other' in 'Sheena' and 'Craig's' construction of their identity. I was positioned in correlation with the 'jealous' media and rival fans, with the participants looking to deny my association with the club and subsequently my opportunity to share the clubs' success. This idea is encapsulated by 'Sheena's' (2012) final comment:

> He's our captain for f***'s sake. He's been at the club his whole life, and put his body on the line week in, week out for us and you can't get over it and support him? I don't care what he's like as a person but when he's wearing the shirt and giving his all he'll get our support and that's how it should be. You protect your own, don't you?

Abramovich: 'I wish he would just f*** off and take his money with him'

As I made my first trip to Stamford Bridge three weeks into the start of the new 2012/2013 season to watch the team play Newcastle United (25 August 2012), it was evident that the club had gone to great lengths to emphasise their status as 'champions' within the culture. As I approached the main gates at the entrance of the stadium, I was met by a huge banner displaying scenes from the Champions League victory celebrations, accompanied by the slogan 'Welcome to Chelsea, home of the European Champions,' a welcome that has been adopted by the public announcer greeting the fans before each home game. Even the club's new kit pays homage to the victory; labelled the 'Champions edition,' the customary white marking had been replaced with gold. While it is customary for fans to get the name of their favourite player printed on the back of their shirt, it seemed poignant that overwhelmingly the fans had opted to get 'Champions 12' printed in homage to the team's success. These initiatives taken by the club's marketing team are highly astute, complimenting my suggestion that the club purposely look to promote themselves as an attraction to a global audience. The banner can almost be interpreted as an advert greeting fans as they enter, reassuring them that they are associating themselves with winners and champions, helping fans to recognise the club's capacity to fulfil their consumer needs. The shirts also indicate that the club are aware of the need of their fans to be recognised as winners, with the gold shirts manufactured to signify their status and giving the fans an opportunity to revel in the team's success every time they wear it.

Adopting these initiatives, the club must have been aware of the backlash they were likely to receive from wider football culture, with popular football blogs particularly quick to judge the tacky, gaudy and self-aggrandising shirts. Indeed, the gold embellishment was used as an example to support the idea that the fans were 'football chavs,' obsessed with status and self-promotion, without class or the cultural capital to back it up (see Ahmed 2004; Hayward & Yar 2006; Walker 2008).

While attacks on chav culture are described by Hayward and Yar (2006: 16) as 'a top down attempt to maintain social order' indicative of the attacks on football's consumer fans made by self-identified traditional fans, it is significant that Cook (2000: 73) suggests alternatively that chav culture can be interpreted as a bottom up assault on the norm of middle-class society. It is my argument that there is self-knowingness in the club's promotion of the gold 'champion' shirts that evokes this idea, particularly Eco's (1976) concept of semiotic guerrilla warfare, the way in which symbols of status can be re-appropriated and knowingly used to antagonise wider cultures. As Aden (1999) argues, fandom is always based on acts of textual and social discrimination articulated via taste, and as previously suggested I argue that Chelsea fans are attracted to the club for the way in which fandom enables them to construct their identity in opposition to wider football culture.

In the previous chapter I analysed the ways in which Dons fans appropriated songs and customs associated with Wimbledon in celebration of their liminality, embracing their role as consumers within the culture. While I argue that the 'Champions edition' kit enables the Chelsea fans, like the Don's fans, to play on their role as football consumers and 'chavs' within the culture, this has not been adopted by the fans as an act of protest, but instead seems to be a clever marketing idea by the club that enables the fans to 'cheer for self' and perpetuate their status as champions, directly evoking the hierarchy that the fans buy into.

Despite the club's Champions League success, three months into the season the decorum of Stamford Bridge changed again. Less than a year after taking over, uniting the fans after AVB's tenure and delivering the best result in the club's history, Di Matteo was sacked after the team's performances were deemed unsatisfactory by Abramovich. It was announced at the same time that former Liverpool boss Rafa Benitez would take over for the remainder of the season. As soon as the news broke I rang 'Jim' and 'Tim' (2012b), the participants I conversed with when Di Matteo was first appointed. Both participants were disgusted with the decision:

Oliver: Have you heard the news?

'Jim': Mate, I am disgusted, truly disgusted. I truly can't believe it. Six months ago he goes and wins us the European Cup and after a couple poor results he's sacked. It's a bloody joke!

'Tim': I have but I can't believe it to be honest with you. I suppose I should never be surprised with Abramovich in charge but it's an embarrassing decision. He's made us a laughing stock again.

Oliver: What about Rafa getting the job?

'Jim': What a bloody joke that is. You have a man that loves the club like Di Matteo and you replace him with someone who has come out and criticised the club and the fans in the press before. Like I say, I'm disgusted. We just won the European Cup, the place has been buzzing every week and this will completely kill it.

'Tim': Its embarrassing, this is the guy that has come out in the press before when he was Liverpool boss and was on about how his team were going to win it for their 'real football fans' and went on this rant calling us a plastic club. I can't stand the guy. Di Matteo was loved here, he was a god and to get rid of him for this guy (Benitez)... Honestly mate, I've had enough of Abramovich now.

Oliver: Really? He makes some very controversial decisions but without his investment the club wouldn't have won any of its success the last few years.

'Tim': I know but I just don't care anymore. His decisions are making the club a laughing stock. Everyone is going to be hammering us again tomorrow and I can't blame them. What more does he want? We won the Champions League, you can't do better than that, but on a whim he goes and fires the most successful manager we've ever had. This is my football club and he's just treating it like his toy. I wish he would just f*** off and take his money with him at this point.

It seems highly significant and indeed emblematic of modern football culture that in my research period the fans' construction of identity had become cyclic. The most obvious indication was in the choice of language used by the participants. Evoking my exchange with 'Fred' (2012), 'Jim' and 'Tim' (2012b) describe the club as a 'joke' with which they are 'embarrassed' to be associated. As suggested, the appointment of Di Matteo was highly astute, encouraging fans to form cohesive bonds with the club after their identity had been 'tarnished' by AVB's 'failure,' while their success in the Champions League enabled them to once again self-identify as winners. The exchange emphasises my argument that despite their almost antagonistic relationship with wider football culture, Chelsea fans are highly concerned about the way in which they are perceived. Now that they feel that their identity has been challenged they again appear vulnerable. Under AVB, 'Fred' (2012) suggested that he felt a sense of embarrassment, that the club's lack of success had tarnished their identification as 'winners.' Ironically, now 'Jim' and 'Tim' (2012b) are embarrassed that having established themselves as winners, Abramovich would do something to harm their status, inviting criticism and supporting the negative stereotypes upheld about the club within wider football culture.

This notion is alluded to by the way in which the fans lament the appointment of Rafa Benitez. While Di Matteo had encouraged the fans to identify as winners again, it is important to note that Di Matteo also provided them with a perfect counter argument to the suggestion that the club prioritised victory and status at the expense of tradition. As 'Tim' and 'Jim' (2012b) indicate, the appointment of Benitez seemingly holds a mirror to Chelsea fans. Accepting Benitez into the community surrounding the club can almost be considered as an acceptance of the idea that he perpetuated, that Chelsea should be considered as 'plastic,' artificial and emblematic of the game's capitalism. Their level of grievance at Benitez's appointment is such that I argue that the fans are fully aware of how it will be perceived in the wider culture, and importantly how the appointment significantly contradicts their claims of legitimacy or self-identity as infallible champions.

With this in mind, it seems significant that 'Tim' (2012b) makes such a point of venting his anger at Abramovich, blaming him for the way in which the club will be perceived in wider football culture. As a fan group that accentuate the importance of winning to their identity, this is significant, as Abramovich has provided the club with the resources that have enabled them to experience success, defining the winning culture that the fans look to identify with. Subsequently I argue that there is a knowingness about the anger directed at Abramovich, in which 'Tim's' (2012b) anger can be interpreted as a ploy to emphasise his 'legitimate' fan identity, demonstrating that he is not a 'plastic' consumer as implied by Benitez.

I strongly doubt that any of the Chelsea fans that I have engaged with throughout the research period would truly want Abramovich to leave the club, particularly as a significant number of the participants admit to being drawn to the club after he took charge, promising them world class footballers, entertainment and the chance to experience victory. Indeed, I argue that the opportunities Abramovich provide the fans to 'cheer for self' are too great for them to truly wish for his departure. While 'Tim' (2012b) makes a passionate case that Abramovich is treating '*his*' club like a 'toy,' I believe he has the relationship the wrong way around. Fundamentally it is Abramovich's club and he has the financial capacity to do with it as he pleases. This corresponds to the astute argument made by 'Fran' (2012) in the previous chapter:

> Fans need to understand that with the big investment in football now, like Abramovich at Chelsea, they, or 'the community,' don't own anything.

> It's Abramovich that buys the players and success, not the fans. Abramovich owns Chelsea, he owns the club, he buys the players, he's the man with all the power there. They love him when they do well, they won loads when they got (Jose) Mourinho, didn't they; he's the man that made the decisions and brought him to the club.

It is the awareness that the fans have of their status within wider football culture that I argue accounts for their attempts to emphasise their engagement with the discourse surrounding traditional football culture, particularly when the team are not giving them reasons to 'cheer for self' on the pitch. However, despite their knowledge of their reputation as consumers within the culture, I argue that the need to 'win' and self-identify as winners always seems to override their attempts to 'legitimise' their identity within football culture or engage in acts of protest. As 'Tim' (2012b) states 'I wish he would just f*** off and take his money with him *at this point*,' a quotation that seems to epitomise my argument. Abramovich was criticised and scorned *at this point* in time when his actions were seen to have affected the club's reputation and the fans' ability to identity as winners.

Positioning himself in opposition to Abramovich and his control of the club, 'Tim' (2012b) takes ownership of the club: 'This is my football club and he's (Abramovich) just treating it like his toy.' As a fan attracted to the club for the way in which it enables him to experience success and identify as a 'winner' within football culture, it could be suggested that the club is in fact his 'toy,' however it is significant that 'Tim' looks to emphasise his deep emotional connection with the club, drawing on the discourse associated with the ways in which traditional fans identify with their clubs (see Crampsey 1990; Imlach 2005; Devine 2012), in opposition to Abramovich's relationship of capitalism.

Notes

1 During my nine months of research I was privy to three changes.
2 Cole cheated on his then-wife and national sweetheart Cheryl Tweedy. Terry had an affair with team mate Wayne Bridge's wife.

Bibliography

Aden, RC (1999) *Popular Stories and Promised Lands: Fan Culture and Symbolic Pilgrimages*. Tuscaloosa. University of Alabama Press.

Ahmed, S (2004) *The Cultural Politics of Emotion*. Edinburgh. Edinburgh University Press.

Bale, J (1998) 'Virtual Fandoms: Futurescapes of Football' Cited in Brown, A *Fanatics: Power, Identity and Fandom in Football*. London. Routledge.

Barker, C (2004) *The Sage Dictionary of Cultural Studies*. London. Sage.

Brimson, D (1998) *The Geezers Guide to Football: A Lifetime of Lads and Lager*. London. Mainstream Publishing.

'ChechMeOut86' (2012) *Napoli vs Chelsea Match Thread*. The Shed End [Website] Available from: http://www.theshedend.com/topic/19626-v-napoli/ (Accessed 22 February 2012).
Cook, J (2000) 'Culture, Class and Taste' Cited in Munt, S *Cultural Studies and the Working Class: Subject to Change*. London. Cassell.
Crampsey, R (1990) *First 100 Years: Scottish League Football*. Edinburgh. The Scottish Football League Press.
Devine, TM (2012) *The Scottish Nation: A Modern History*. London. Penguin.
Doyle, P (2011) *Chelsea Appoints Andre Villas Boas on Three-year Deal*. Footy Tube [Website] Available from: http://www.footytube.com/news/guardian/chelsea-appoint-former-porto-coach-andre-villas-boas-on-three-year-deal-L9179 (Accessed 11 January 2013).
Dyer, R (1999) 'The Role of Stereotype' Cited in Marris, P & Thornhan, S *Media Studies: A Reader*. Edinburgh. Edinburgh University Press.
Eco, U (1976) *A Theory of Semiotics*. Indiana. University of Indiana Press.
Fiske, J (1992) 'The Cultural Economy of Fandom' Cited in Lewis, L *The Adoring Audience*. London. Routledge.
Fynn, A & Davidson, H (1996) *Dream On: A Year in the Life of a Premier League Club*. London. Simon & Schuster Press.
Hayward, K & Yar, M (2006) The 'Chav' Phenomenon: Consumption, Media and the Construction of a New Underclass. *Journal for Crime, Media and Culture* 2 (9) 10–28.
Hills, M (2002) *Fan Cultures*. London. Routledge.
Hutchinson, R (1997) *The Toon: A Complete History of Newcastle United*. Edinburgh. Mainstream Publishing.
Imlach, G (2005) *My Father and Other Working-Class Football Heroes*. London. Yellow Jersey Press.
Ingle, S (2005) Football Fans Are Idiots. *The Guardian* [Website] Available from: http://www.theguardian.com/football/2005/sep/02/sport.blueprintforabetterfootball (Accessed 23 October 2011).
Jameson, F (1991) *Postmodernism or the Cultural Logic of Late Capitalism*. London. Verso.
Lancaster, K (2001) *Interacting with Babylon 5*. Austin. University of Texas Press.
McNulty, P (2012) *Time Waits for No Man at Stamford Bridge*. BBC Sport [Website] Available from: http://www.bbc.co.uk/blogs/legacy/philmcnulty/2012/03/wealth_and_honour_waits_for_no.html (Accessed 5 March 2012).
Neville, G (2012) I Know It's Cliché but Chelsea's Name was Always on the Cup. *The Daily Mail* [Website] Available from: http://www.dailymail.co.uk/sport/football/article-2146986/Gary-Neville-I-know-cliche-Chelseas-cup.html (Accessed 14 October 2014).
Pearson, G (2012) *An Ethnography of English Football Fans: Cans, Cops and Carnivals*. Manchester. Manchester University Press.
Rolls, T (2014) *Chelsea Fans Blame Price for Empty Stadium*. BBC Sport [Website] Available from: http://www.bbc.co.uk/sport/0/football/29872408 (Accessed 19 November 2014).
Sandvoss, C (2005) *Fans*. Cambridge. Polity.
Sennett, R (2006) *The Culture of the New Capitalism*. London. Yale University Press.
Thornton, S (1995) *Club Cultures: Music, Media and Subcultural Capital*. Cambridge. Polity.
Vass, J (2003) *Cheering for Self: An Ethnography of the Basketball Event*. Indiana. IUniverse.

Walker, J (2008) Chav: The Emergence of a New Identity. *Interstice: Journal of Literature and Culture* 1 (1) 1–12.
Williams, J (2000) 'The Changing Face of Football: A Case for National Regulation' Cited in Mitchie, J et al *Football in the Digital Age: Whose Game is it Anyway?* London. Mainstream Publishing.

Chapter 7

'IN-GER-LAND'

Ethnography in the pub

While the preceding chapters document the unique ways in which consumer fans enact fandom in relation to the specific culture of their club, the chapters present a commonality between the ways in which the fans construct their identity. I argue that the fans engage in a process of complex discursive negotiation, constructing their identities by drawing on the discourses that continue to surround the culture, 'capitalism' and 'tradition,' informed by the cultures of their club. My argument is that the fans' levels of engagement and understanding of these discourses produce different expectations of how they *should* identify as fans. Indeed, I argue that fans construct their identity based on their different perceptions of what is *expected* of them within the culture.

I document the way that participants self-identify as consumers within the culture, 'buying into' the culture of their club for the way in which it is seen to address their consumer need, yet as indicated the fans' identification as consumers does not mean that they fail to identity with discourse of the game's tradition. In each chapter I acknowledge the ways in which participants similarly construct their identity in opposition to the culture of their club to enact a fandom culturally recognised and associated with traditional football culture. The more I considered my data, the more I started to pick up on this tension. It became increasingly apparent that the participants exercised interactive and flexible fan identities that manifest in their relationship with the culture of their clubs, choosing to identify and distance themselves from it interchangeably based on their individual expectation of the *type* of fandom that each situation required.

Acknowledging this trend in my data I felt compelled to conduct further research, taking my work into 'extra time.' While presenting a unique insight into the ways in which self-identified consumer fans construct their identity, I was keen to assess the way in which self-identified 'traditional fans' enact identity, to see if they engage in similar discursive negotiations and to assess whether their identity is similarly shaped by their expectations of what it means to be a 'traditional fan.' I believe that the inclusion of this chapter operates to further explicate the nuances of identity within contemporary football culture while similarly helping to promote cohesion between 'consumers' and 'traditional' fans within the culture. I looked to achieve this by approaching both self-identified fan groups with methodological parity, conducting further ethnography within 'MG's,' a popular sports bar in Norfolk, England.

Contextualising the pub as an arena

The historical literature documents the affinity between the public house (pub) and football culture (see Williams 2000; King 2002; Hopcraft 2006). This literature predominantly describes the ritualistic significance that the pub has had in the life of the fan, providing them with 'the holy trinity, beer, football and male bonding' (Weed 2008: 189), a space to read about football, talk about football and meet with friends before attending matches. However, since the sale of television rights to BSkyB in 1992 and the implementation of stadia modernisation in correlation with the Taylor Report, much of the contemporary literature has argued that the role of the pub within the culture has developed, the pub described as a venue in itself to watch live matches (Brimson 1998; Bale 1998; Williams 2000; Weed 2008). Much of this contemporary literature argues that the pub provides the 'traditional' fan with a 'more authentic' alternative to the modern stadium, with the pub on match days becoming the preferred space of the 'traditional fan.'

Citing evidence from market information source Mintel and Keynote, Weed (2008) outlines the contemporary popularity of pub fandom in England. He suggests that in 2002 9.1 million chose to watch live football in the pub, a figure notably higher than the 8.7 million that paid to attend a match in the modern stadium. This figure is equivalent to 19% of the population. Taking into account the increasing popularity of the pub as a regular venue to watch live football, this chapter explores pub fandom as a unique cultural experience.

The first literature that acknowledged the changing role of the pub within football culture described the fans' patronage in terms of necessity. With the sale of Premier League broadcasting rights to BSkyB and the relatively low penetration of satellite and cable TV services, Weed (2008) estimates that between 5% and 8% of the population would have been able to access the first year of BSkyB's Premier League coverage at home. It is suggested that this led to an increase of fans keen to watch live matches but deterred by the modern stadium, being forced to watch matches in the pub. The idea of 'necessity' still surrounds the pub in the suggestion that the increased ticket prices and the wider gentrification of the game has made attending live matches virtually impossible for 'traditional' working-class fans. Weed (2008) estimates that over a third of men in the UK visited the pub to watch a live game for the 2011/2012 season due to the way that it is said to afford a 'participatory fandom' indicative of the terraces.

I argue that this discourse surrounding pub fandom produces certain expectations for fans that are fundamentally different to those of the modern stadium. To refer back to the quote from Ken Bates (cited by King 2002), he argues that consumer fans expect the modern stadium to reflect football's assimilation with modern leisure industries, expecting a level of comfort and amenity, a proposition that is vindicated by the participants in the previous chapters describing the ways in which the modern stadium addresses their needs as consumers. Conversely the construction of the pub as a 'traditional space' evokes the image of the terraces as encapsulated by Hopcraft (2006: 188): 'trapped for a couple of hours in a swaying crush of bodies, frequently forced off his feet in a delirious surge of mass movement, coming away with bruises and stains.' I argue that this construction of the pub helps to produce certain expectations about the demographic attracted to the pub, the atmosphere and the types of behaviour expected, making the pub attractive to a generation of fans enticed by collective images of revelry and the idea that the pub allows the enactment of a 'more authentic,' participatory fandom, outlawed in the modern stadium.

With the growing popularity of pub fandom and the proliferation of literature that describes the pub as a legitimate alternative to the modern stadium, this chapter approaches the pub as stadia in its own right. Accordingly, ethnography was conducted in the same manner as the previous chapters, in which 'MG's,' a popular pub for sports in Norfolk, England, was selected as a site for analysis. The impetuous for this selection was inspired by a fortuitous encounter with my neighbour 'Toby' (2012), who invited me to join him and his group of friends to watch England's Euro 2012 matches.[1] This provided me with access to a regular venue from which to conduct my research as well as the opportunity to engage with him and a group of his friends, self-identified traditional fans, as a 'complete participant' (Reed-Danahay 1997; Bryman 2008; Scott-Jones & Watt 2010). In correlation with the previous chapters I positioned myself within the 'arena' to observe the behaviour of his group as well as the wider patrons of the pub, sharing their sensory experience. Like my research in the modern stadium, I complimented my observations with a series of semi-structured interviews, conducted both with 'Toby' and his friends as well as other 'pub fans' attracted to 'MG's' for the tournament. While the use of ethnography enabled me to consider the pub as a legitimate venue in its own right, the method helped to maintain the continuity of my work to ensure my comparisons between the collective identities and experiences that I documented in each chapter are as valid as possible.

Like the fans within the stadium, the patrons that frequented the pub provided me with a self-selecting research sample. In my attempt to maintain methodological parity, I conducted eight semi-structured interviews concomitant with each chapter, with eight conducted throughout the tournament. Interviews were again guided by an inventory and conducted largely before kick-off, however on particular occasions when I encountered something interesting while the match was in progress, I purposefully looked to engage with the discerning participants at a suitable stop in play, half-time or upon the final whistle. Concomitant with my in-stadia ethnography, participants were fully informed about the aims of the research, consent was obtained and anonymity was assured.

Invited to the pub by 'Toby' (2012), the chapter similarly features extracts from informal conversations that I had with members of his group. Again, the behaviour of the group was occasionally reprehensible, but I did not intervene. I justify this in the methodology chapter by suggesting that the motivations underpinning these incidents relate to the participants' fan identity or importantly their *expectations* of how to enact and articulate their identity. This seems explicit in relation to 'Toby' and his friends; I believe that there was a strong level of performativity to our exchanges with the group acting in a way that related to their expectations of what constituted 'traditional' fan identity. Again, while unpleasant I argue that the more unsavoury elements of the group's fan performance provided me with a valid insight into the way in which the group looked to construct their identity.

While an analysis of pub fandom around a specific team would have enabled me to compare the way in which collective identity is enacted in contrast to the modern stadium, I opted to conduct my research around England's Euro 2012 campaign. There is a range of ethnographic research that analyses the role of the pub in screening major international tournaments (Bale 1998, Brimson 1998; Weed 2008); in keeping with much of the literature these studies position the pub as the space of 'traditional' fandom. However, it is poignant that a different strand of literature, written by authors that do not self-identify as traditional fans, frame international matches as contests that attract more 'casual' fans whose interest is promoted by a sense of national collectivity and sporting occasion (Carrington 1998; Bondy 2010; Brown 2014). These texts similarly suggest that fans are attracted to the pub to watch live matches, but not for its association with the game's traditional culture, but to experience a sense of 'togetherness' and collectivity that the semi-public nature of the pub facilitates. Carrington (1998: 109) suggests that different agents prompt this 'casual' fandom: 'the media,' 'neighbours' and 'work mates.'

The different ways in which international matches are said to attract different 'types' of fans emphasises the discursive *construction* of the pub as a 'traditional' space. The different literature surrounding international matches indicates that there is nothing 'natural' about the relationship between the pub and traditional fans. This tension suggests that different agents frame the football event in a manner that produces different expectations for fandom. With this in mind I rationalised this choice with the idea that international matches would provide me with the opportunity to consider the ways in which 'traditional fans' construct their identity, and construct the pub as a 'traditional' space.

Despite my intentions to frame the pub in the same way I consider Carrow Road, Stadium MK or Stamford Bridge, there are fundamental differences that the different discourses surrounding international matches alludes to. Fans from the previous chapters indicate that they share a collective identity that is engendered by the culture of their club. While the literature describes those that frequent the pub as 'pub fans,' the different ways in which the pub is framed indicates that patrons are not likely to share a collective identity in the same way as the fans suggest in the previous chapters. For example, while both strands of literature describe how fans are attracted to the pub to watch international matches, they indicate that the fans have different expectations for fandom that are framed by different agents. While the Snake Pit fans may enact a different fandom to the family fans that I engaged with at Norwich City, it is important to note that their fandom is still prompted by their shared engagement and negotiation of the culture of their club. Conversely the appeal of the pub is said to derive from the fact that it does not operate with a unified culture, something that becomes apparent for the tournament, with the pub attracting fans with different identities and expectations for fandom.

The screening of England's Euro 2012 matches at 'MG's' attracted a particularly diverse clientele, challenging the 'traditional' construction of the pub. The international matches that I experienced at 'MG's' seemed to attract both self-identified 'traditional' fans (traditional football culture) and 'casual fans' (football's capitalism). Observing the interaction between the different types of fans enabled me to assess the negotiation that I have referred to through this book, with the 'traditional' fans' expression of identity tempered by the presence of 'consumer' or 'casual' fans within the pub. Indeed, the presence of 'casual' fans within the pub seemed to compromise the group's expectations of the pub as a 'traditional' venue, emphasising the way in which their fandom is enacted in negotiation but also the way in which their expectations for fandom had been constructed in a highly specific way.

''MG's' is quality … it's just like the darts'

A couple of hours before England were set to kick off their campaign against France (11 June 2012) I caught 'Toby' (2012) my neighbour coming out of his house in a Hawaiian shirt with an inflatable guitar. I did not consider that he was going to watch the match.

Oliver: You are out of work early, are you going to a party?

'Toby': Yeah, kind of, I'm going to 'MG's' to watch the England game. I booked the afternoon off, so I can get down there early and get a good spot.

Oliver: I love the shirt. Is it fancy dress down there?

'Toby': Haven't you been down to 'MG's' for the footy? It's like a massive party, the place is always packed out and it's a right laugh. You know, like at the darts at Ally Pally (Alexandra Palace) when you see everyone in the crowd all pissed up in fancy dress? It's like that down there. I made an event on Facebook, so all the boys are coming down for it. You can come if you want.

From our initial conversation, it appeared that 'Toby' (2012) was keen to emphasise the carnival of 'MG's,' the football event providing him with the opportunity to 'get pissed,' 'dress up' and engage in a collective revelry, something that Bale (1998) indicates is synonymous both with the terraces and, contemporarily, the 'virtual terraces' of the pub. The exchange suggests that 'Toby' identifies with this discourse surrounding the pub, with the culture of 'MG's' central to his fan identity. The exchange provides an early indication of 'Toby's' conception of 'traditional' football culture. In Chapter 2, I document how 'traditional' football culture is historically associated with the game's bureaucracy, in which fandom was defined by 'communal representation,' 'family lineage' and 'emotional attachments' (see Crampsey 1990; Imlach 2005; Devine 2012). However, 'Toby's' conception of traditional football culture, like the Snake Pit fans at Norwich City, seems to be influenced by the contemporary texts that associate traditional football culture with the participatory fandom of the terraces.

By making this association between the pub and the terraces I argue that these texts produce certain expectations about the demographic attracted to the pub and the atmosphere. The exchange with 'Toby' (2012) supports this idea: he alludes to 'MG's' androcentric culture, 'all the boys are coming down,' and how the venue is 'always packed' and promises to be 'a right laugh,' in which he forms associations between the revelry of the pub on match days and the darts at Alexander Palace, an event with a similar raucous culture. This association seems poignant; while 'Toby's' fandom is indicative of a 'traditional fan identity,' with the revelry that he associates with the pub evocative of the nostalgic depictions of the terraces, he does not make this association, instead describing his motivations for fandom in relation to the opportunity that matches provide him to 'get pissed' and be part of a 'massive party,' rather than the conscious continuation of a cultural tradition.

While the discourse that presents the pub as 'traditional space' may have been produced with the intention of maintaining traditional terrace culture, this does not necessarily mean that this discourse will be internalised by the fans and imparted into their fan identity. While 'Toby' (2012) identifies with the culture of the pub and its carnivalistic affordances, there does not seem to be a political or transgressional element to his fandom. While the literature describes those that frequent the pub as 'traditional fans,' Toby does little to identify as such, instead presenting himself as a fan of the culture that the pub represents. This notion is vindicated by the way in which he assimilates the pub experience to the darts at Alexander Palace rather than the terraces.

The previous chapters document the way in which fans from Norwich, MK Dons and Chelsea heavily identify as fans, with the culture of their club central to their fan identity. Similarly, this exchange indicates that the culture of the pub is foundational to 'Toby's' (2012) identity. Like the fans that I have engaged with in the previous chapters, I argue that the pub addresses his individual need, providing him with the opportunity to experience a participatory fandom with like-minded people. Like the Snake Pit fans, I argue that his desire to enact a fandom that is incongruent with the modern stadium emphasises the way in which his fandom is enacted in negotiation, with his identity informed by his understanding of commercial football culture and his expectation of the pub as a traditional, carnivalistic space.

'For f*** sake I put all the details up on Facebook'

Disregarding a couple of family groups that subsequently left upon finishing their meals at the pub, we were the first to arrive at 'MG's' for the match.

'Toby' (2012) was satisfied that his objective of securing a 'prime position' had been achieved, claiming a space at the back of the venue. Pearson's (2012) ethnography of Blackpool fans describes the measures fans would take to get time off work to attend away days and the premium they placed on the 'perfect spot' within the terraces, like 'Toby,' arriving early to ensure that they secured the best place within the stand. 'Toby' seemed aware of this ritual and was satisfied he had taken the time off to 'mark his territory' with an England flag. After twenty minutes without any of his friends turning up and few England fans taking their place, he started to get agitated that his friends did not share his commitment to the ritual.

The following quotes emphasise the significance 'Toby' (2012) places on the collective experience of the pub and the way that his expectations as a fan are associated with the shared recognition and identification of his friends:

> I can't believe none of them have turned up yet. I told them I was going to get down here early and it looks like they can't be bothered. They better dress up or I am going to be really pissed off.
>
> I can't believe how quiet it is, this place is normally packed. We are going to look like right pricks if it's empty and we are here dressed up trying to party on our own.
>
> I don't get it, it's England's first game and I thought everyone would be down here. Everyone was buzzing about it on Facebook, and now it looks like they can't be arsed. I took time off work and everything for f*** sake, but where are they? Probably sat on the sofa shovelling s*** into their mouths.

Like many of the heavily identified fans that I discuss in previous chapters, 'Toby' (2012) looks to legitimate his fan identity, emphasising the commitment that he has made 'taking time off work,' 'getting down early' and organising the meet up on Facebook, accentuating his commitment by framing himself akin to the Blackpool fans Pearson (2012) describes. In his self-affirmation it is notable that 'Toby' recalls the argument posed against 'modern football fans,' insinuating that those that do not share his commitment or 'can't be arsed' have a passive, less authentic fan identity (see Bale 1998; Brimson 1998; Hopcraft 2006; Weed 2008). This notion is particularly explicit in his anger at those 'buzzing about' the match on Facebook but who seemingly can't be bothered to engage in active fandom. 'Toby' draws on the discourse that juxtaposes (his) participatory fandom with passive consumer fans, as encapsulated by the idea that his friends are 'probably sat on the sofa shovelling s*** into their mouths' ('Toby' 2012), in which he draws upon the discourse that describes the lethargy of armchair fans, emphasising their passivity, 'sat on the sofa,' and ill-consumption, 'shovelling s*** into their mouths.'

While the quotes indicate that 'Toby' (2012) has an understanding of the debates within football culture, I argue that his grievance is multifaceted; while he attempts to create distinction between 'traditional' and 'consumer' fans, he similarly highlights the importance of collectivity to his fan identity. His desire for communality is emphasised throughout the exchange: 'I can't believe none of them have turned up yet,' 'I can't believe how quiet this place is,' 'this place is usually packed' and 'I thought everyone would be down here.' Large crowd numbers are synonymous with a 'good experience,' both within the terraces and within the virtual terraces of the pub. Hopcraft (2006: 188) describes how the kinetic and sensual experience of the terraces were at their optimum when the fan was part of an enthused crowd, 'packed in, swaying and singing in unison,' while Brimson (1998: 166) describes the appeal of the pub in terms of the sociality of 'the same group of geezers' packed into the pub together. 'Toby' (2012) acknowledges the centrality of the crowd to traditional football culture, framing it as a vital part of his identity. Citing the importance of the crowd helps 'Toby' frame his identity as a traditional fan. As Brimson (1998) suggests, crowds have a transformative ability, with their convergence and collective need transforming the pub into stadia in its own right. 'Toby' (2012) seems aware of this, fearful that 'MG's' may not fulfil his need: 'We are going to look like right pricks if it's empty and we are here dressed up trying to party on our own.'

I argue that parallels can be established with the Norwich City fans that I engaged with in the Snake Pit. The fans seemed fully aware of the traditions of football culture and, like 'Toby' (2012), imparted effort to try and replicate elements of terrace culture in their fan performance in attempts to combat what they perceived to be the inauthentic family image of the club. It is my argument that the identity of the Snake Pit fans is complex, with their identity influenced by their expectations of how they thought they *should* act as traditional fans and subsequently how the club's family fans interpret their fandom. Similarly, I argue that it is the effort made by 'Toby' (2012) to enact a traditional fan identity, to actively foster collectivity and transform 'MG's' into a traditional space that emphasises his expectations for fandom and importantly his desire to be recognised as a traditional fan. Like the Snake Pit fans, I argue that it is his expectations of what it means to be a traditional fan and his desire to be recognised as such that informs his performance. While the Snake Pit fans construct their identity in opposition to Norwich's wider fan culture, significantly 'Toby's' (2012) fandom requires the transformative power of the crowd and the convergence of like-minded people to authenticate his identity. Here the fact that it was an international tournament becomes significant. As suggested, international matches are said to attract more casual fans, yet the pub requires the convergence of like-minded fans to transform it into a traditional space. In this context casual fans threaten the transformability of the pub, and 'Toby' seemed aware of this, desperate for his friends to join him to frame the culture and dictate the identity of the pub, enabling him to enact his fan identity.

This need for recognition is alluded to throughout the exchange, with 'Toby' (2012) 'marking his territory' with an England flag and encouraging his friends to 'dress up,' helping their self-identification, making the group distinct from other groups, particularly the casual fans within the pub. While Brimson (1998) indicates that pub fandom mirrors the terraces in the way in which the same group of 'geezers' naturally congregate together, this research indicates that the congregation of the lads and their colonisation of the venue was not a spontaneous continuation of terrace culture, but a result of significant effort on 'Toby's' (2012) behalf to actively foster collectivity, to engineer an experience in keeping with his expectations of the terraces. After finally losing patience, he decided to call his friends, reminding them of their promise to join him: 'you better be on the way and don't bother coming if you're not dressed up' ('Toby' 2012). This quotation seems to encapsulate my argument about 'Toby's' fandom, in which it is seemingly redundant if enacted individually or if the collective identity of his friends as 'traditional fans' is not recognisable to the wider patrons of the pub.

'Everything you need is here and we know it's going to be a good time'

I argue that 'Toby's' (2012) choice of 'MG's' as a venue was not born out of necessity or that his identity developed spontaneously from engaging with like-minded people within the pub (see Bale 1998; Brimson 1998; Weed 2008), but instead, like the fans from the previous chapters, I believe that his identity is constructed in negotiation, with the discourse surrounding the culture, informing his choice of 'MG's' as an arena for the way in which it meets his needs as a fan. As Sandvoss (2005: 33) argues, choices of fandom are based on the object's capacity to carry meanings that articulate the fan's sense of identity. I have suggested that 'Toby' (2012) has an understanding of commercial football culture, with his identity constructed in opposition as insinuated by the way in which he compares his active fandom, 'taking time off work' and 'securing a prime position' ('Toby 2012'), to the perceived passivity of his friends, 'probably sat on the sofa shovelling s*** into their mouths' ('Toby' 2012). Indeed, I argue that his patronage of 'MG's' and his willingness to transform the venue reflects his negotiation of the discourses surrounding both commercial and traditional football culture, with his choice of 'MG's' as a venue reflecting his intention to position himself as a traditional fan.

While the pub is predominantly presented as a traditional venue, I think that it is important to recognise it as a central part of contemporary football culture. With this being said, while the pub is said to have its own culture, my initial exchanges with 'Toby' (2012) indicate that it would be naive to suggest that the pub operates in a vacuum, independent of capitalist football culture. Indeed, it is of note that Weed (2008) describes how a whole industry has developed around pub fandom, with pubs aggressively marketing themselves as venues to watch live matches. Weed (2008: 79) indicates that pubs increasingly rely on match days to cover losses they incur throughout the week. Similarly, like the 'consumer fans' from the previous chapters, I argue that 'Toby's' (2012) patronage of 'MG's' relates to the group's needs as (traditional) fans. An exchange I had with him and his friend 'Chad' (2012) builds upon this idea, in which the pair implicitly describe their fandom as a product of consumer choice:

Oliver: So why do you guys like coming here ('MG's') for matches?

'Toby': It's quality, look at it. There's loads of floor space to pack people in, it's a big screen, it's cheap beer. Trust me come kick off it will be bouncing.

'Chad': The atmosphere is class, the low ceiling is good for the sound, so it keeps all the noise in. It's like how you see on the films, you know, like with beer flying everywhere and people jumping about. It's great to be part of it.

'Toby': He's right. I work around the corner so came to watch one of the Champions League matches and it was full of United fans. I'm a Norwich fan, but f*** me the atmosphere was good. I was like, I want a bit of that, you know. It was something I wanted to be part of.

Oliver: You haven't been tempted to check out any of the other pubs around here?

'Chad': What's the point? Everything you need is here and we know it's going to be a good time. 'Toby' said it was quality and it's right on our doorstep.

'Toby': We've been coming here for a while now. There's a bunch of us and we always dress up and that, so people know us here. We don't need to try anywhere else.

Both 'Chad' (2012) and 'Toby' (2012) are keen to vindicate their choice of 'MG's' as a venue to watch football matches, 'Chad' (2012) suggesting that the venue provides them with 'everything they need' and 'Toby' (2012) arguing that they 'don't need to try anywhere else.' Indeed, the entire conversation revolves around the participants' appraisal of the venue, outlining the ways in which 'MG's' corresponds to traditional images of the terraces. The participants outline how the structural orientation of 'MG's' helps the pub transformation with the 'big floor space to pack people in,' 'the big screen,' 'the cheap beer' ('Toby' 2012) and the 'low ceiling' that 'keeps all the noise in' ('Chad' 2012). Bale (1998) in his ethnography of pub fans notes how fans favored pubs with big standing areas, as the experience of a large crowd packed in together is indicative of the terraces. The image 'Chad' (2012) creates of 'beer flying everywhere and people jumping about' corresponds to Hopcraft's (2006) description of the terraces, in which he describes the kinetic and sensory experience. While Bale (1998) makes connections between the participatory nature of the pub and the terraces, the participants similarly form associations between the atmospheres. The participants in Pearson's (2012) ethnography celebrate the sensory experience of the terraces, in which fans describe the lingering smell of beer, and the 'deafening roar' so loud 'you couldn't hear the person next to you.' 'Chad' and 'Toby' seem to identify with this discourse, citing the significance of 'beer flying everywhere' ('Chad' 2012) and importantly, like Pearson (2012), the low ceiling that helped to amplify the noise and generate atmosphere.

While the exchange illustrates the way in which 'MG's' resembles the experience of the terrace, meeting the fans' collective need, I argue that the exchange also emphasises their individual needs as fans, demonstrating the complexity of their identity. While their assimilation of 'MG's' with the terraces demonstrates their knowledge of terrace culture, it is poignant that 'Chad' (2012) compares the experience to 'like how you see on the films,' indicative of the way in which 'Toby' (2012) had previously compared the experience to the darts. Despite making association between 'MG's' and the terraces, it is poignant that, again, 'Chad' (2012) does not explicitly correlate the experiences, instead comparing it to his expectations of terrace culture, comparing it to that which he has encountered on the screen. While there has been an upsurge in nostalgic literature produced by self-identified traditional fans documenting the culture of the terraces, as suggested there has similarly been a proliferation of films[2] that look to profit from the nostalgia surrounding the terraces but, like the literature, helps to maintain the aura associated with the game's traditional culture and contribute to the discourses that frame the traditional fan experience.

While the nostalgic texts help to maintain the centrality of the game's traditional culture, it is important to recognise that, like the pub, a whole industry has developed around the preservation of the culture, with the texts attractive to fans like 'Chad' (2012) and 'Toby' (2012) who identify with the nostalgic images that they produce. Subsequently I argue that, like the fans from the previous chapters, the participants' fandom reflects the complex ways in which fans are positioned as consumers within football culture. While traditional discourses encourage fans to stand in opposition to modern football culture, to boycott the modern stadium and distance themselves from the 'passive' 'corporate dupes' that frequent them, they similarly encourage fans to 'buy into' the images and culture of the terraces that they present. 'Toby's' (2012) description of his first experience of 'MG's' encapsulates this idea. Despite his lack of identification with the majority of the fans within the pub, 'Toby' (2012) a 'Norwich fan', 'MG's' 'full of United fans,' he still indicates that he identified with the culture and atmosphere within the pub, with the experience appealing to his sense of (consumer) need. Indeed, the following quotation is indicative of the identification that fans have as consumers in which their needs are addressed in their identification with capitalist texts (see Jameson 1991; Fiske 1992; Hills 2002; Barker 2004; Sandvoss 2005).

> It was full of United fans. I'm a Norwich Fan, but f*** me the atmosphere was good. I was like, *I want a bit of that,* you know. It was something *I wanted to be part of*.
>
> ('Toby' 2012, emphasis added)

It is feasible to suggest that his engagement with the discourse surrounding the pub as a traditional space helped condition his identification and prompted his desire to engage with the experience that he encountered, producing his expectations of what it means to be a traditional fan. Even though the pub was 'full of United fans' ('Toby' 2012), people he did not share an affinity with, the atmosphere conformed to his ideas of a traditional fan experience, something he 'wanted to be part of' ('Toby' 2012). In this context the exchange can almost be read as a check list, with the participants both acknowledging the ways in which 'MG's' conforms to the culture of the terrace while also addressing their (consumer) needs, with both participants indicating that it is close to home, 'it's right on our doorstep' ('Chad' 2012) and 'I work just around the corner' ('Toby' 2012), that it provides refreshment, 'it's cheap beer' ('Toby' 2012), and that they feel part of the community that has formed around the venue, 'we've been coming here for a while now. There's a bunch of us and we always dress up and that, so people know us here' ('Toby' 2012).

Despite their identification with 'MG's' for the ways in which it opposes the modern stadium, I argue that the needs of the group correlate to those of the consumer fans that I discuss in the previous chapters. It seems significant that given the choice of pubs within the region the fans remain loyal to 'MG's' as a venue. Again, I argue that this sense of loyalty and repeat patronage can be assimilated with the fans from the previous chapters.

Having previously considered the way in which the fans' identity draws on their understanding of the game's traditional culture, it is ironic that despite their attempts to position themselves in opposition to contemporary football culture, the things that inspire their fandom correlate to the choices informing the fandom of the 'consumers' discussed in the previous chapters, notably the importance of collectivity (Norwich), the significance of the locality and the way in which it aids the formation of community (MK Dons) and the importance of hierarchy and distinction (Chelsea). While the previous chapter indicates that the culture of each club helps to foster a unique collective identity among their fans, it seems poignant that elements central to the collective identity of each group also inform 'Toby' (2012) and 'Chad's' (2012) fan identity yet, unlike the fans from the previous chapters, it is significant that 'Toby' (2012) and 'Chad' (2012) do not consider this negotiation or engagement with the game's consumerism in our discussions.

'I can't spend the whole day worrying about football'

After the necessary phone calls had been made, 'Toby's' (2012) friends slowly started to arrive; with just over an hour to kick-off the 'whole band' had turned up. 'Toby' was joined by seven of his friends, all dressed in Hawaiian shirts, each with their own inflatable instrument. Having engaged in conversation with 'Toby' and 'Chad' (2012), gaining an insight into the way in which they articulated their fandom ,I was keen to engage with other members of the group to see if they identified as 'traditional' fans in a similar manner, the significance they placed upon collectivity and their conception of 'MG's' as a venue.

Oliver: It's good you guys could make it. 'Toby' was worried that you weren't coming.

'Wayne': He needs to have a drink and calm down. We told him we were coming after work. I can't just take the day off like him, and spend the whole day worrying about football.

'Owen': It's meant to be a laugh; I don't know why he takes everything so seriously.

Oliver: He was saying he created an event about this on Facebook and had been trying to organise the meet up for a few weeks.

'Wayne': Yeah, he did. I don't see the point though; we come down for matches anyway. We usually send some texts round or whatever the night before, so I don't get why this has been turned into some big event.

'Owen': He's given it the big build up and tried to get us all down early, but I don't get the point. It's meant to be a laugh.

'Toby' (2012) suggests that the collective identification of the group is central to his fan identity, yet this exchange indicates that 'Wayne' (2012) and 'Owen' (2012) have a different fan identity to 'Toby' (2012) and 'Chad' (2012). This is encapsulated by 'Wayne's' (2012) suggestion that unlike 'Toby' he has more important things to do than 'spend the whole day worrying about football.' While 'Toby' (2012) previously emphasises the effort that he put into organising the event, both 'Owen' (2012) and 'Wayne' (2012) ridicule his efforts, insinuating that the organisation of the event dampens the experience, as 'Owen' (2012) suggests: 'I don't get the point. It's meant to be a laugh.' 'Wayne' (2012) similarly questions why it has been 'turned into some big event.' Previously I compared 'Toby's' (2012) fandom to that of those within the Snake Pit, in which his understanding and expectations of terrace culture prompts him to try and construct the culture of the pub. It was my argument, both in the context of the Snake Pit fans and with 'Toby' (2012), that it is their effort in presenting themselves as traditional fans that emphasises the complexity of their fan identity in which they demonstrate their understanding of both contemporary and traditional football culture. Indeed, I argue that 'Toby's' (2012) attempts to manufacture the experience of the pub relates to his understanding of the way in which international matches are considered to attract more casual fans, emphasising his understanding of the debates with contemporary football culture. 'Owen' (2012) and 'Wayne's' (2012) comments, on the other hand, indicate that they do not share 'Toby's' (2012) engagement, indicating that his efforts in fact lessen their sense of enjoyment, with 'Owen' (2012) bemoaning the fact that 'It's meant to be a laugh.'

'Wayne' (2012) poses the question 'I don't get why this has been turned into some big event;' this seems poignant. If members of 'Toby's' (2012) group regularly congregate at the pub on match days anyway, indicative of the spontaneous process that Brimson (1998) describes, then why did 'Toby' (2012) feel the need to create an event and accentuate the effort he had made to foster a sense of collectivity? I argue that one possibility could have been 'Toby's' (2012) desire to impression manage, with his performance influenced by my presence as a researcher. If, as I argue, the identity of the group and the recognition of the group are foundational to his fandom then my research may be seen by 'Toby' (2012) as a platform to promote his identity, with my work helping to vindicate and reflect his identity. 'Toby' (2012) was very welcoming to me, inviting me to share the experience of his group; this may have been due to my use value, with the idea that my acknowledgement of the 'traditional' identity of the group could help validate his sense of identity.

This still leaves the question that if the fans 'spontaneously' congregated for football matches together anyway, why would 'Toby' (2012) go to the effort of turning England matches into an event? As previously suggested, 'Toby' (2012) seems aware of the way in which England matches attract a more diverse, casual crowd, challenging the discursive construction of the pub as a 'traditional' space. As previously indicated, I argue that 'Toby's' (2012) fandom relies on the collectivity of the crowd and the shared identification of the group to transform the pub into a traditional space. With the perceived threat of the casual fan to the pub I argue that 'Toby' may have felt a need to actively bring together a large group to ensure that 'MG's' housed the correct 'type' of fan necessary for it to maintain its 'traditional' character, complimenting my argument that 'Toby' (2012) can be considered as an agent of the football event, working to frame the fan experience and culture of the venue.

This may account for the emphasis 'Toby' (2012) placed on the fancy dress, to ensure that the group were recognisable as a collective but also to maintain their interest, as the exchange above indicates that some of his friends did not share his motivation for fandom. This notion is supported by an exchange with other members of the group in which they indicate that they do not possess a particularly strong awareness of the debates surrounding football culture and, surprisingly, a lack of awareness concerning the England team:

Oliver: So why do you think 'Toby' made the 'event' on Facebook to try and get people down here for the matches? Don't you normally watch matches together?

'Simon': I'm not sure really. I've come with them for a couple of Premier League games and it's always been pretty lively, but it's not like I come here every week or anything. 'Toby' and me haven't watched that much football together to be honest, but we've been going to the darts the last few years and that's quality. 'Toby' was saying that this is like that, you know, with us all wearing fancy dress and just drinking; he said the atmosphere was like that so I'm well up for it.

Oliver: So by coming together in your fancy dress and everything you are hoping to recreate the experience that you had together at the darts?

'Bob': Yeah, if the drinks are flowing and we can get the singing going then, yeah, it'll be just like it I reckon. Let's face it, England are pretty s***, so you've got to have fun with it, don't you? Everyone goes to the darts to get pissed and have a laugh. I don't think people care who wins or anything; it's just a day out with your mates.

Oliver: So are you saying that you are not too bothered about the score today or England winning? There has been a lot written about the pub suggesting that it has become the place where the heavily identified or 'traditional' football fan goes to watch games.

'Simon': No, it's not that we don't care about the result, but it's not like it's the most important thing, you know? You come to have a good time and the result is what it is, you know? Obviously you want England to win, but like he said, we never win 'Jack.' Like, I don't think Bale is in the squad, or Beckham. It's a joke. I think most people that come here are up for a laugh and want a drink. If people were really into it, they would be out there for the tournament, wouldn't they?

Once again, 'Simon' (2012) and 'Bob' (2012) indicate that their fandom revolves around the opportunity that it provides them to 'have a laugh,' 'dress up' and 'get pissed.' While these behaviors are continually associated with the terraces, again it is poignant that the pair do not form this correlation, instead accentuating their desire to replicate the experience of being at the darts. This suggests that their fandom is non-politicised. Throughout the exchange the pair indicate that unlike 'Toby' (2012) they have little knowledge of the arguments surrounding football culture, suggesting those traditional fans 'really into it' would be at the tournament. These remarks demonstrate that the participants are not aware of the debates happening within the culture, with match attendance considered to be economically impractical and ideologically unappealing to traditional fans (see Brown 1998; Williams 2000; Walsh & Giulianotti 2001; King 2002; Pearson 2012). Similarly, the reference to Welsh International Garth Bale and the retired David Beckham suggest that the participants have a limited interest in the England team, or that the team achieves success.

I argue that 'Toby' (2012) and 'Chad' (2012) create an impression of 'MG's,' describing the way in which it meets the need of their group as a traditional fan, however the exchange with 'Simon' (2012) and 'Bob' (2012) challenges the collective identity of the group, with the exchange compromising their identity as traditional fans and similarly challenging the construction of the pub as a traditional space, accentuating the idea that the pub similarly attracts casual fans that do not identify with the football event, 'Bob' (2012) suggesting that 'people don't really care who wins,' and 'Simon' arguing that the result is 'not the most important thing.' While 'Toby' (2012) emphasises the effort imparted to book time off work, arrive early at the venue and organise the 'event' in a manner that frames his traditional identity, the exchange indicates that the participants do not perceive his actions this way, with 'Simon' (2012) 'not sure' why he would go to the effort of staging a 'piss up,' or as 'Bob' (2012) suggests, for a 'casual day out with your mates.' This indicates that the pair do not even assimilate the experience of 'MG's' with terrace football, with the participants suggesting that the tournament merely provides them with an opportunity to engage in a collective celebration or as 'Bob' (2012) maintains, an experience like the darts, a chance to 'get pissed and have a laugh.'

The responses of the participants produce a tension. While 'Toby' (2012) and 'Chad' (2012) acknowledge how England matches attract more casual fans, keen to present the identity of their group and frame the culture of 'MG's' in opposition, it is problematic that 'Simon' (2012) and 'Bob' (2012), while identifying with the rituals of the terraces, the 'piss up' and 'having a laugh,' implicitly identify as casual fans. It is poignant that 'Bob' (2012) explicitly describes the meet up as a '*casual* day out with (his) mates' while 'Simon' (2012) suggests that he has gone with the group to watch 'a couple of Premier League games' 'but it's not like I come here every week or anything.'

I had previously provided the group with the opportunity to acknowledge the association of the pub with the terraces and traditional fandom by posing the following comment: 'There has been a lot written about the pub suggesting that it has become the place where heavily identified fans go to watch games,' yet the pair ignored my prompt, with 'Simon' (2012) suggesting that he had been drawn to the pub by the way in which 'Toby' (2012) associates it with the experience of the darts: "Toby' was saying that this is like that, you know, with us all wearing fancy dress and just drinking; he said the atmosphere was like that so I'm well up for it.' This seems significant. While 'Toby' (2012) accentuates the collective identity of the group, 'Simon' (2012) suggests that 'Toby' (2012) had looked to foster a shared experience around the event by describing the experience of 'MG's' in a manner that produced certain expectations for the event. In this context association can be formed to the way in which the existing literature constructs pub fandom, producing discourse that speaks to a demographic like 'Toby' (2012) with certain (consumer) needs. This vindicates my argument that both the literature and 'Toby' (2012) draw upon these discourses with similar intentions, acting as agents framing pub fandom to their audience in a manner that enables the continuation and validation of their identity and culture.

'You've got to build atmosphere and get people in the mood to get things going'

Sandvoss (2005) argues that fandom is the process of buying into a text and forming an emotional connection with it. In doing so he suggests that the way in which fandom is enacted accentuates fandoms assimilation with capitalism. Correspondingly I argue that 'Toby' (2012) looks to foster this relationship between his friends and 'MG's,' encouraging them to 'buy into' the culture of the pub that he presents, appealing to their consumer needs. While members of the group suggest that they have different identifications with the pub and thus different consumer needs, he manages to draw upon the same 'catch all' logic of capitalism in orchestrating the collective image of the group. Again, this emphasises the way in which fans are both positively and negatively framed as consumers, with 'Toby' (2012) drawing on the discourses of consumerism to create the impression that his group ironically opposes the game's capitalism. This seems to accentuate the way in which the participants enact their identity in negotiation with 'Toby's' (2012) understanding of the game's capitalism, both prompting and encouraging him to frame the experience of the pub, and his friends' engagement with wider leisure industries, particularly with films and the darts informing their expectations of the terraces. This relates once again to Cavicchi's (1998) argument that fans create community not through shared experiences but through a mutual shared expectation of experience.

I looked to address the different expectations of the group with 'Toby' (2012):

Oliver: You were saying earlier that the group of you all come down for the football. I was just speaking to 'Simon' and he was saying that they aren't particularly regulars with you.

'Toby': Yeah, they don't come down all the time, but he's come a few times and likes the atmosphere and gets involved. He's here today though, so that's the main thing.

Oliver: Yeah, he seems pretty up for it, but more because he thinks it's going to be like the darts than the match itself.

'Toby': [Laughs.] That's because I told him it was like the darts. We always have a good time at Ally Pally so I thought that it would get him going, you know.

Oliver: But why do you need to get him going? You were saying before that it is a good place to watch matches and that it has a good atmosphere.

'Toby': It does but it's important to keep it up, you know. You've got to build atmosphere and get people in the mood to get things going.

Initially 'Toby' (2012) tries to present 'Simon' (2012) as a traditional fan, suggesting that like the heavily identified members of the group he 'likes the atmosphere and gets involved,' creating a distinction between 'Simon' (2012) and the image of the 'passive' casual fan. While initially validating his fan identity, it seems poignant that he then looks to distance 'Simon' (2012) from the group, seemingly aware that his remarks may harm the group's collective identity, suggesting that 'he's come a few times' before continuing again to validate his identity, suggesting that he is 'here today though, so that's the main thing.' This compliments my argument that 'Toby' (2012) is cautious in the way in which he manages the identity of the group, constantly negotiating the discourses surrounding the culture in his perpetuation of their identity. In this sense his performance can be assimilated with that of the Chelsea fans that I engaged with in the previous chapter. I argue that their fandom is constantly in flux depending on the status of the club in the wider culture and the success of the team on the pitch.

Distancing 'Simon' (2012) and his 'casual' fandom from the group helps to solidify his identity and the status of the group as traditional fans, while similarly the fact that he is with the group helps to authenticate his identity by affiliation. Indeed, this tension is evidenced by the way in which 'Toby' (2012) purposefully told him that the experience was like that of the darts, with the idea that it would 'get him going.' I questioned that if 'MG's' is as he suggests, a place in which traditional fans congregate, why was it necessary to try and encourage his fandom and frame his expectations of the event? His response to my query seems to provide the answer:

Oliver: But why do you need to get him going? You were saying before that it is a good place to watch matches and that it has a good atmosphere.

'Toby': It does but it's important to keep it up, you know. You've got to build atmosphere and get people in the mood to get things going.

While indicating that it has a good atmosphere 'Toby' (2012) suggests that it is important that it stays that way, alluding to the idea that he encouraged the participation of his friends to maintain the atmosphere of the pub. The idea of 'building the atmosphere' of 'MG's' and managing the culture of the pub relates not only to his desire to enact terrace culture but also to the way in which it is suggested that England matches attract casual fans. While collectivity is vital to transform the pub, to give the pub its traditional identity, the right type of fan is required. 'Toby's' (2012) friends fit the demographic of the traditional fan and strongly identify with facets of the culture which 'Toby' (2012) valued, namely the feeling of collective revelry, the party atmosphere and the idea of 'getting pissed.' In their adherence to this profile his friends are vital to the transformation of the pub in the sense that they help to maintain its culture and identity.

In this context the fancy dress 'Toby' (2012) demanded becomes poignant. To 'Simon' (2012) it is attractive as he associates it with the experience of the darts, however it is also a way of creating a collective identity for the group, ensuring that their association was obvious to other patrons of the pub. In this way the casual association of 'Simon' (2012) and 'Bob' (2012) could similarly be obscured by their affiliation to the group with their identity stratified by properties of their fandom such as the singing, drinking and raucousness associated with the profile of the traditional fan. In this context, even if the pub did attract more casual fans, the collectivity of the group would continue to enable them to transform the pub into a traditional space and differentiate themselves from casual fans.

'If you are looking at football fans why are you running around with that lot?'

With all of 'Toby's' (2012) group taking their place in 'MG's' an hour before kick-off, the pub slowly started to fill up, with more fans turning up the closer it got to the match. Despite the fact that it was England's first game of the tournament, the pub was roughly three quarters full. Several observations could be made about the demographic. The majority of fans were male, as the game started I counted eleven women in attendance, and most of the fans seemed to be in groups, there were very few fans on their own. With kick-off at 5pm, there were fans that had come straight from work, with several wearing suits and office attire. The pub also seemed to attract two distinct age bands: those that were the age of 'Toby's' (2012) group, in their late teens to early thirties, and middle aged fans aged forty plus.

My exchanges with 'Toby's' (2012) group indicated that the participants had not experienced the terraces first hand and subsequently that their expectation of the terraces and their desire to enact its rituals had been prompted by the discourse framing the culture. My exchanges with the group compliment the idea that the pub has become attractive to a new generation of fans (see Bale 1998; Brimson 1998: King 2002; Weed 2008). However, it is important to remember that the literature argues that the pub originally functioned to accommodate 'disenfranchised traditional fans' who had been outlawed from the modern stadium (Bale 1998; Weed 2008). Observing the demographic within the pub and taking the literature into account, I questioned whether the middle aged fans within the pub could be identified as this diasporic group with their age and group association helping them fit the profile. Like 'Toby's' group, they consumed beer and engaged in chants of 'IN-GER-LAND' and 'Football's coming home.'

While the atmosphere and demographic within 'MG's' resembled the description of the terraces, it was poignant that there were disconnects between the groups within the pub, particularly between 'Toby's' (2012) group and the middle age participants. While both 'Toby' (2012) and the literature associated with the pub describes the importance of collectivity to the identity of the traditional fan and the transformation of the venue, I argue that the pub did not seem to cohere in the same way in which historical accounts depict the terraces (see Crampsey 1990; Hutchinson 1997; Hopcraft 2006).

Weed (2008) describes the traditional stadium as a microcosm of the town, with terraces akin to individual neighborhoods, each with their own customs, indicative of the inhabitant's position within the community. While the pub is transformed into a terrace by the convergence of likeminded individuals, the pub does not account for the different communities formed within the terraces, with the pub providing fans with a single space. The semi-public nature of the pub ensures that they attract a mix of people, making it difficult for patrons to re-create the idiosyncrasies of the different communities within the terraces or to create the idea of hierarchy that was established in the stadium. While I have previously argued that 'Toby' (2012) looks to create his identity in opposition to modern 'consumer fans,' my observations indicate that fans within the pub similarly look to create distinction between themselves, perhaps indicative of their attempts to re-establish this idea of distinction within the terraces, with different groups within the pub engaging in different forms of fandom. Indeed, articulations of traditional fan identities were enacted in different ways by 'Toby's' (2012) friends and the middle aged fans within the pub.

With 'Toby' (2012) arriving early to get 'the best spot,' his group was positioned towards the back of the venue, equipped with their inflatable instruments. This helped the group's self-identity, the instruments corresponding to their role, assuming the duty of 'house band,' regularly trying to create chants and encouraging other patrons within the pub to join them. As the match began, chants of 'IN-GER-LAND' filled the pub, with the low ceiling helping to generate an impressive atmosphere. Yet, with the match a stalemate and England struggling to produce chances, the group were finding it harder to inspire participation or as 'Toby' (2012) previously suggested to 'generate atmosphere.' 'Owen' (2012) tried to start a song about 'Steven Gerrard' with little response from the other patrons. A few minutes later, French playmaker Frank Ribery went down injured, prompting 'Toby' (2012) to start a chorus of 'Dig a hole and f***ing bury him,' which again received minimal response from the crowd. Aggrieved by the lack of participation 'Toby' (2012) vented his frustration, 'my god this is embarrassing, it's a pub for f*** sake.'

'Toby's' (2012) rant illustrates both his expectations of pub fandom and his desire to enact a particular type of fandom, shocked that more patrons were not joining in with his chants and angry that the lack of participation from the other patrons compromised the 'traditional' pub experience that he had promised his friends. As previously suggested, I believe that 'Toby' (2012) was keen to promote the experience of 'MG's' to me to validate his identity as a traditional fan, yet despite the effort he put into organising the event and 'generating atmosphere,' the collective party he depicted was localised. Similarly, it seems significant that while there was chanting in the pub, it was the chants that his group had tried to start that were ignored by the wider patrons. I have argued that 'Toby' (2012) can be considered as an agent working to 'sell' the experience of the pub to his group, yet it is significant that his attempts to dictate the fan experience and the atmosphere within 'MG's' extended only to his group and not the wider collective. This seems to demonstrate the lack of cohesion within the pub vindicating my argument that the fans had different expectations for fandom.

With Rooney hitting a shot just past the post, the group started chanting his name, 'Rooney, Rooney, Rooney.' This prompted a response from a middle aged fan in front of the group, 'Alf' (2012), who turned to engage with 'Toby's' (2012) group: 'Christ lads, pack it in for a bit, we are getting f***ing headaches.' Associations can be made with the encounter between 'Jack' (2012) and 'Tom' (2012) discussed in Chapter 4, with 'Tom' reprimanding 'Jack' for giving his son 'Ben' (2012) a running commentary: 'Just keep it down. He has eyes, doesn't he? Let him watch the game and let us watch it without you prattling for the last ten minutes, I'm getting a bloody headache' ('Tom' 2012). Even the use of language is similar with both participants suggesting the constant noise of their adversary was giving them a headache. In the corresponding chapter, I suggest that 'Tom's' (2012) fandom was incongruent with the family culture of the club. Indeed 'Jack' (2012) called him a 'dinosaur,' indicating that he was out of touch with the modern game and that he should 'bugger off to the Snake Pit,' the stand that houses the traditional Norwich fans. While 'Tom' (2012) and 'Jack' (2012) had different fan identities, both of the groups within the pub self-identified as traditional fans. This compliments my argument that the different groups within the pub had different expectations for fandom.

On the thirtieth-minute mark England scored, there was a roar of excitement within the pub with beer flying into the air, a scene envisaged earlier by 'Chad' (2012) 'like what you see in a film.' In that moment, 'Bob' (2012) and 'Toby' (2012) bounced from the back of the venue towards the group that confronted them earlier, jumping up and down and slapping them on the back. While a couple of the group took it in good spirits punching the air and hugging the participants, 'Alf' (2012) notably gave 'Bob' (2012) a shove, telling him to 'f*** off.' While the participants in our early exchange emphasised the collective revelry of the pub, again 'Alf' (2012) rejected their fandom.

I was keen to talk to the group to establish their opposition to 'Toby's' (2012) group and looked to engage in conversation with them after the match. At first, I was treated with a level of hostility due to my perceived association with the group yet after explaining my research, 'Mark' (2012), while unwilling to have a proper discussion, offered me some advice:

> If you are looking at football fans why are you running around with that lot? I've been going to matches since I was a kid, I used to stand on the Kop every weekend. Then a bunch of kids in fancy dress who have watched too many Danny Dyer films try and tell me how to act … bloody kids.

The way that 'Mark' (2012) dispels the identity of the group can be assimilated to the way in which 'Craig' (2012) looked to reject the identity of the MK Dons fans that I engaged with:

> As if you're looking at 'Franchise United.' If you are researching football fans why are you looking at them? They aren't even a real football club, they don't have *real fans*. No one takes them seriously, do they?

Both 'Mark' (2012) and 'Craig' (2012) question the legitimacy of researching their fan identity, insinuating that both groups are incongruent with 'real' football culture. In doing so both participants look to legitimate their fandom in opposition, with 'Mark' (2012) emphasising his status as a 'proper' fan 'stand(ing) on the Kop every weekend.' While this vindicates my suggestion that the older patrons within the pub may have first-hand experience of the terraces, 'Mark' (2012) draws on this to distance himself from the group's aspirations to enact a 'second-hand' fandom, mocking their desire to be part of the culture as insinuated by reference to 'Danny Dyer films.' Indeed, it is poignant that 'Chad' (2012) previously suggested that his desire to enact a traditional fan identity was promoted by watching films. 'Mark' (2012) positions the group as consumers within the culture, while, conversely, he has lived the experience. In doing so it seems poignant that he mobilises the discourse surrounding the 'active' traditional fan and the 'passive' consumer. The tension between 'Alf' (2012), 'Mark' (2012) and 'Toby's' (2012) group demonstrates the way in which the concepts of 'traditional fandom' and the culture of the pub are constructed by different groups. Indeed, I argue that their identity is the product of different discursive negotiations, complimenting Sandvoss' (2005: 42) argument that 'the object of distinction in fandom is no longer the text but the meaning that is constituted in the interaction between the text and reader.'

The literature celebrates the autonomy of the pub, that as a semi-public space it operates without regulation in contrast to the modern stadium (see Bale 1998;

Brimson 1998; Weed 2008). Contrarily I argue that the pub still has a hegemonic culture and is similarly exclusionary with a culture that, like the stadium, is maintained and reinforced by the behaviour of those that are occupying its space. I return to the idea of hierarchy in which the confrontation between 'Toby' (2012) and 'Mark's' (2012) group corresponds to the distinction that Weed (2008) associates with the terraces and the different ways in which it is mobilised by the group in their expectations of fandom. 'Toby' (2012) was keen to legitimise himself as a traditional fan, creating distinction between himself and modern consumers with his fandom based on an expectation of how he should enact fandom in opposition. It seems poignant that he values the revelry associated with the terraces, aware that such fandom has been outlawed from the modern stadium. On the other hand, 'Mark' (2012), as a fan with experience of the terraces, seems keen to create distinction between his group and what he perceives to be 'Toby's' (2012) mimetic attempts at authenticating himself within the culture. Cook (2000) describes mimesis as the process in which those at the top of the hierarchy determine what is good taste, and those lower down imitate what has been decided by those above them, further suggesting that mimesis 'comes from the desire to emulate what is felt to be superior,' yet it really 'works to reinforce social hierarchy' (Cook 2000: 107). I argue that this emphasises 'Toby's' (2012) engagement with the game's consumerism as much as it does the game's traditional culture, his sense of fandom and the experience that he sells to his group, reflecting his perception of what it means to be a traditional fan.

'Mark's' (2012) attempts to create distinction between the groups similarly corresponds to Weed's (2008) argument that the terraces were organised hierarchically with different terraces resembling the fan identity of the inhabitants. The pub does not enable this sense of separation and consequently I suggest that 'Mark' (2012) looks to create distinction in his fan performance, positioning the group as 'kids' that should know their place. In this context it could be argued that the pub resembles the modern stadium as much as it does the terraces. Like the modern stadium, I argue that participants are attracted to the pub by the different ways in which it is imagined to meet their needs, and, like the modern stadium, I argue that the pub operates with a culture that is regulated and enforced by hegemony, in this context the middle aged fans with first-hand experience of the terraces.

'This is a football match not a family day out'

England's second match of the tournament was against Sweden. With the relative success of the first match, the more favourable kick-off time and the expectation in the media that England would win, 'MG's' housed a larger crowd, yet significantly the demographic had changed. While there were notably fewer groups of middle aged men, the pub had attracted more family groups, with a significantly larger number of women and children in attendance.

The group seemed relatively unhappy about this, with 'Toby' (2012) emphasising the need for the group to make sure that the atmosphere was right. While the terraces are celebrated by much of the literature as the 'authentic' way to experience live football, there is a minority voice that argues that the terraces were fundamentally dangerous, threatening and uncomfortable, in which they were largely unsuitable for women and children (see Armstrong & Harris 1991; Horrie 1992; Giulianotti 1993; Hopcraft 2006; Stott & Pearson 2007). As suggested, while the public house is largely celebrated for enabling the continuation of the positive facets of terrace culture, the group took it upon themselves to facilitate the recreation of its less favorable attributes. I argue that this relates to the participants' expectations of the terrace experience and the way that is was challenged by what they perceived to be more casual fans.

The match started similarly to the France match, with 'Toby's' (2012) group starting chants and the rest of the patrons joining in. The participation was greater than the previous match with the children in attendance eagerly looking to join in. 'Toby' (2012) had previously described the need to maintain the atmosphere within the pub despite the attendance of casual fans, yet unlike the previous match, his chants were encouraging the participation of the crowd, firing their enthusiasm. At half time I engaged with 'Toby' to assess his enjoyment of the first half.

Oliver: It's buzzing in here today; there are way more people than the other night and everyone is joining in with your songs.

'Toby': See, I told you it was quality! There weren't enough people (the other night) but this is what it's like when it's jumping.

Oliver: It's a different crowd too, a lot more families and children.

'Toby': That's why the atmosphere is so good today. We have had to step it up and make sure the place keeps its atmosphere.

Oliver: They are helping to build the atmosphere, you can hear the kids singing along.

Initially the group seemed to disregard the attendance of the more casual fans, with 'Toby' (2012) insinuating that their group's attendance helped to improve the atmosphere, using it as another excuse to emphasise their group's status, that the attendance of casual fans had encouraged the group to 'step it up.' 'Toby' (2012) seemed surprised that the casual fans were joining in with his group's chants and then seemed to recognise the implications of this.

After half time, the group noticeably started to sing more crude songs, subjecting a young female glass collector to choruses of 'get your tits out for the lads;' this time they were alone in song. Later 'Bob' (2012) started to chant 'Two World Wars and one World Cup,' a song that was met with disapproving glares from families nearby. After the referee failed to call for a foul on Lampard, 'Chad' (2012) started screaming, 'f*** off, you c*nt.' This was met with anger, with a few fans turning to remonstrate with him, which resulted in the group targeting a particularly angry women and subjecting her to a chorus of 'sit down, shut up.' What had been a party atmosphere had turned into something nasty and

I was wary of my contribution to this, with the conversation I had with the participants at half time seemingly prompting their more aggressive, confrontational fan performance.

I broached this with 'Toby' after the match:

Oliver: That turned nasty pretty quick guys, what was that about?
'Toby': There were just too many families trying to hi-jack the match. I was getting pissed off and thought we needed to get the atmosphere going again.
Oliver: But at half time we were saying how good the atmosphere had been.
'Toby': Yeah, but it was f***ing soft. This is a football match not a family day out. I said there were more people, but the kids were killing it; we are not bloody kids' entertainers.
Oliver: Of course not, but you don't have to ruin it for them either.
'Toby': They were ruining it for us though. Why should we act a certain way and not do what we want just because a bunch of kids are here? It's a pub, why would parents bring kids to a pub to watch football? They know everyone's going to be drinking and f***ing around, it's not a place for them.

The idea that it is not a 'place for (children)' seems poignant, drawing on 'Toby's' (2012) expectations of the traditional pub experience and the way that he framed the experience in our initial conversations. I fear that the exchange we had at half time may have prompted him to consider the way in which the engagement of the casual fans with his group's performance may have tarnished their identity and the status of 'MG's' as a traditional space. The exchange demonstrates 'Toby's' (2012) attempt to re-establish the identity of the group as traditional fans, and the traditional culture that he associated with the venue. In doing so 'Toby' (2012) questions the sensibility of bringing children to a pub, the home of the traditional fan, in the same way in which 'Aaron' (2012) questions the sense in allowing children into the Snake Pit in Chapter 4:

Oliver: There are quite a lot of kids around the Snake Pit; the chant was hardly 'family friendly.'
'Aaron': Mate, it's the Snake Pit, they shouldn't be there if they can't handle swearing. What do they expect?

'Aaron' (2012) seemed surprised by my question, with the retort 'What do they expect?' directed at me, the intonation in his voice putting emphasis on the fact that it was the Snake Pit. Similarly, 'Toby' (2012) looked to draw upon the discourse associated with the pub, suggesting that its culture was inappropriate for children and, like 'Aaron' (2012), that the group should not curtail their behaviour in a 'traditional' space. Like 'Aaron' (2012), I argue that there was a knowingness in 'Toby's' remarks, with his response influenced both by my questions at half time and more widely by his knowledge of commercial football culture and the expectation that as a traditional fan he should oppose 'casual fans' that embody it.

The group, looking to distance themselves from the family fans within the pub for the way in which they are perceived to be incongruent with the pub's traditional culture, adopted the role of the hegemon to reject the fandom of the casual fans in the same way in which the middle aged fans, 'Alf' (2012) and 'Mark' (2012), looked to create distinction between themselves and 'Toby's' (2012) group at the previous match. In both contexts, the group perceived to be 'casuals' or inauthentic were rejected for the way in which their attempts to 'buy into' traditional football culture were seen to compromise the identity of the self-identified hegemons, and the culture of the pub. This vindicates my argument that traditional fandom is enacted by negotiating the game's capitalism as much as it is in understanding the discourse associated with the game's traditional culture.

As this chapter argues, the fandom of 'Toby's' (2012) group relates to their sense of need, particularly their desire to disassociate themselves from their game's capitalism. However, as suggested throughout the chapter, I argue that the fans similarly engage in a consumptive relationship with football's traditional culture, engaging with the discourse surrounding the terraces to construct their identity in line with their expectations of what it means to be a traditional fan. 'Mark' (2012) alludes to this idea in his rebuke of the group as consumers, suggesting that they have been attracted to the pub for the way in which it enables them to engage in an experience reminiscent of a 'Danny Dyer movie.'

In the previous chapters I argue how fandom through consumption enables fans to 'buy into' the culture of their club, yet unlike the modern stadium I argue that fans are attracted to the pub by their expectations of its 'traditional culture,' for the way in which pub fandom is said to oppose the game's capitalism. While the culture of each club is carefully cultivated to address the fans' consumer needs, the culture of the pub is defined as a 'traditional space' by self-identified traditional fans keen to maintain the aura and sense of authenticity associated with 'traditional' football culture and the images of the terraces.

The discourse associated with the pub operates to attract a different demographic to the modern stadium, producing different expectations for fandom, however my research indicates that the identity of pub fans is similarly complex and enacted in negotiation. The fans that I engaged with in the previous chapters largely self-identified with the culture of their clubs, positioning themselves as consumer fans constructing their identity in negotiation of the discourse associated with the game's traditional culture. Similarly, I argue that 'Toby's' (2012) group identify with the discourse surrounding the pub to position themselves as 'traditional fans,' yet it is clear that their understanding of the game's capitalism and their perceived need to oppose it as 'traditional fans' influences their fandom. Once again, this indicates that their identity is constructed in negotiation and influenced by their expectations of what it means to be a specific 'type' of fan.

Notes

1 France Vs England (11 June 2012); Sweden Vs England (15 June 2012); England Vs Ukraine (19 June 2012); England Vs Italy (24 June 2012).
2 See *The Football Factory* (2004); *Green Street* (2005); *Cass* (2008); *The Firm* (2009); *Away Days* (2009).

Bibliography

Armstrong, G & Harris, R (1991) Football Hooligans: Theory and Evidence. *Sociological Review* 39 (3) 427–458.

Bale, J (1998) 'Virtual Fandoms: Futurescapes of Football' Cited in Brown, A *Fanatics: Power, Identity and Fandom in Football*. London. Routledge.

Barker, C (2004) *The Sage Dictionary of Cultural Studies*. London. Sage.

Bondy, F (2010) *Chasing the Game: America and the Quest for the World Cup*. Boston. Da Capo.

Brimson, D (1998) *The Geezers Guide to Football: A Lifetime of Lads and Lager*. London. Mainstream Publishing.

Brown, A (1998) *Fanatics: Power, Identity and Fandom in Football*. London. Routledge.

Brown, O (2014) Football Fans Ticket Price Protest Doomed to Failure. *The Telegraph* [Website] Available from: http://www.telegraph.co.uk/sport/football/competitions/premier-league/11032422/Football-fans-ticket-price-protest-doomed-to-failure.html (Accessed 20 November 2014).

Bryman, A (2008) *Social Research Methods*. New York. Oxford University Press.

Carrington, B (1998) "Football's Coming Home,' but Whose Home? And do we Want it?' Nation, Football and the Politics of Exclusion' Cited in Brown, A *Fanatics: Power, Identity and Fandom in Football*. London. Routledge.

Cavicchi, D (1998) *Tramps Like Us: Music and Meaning among Springsteen Fans*. Oxford. Oxford University Press.

Cook, J (2000) 'Culture, Class and Taste' Cited in Munt, S *Cultural Studies and the Working Class: Subject to Change*. London. Cassell.

Crampsey, R (1990) *First 100 Years: Scottish League Football*. Edinburgh. The Scottish Football League Press.

Devine, TM (2012) *The Scottish Nation: A Modern History*. London. Penguin.

Fiske, J (1992) 'The Cultural Economy of Fandom' Cited in Lewis, L *The Adoring Audience*. London. Routledge.

Giulianotti, R (1993) 'Soccer Casuals as Cultural Intermediaries' Cited in Redhead, S *The Passion and the Fashion*. Aldershot. Avebury.

Hills, M (2002) *Fan Cultures*. London. Routledge.

Hopcraft, A (2006) *The Football Man: People and Passion in Soccer*. London. Aurum Press.

Horrie, C (1992) *Sick as a Parrot*. London. Virgin.

Hutchinson, R (1997) *The Toon: A Complete History of Newcastle United*. Edinburgh. Mainstream Publishing.

Imlach, G (2005) My *Father and Other Working-Class Football Heroes*. London. Yellow Jersey Press.

Jameson, F (1991) *Postmodernism or the Cultural Logic of Late Capitalism*. London. Verso.

King, A (2002) *The End of the Terraces: The Transformation of English Football in the 1990's*. London. Leicester University Press.

Pearson, G (2012) *An Ethnography of English Football Fans: Cans, Cops and Carnivals*. Manchester. Manchester University Press.
Reed-Danahay, D (1997) *Auto/Ethnography: Rewriting the Self and the Social*. Oxford. Berg.
Sandvoss, C (2005) *Fans*. Cambridge. Polity.
Scott-Jones, J & Watt, S (2010) *Ethnography in Social Science Practice*. London Routledge.
Stott, C & Pearson, G (2007) *Football 'Hooliganism', Policing and the War on the 'English Disease.'*. London. Pennant Books.
Walsh, A & Giulianotti, R (2001) This Sporting Mammon: A Normative Critique of the Commodification of Sport. *Journal of the Philosophy of Sport* 28 (1) 53–77.
Weed, M (2008) Exploring the Sport Spectator Experience: Virtual Football Spectatorship in the Pub. *Soccer and Society* 9 (2) 189–197.
Williams, J (2000) 'The Changing Face of Football: A Case for National Regulation' Cited in Mitchie, J et al. *Football in the Digital Age: Whose Game is it Anyway?* London. Mainstream Publishing.

Chapter 8

Conclusion

They think it's all over

This book started with the premise that consumer fans are trapped within the discourse of representation. I argue that agents of the game's capitalism position consumer fans positively as consumers, in which their fandom is presented as something to be garnered from a transaction. At the same time, I argue that consumer fans are negatively framed as consumers by self-identified traditional fans that resent their consumer attempts to 'buy' into the popular images of fandom upheld and disseminated by football's capitalist industries.

Through both positive reinforcement by agents of the game's capitalism and rejection by agents of the game's traditional culture, I initially outlined the way in which the identity of consumer fans was explicitly framed in relation to their status as consumers. It is my argument that this ignores the idiosyncrasies of their identity. As indicated, while consumer-oriented cultural studies analyse the multilateral power relationship between both producers and consumers of capitalist texts (see Jameson 1991; Fiske 1992; Hills 2002; Barker 2004; Sandvoss 2005), football culture operates in opposition to this premise with much of the literature, particularly the texts written by self-identified 'traditional' fans (see Bale 1998; Brimson 1998; Burgess 2005; Conn 2005; Imlach 2005), denying consumer fan subjectivity.

Taking this into account, I argue that consumer fans are defined as an exploited mass, as corporate dupes and victims of what Marx described as 'false consciousness,' hollow ersatz to the lost emotional qualities of traditional football culture. The idea that consumer fans are victims of a false conscious epitomises the hierarchy that defines contemporary football culture. The implication is that self-identified traditional fans that largely define the identity of consumer fans within football culture can do so due to their higher perception and 'authentic' relationship to football culture unmediated by capitalism. Not only does this naturalise the 'traditional' relationship between working-class fans and football culture, helping to maintain the aura associated with traditional fan identities, but this notion of hierarchy is similarly represented in the way in which football culture is studied and analysed, with the game's traditional culture and the identity of the traditional fan taken as a 'natural' starting point for research.

Consumer fans are 'othered' for reflecting the processes that have led to changes within football culture, without considering the nuances of their fan identity. As indicated throughout my research and explicated with 'Toby' (2012) and his friends in the previous chapter, self-identified traditional fans frame their identity in opposition to the game's capitalism and their perception of the consumer fan. This raises a poignant question. 'Toby' (2012) indicates that he constitutes his identity in negotiation of the discourses associated with both the game's capitalism and traditional culture. In this context I posed the question, why is it taken for granted that consumer fans do not engage in a similar process of negotiation, engaging with both capitalist and traditional discourses in the process of their identity formation? This inspired my research question. What does fandom mean to consumer fans and how do they articulate their own identity within football culture?

To develop a more nuanced understanding of contemporary football culture and to contribute to consumer-oriented cultural studies that look to understand the agency and motivations of consumers (see Jameson 1991; Fiske 1992; Hills 2002; Barker 2004; Sandvoss 2005; Lash 2007), my research has endeavoured to analyse how consumer fans understand the way in which they are positioned within football culture, how they articulate and understand their fan identity and how they negotiate the ways in which they are represented. In doing so each chapter draws upon unique data from ethnographic research to analyse the way in which fans of different clubs understand and respond to their representation within football culture, both by their club as an agent of the game's capitalism and agents of the game's traditional culture. Subsequently this research can be considered as a study of consumerism and pleasure, unique in taking the game's modern capitalism as a starting point, operationalising football culture as a 'capitalist text.'

While I argue that the participants that I engage with enact different identities in relation to the culture of their club, there is a commonality in the ways in which the participants conceptualise their identity as consumers. Positioned positively as consumers by agents of football's capitalism, such as the chairmen of their club, the FA and football's affiliated companies, then negatively as consumers by agents of the game's tradition, particularly self-identified traditional fans, my research indicates that the consumer fans define themselves as *active* consumers.

Self-identified traditional fans that I engaged with, such as 'Joe' (2011) (Chapter 4) and 'Toby' (2012) (Chapter 7), explicitly framed their identity in opposition to their perception of the identity of the consumer fan. The pair's arguments against the consumer fan correspond to the discourse of the popular literature (see Brimson 1998) that criticises consumer fans for 'buying into' the popular image of fandom upheld and disseminated by football's capitalist industries, without understanding the traditions of the culture. While my research indicates that participants engage in active consumer relationships with their clubs, identifying the ways in which the culture of their club meets their individual consumer needs, I argue that consumer fans similarly 'buy into' the game's traditional culture, negotiating its discourse and using it as a resource in the substantiation of their identity. This challenges the simplistic binary that has been created between the 'traditional fan' and 'modern consumer' that still looms over contemporary football culture.

In each chapter participants demonstrate their understanding and acceptance of the game's capitalism, articulating the ways in which the culture of their club corresponds to their consumer needs. My research indicates that consumer fans similarly engage with football culture's traditional discourses, leading me to argue that their identity as consumers extends beyond their relationship with their club. Indeed, I argue that the fans' consumption of the game's traditional culture works in the same way in which the participants' identify with the culture of their clubs, with traditional football culture becoming a resource that fans can draw upon in the substantiation of their identity.

This idea is epitomised by the identity of the MK Dons fans that I analysed in Chapter 5. The chapter argues that the Dons fans actively engage with the traditional culture associated with Wimbledon, appropriating the traditional rituals associated with the club to actively emphasise their status as consumers within football culture, playing on the fact that the club has 'consumed' the identity and community of Wimbledon. I argue that fans of the Dons appropriate the traditional culture of Wimbledon in self-aware celebrations of their own liminal status within football culture to emphasise their collective identity as consumer fans of a franchise football club.

This leads to my argument that the identity of the participants that I engage with is influenced by their expectations of how they *should* enact fandom. Again, using the MK Dons fans to punctuate my argument, I believe that the knowing performance of the Dons fans challenges the expectations that their rivals have about them. The idea being that as 'passive' consumers of a 'franchise' football club they should not understand or engage with the game's traditional culture. The way in which the Dons fans enact traditional rituals associated with Wimbledon not only emphasises their identity as consumers but also challenges the rival fans' power of definition, enabling the Dons fans to subvert the expectations they have of their identity.

This book argues that consumer fans' levels of engagement and understanding of both the game's modern capitalism and its traditional culture enables them to enact different types of identity. Rather than being trapped within discourses of representation, my research indicates that consumer fans engage in processes of complex discursive negotiation, constructing their identities at the juncture of the hegemonic discourses that surround the culture, consumerism and tradition, but also their individual understanding of how they are expected to enact fandom. In the context of the Dons, I argue that the fans' understanding of the culture of the club and the way in which the club are perceived within football culture motivates them to enact fan identities that challenge the expectations of them upheld within football culture. The fans' understanding of the business process that lead to the creation of the club demonstrates their understanding of the capitalist orientation of the club and its operation as a leisure industry. Similarly, their active appropriation of the traditional rituals associated with Wimbledon demonstrates their engagement with traditional football culture. The fans are aware that it is their ability to negotiate the discourse surrounding traditional football culture that challenges expectations, particularly the idea that they are passive consumers. Chapter 5 argues that the Dons fans experience pleasure from this. Indeed, throughout this book I document the ways in which participants experience pleasure in negotiating expectations rival fans have of their identity.

While I outline how fans construct their identity in negotiation of their status as consumers, I acknowledge that this could be seen as problematic; the fans' adherence to both hegemonic discourses surrounding the game could be seen as demonstrative of the limited boundaries for identity formation within football culture. I would argue that the fact that the participants are able to negotiate these discourses indicates that consumer fans are starting to enact their own unique, hybrid identities within the culture, encouraging us to reconsider the scope of representation within contemporary football culture.

As suggested, my research indicates that consumer fans substantiate their identity at the juncture of the discourses surrounding football culture, in negotiation of the game's capitalism and tradition. In doing so I argue that fans actively attempt to expand the boundaries of representation with their identity oscillating between affirmation and rejection of these discourses. I interpret this as the participants' attempts to engineer their own representational space within football culture, a culture that largely struggles to accept and adapt to the changes that they represent. Thornton (1995: 201) argues that understanding culture is fundamentally a question of epistemology and my research vindicates my argument that it is necessary to analyse football culture with new epistemological approaches. I have looked to do this by adopting a consumer-oriented cultural studies approach, taking into account the unique ways in which consumer fans engineer their own frames of representation within contemporary football culture.

It is significant that the participants that I engaged with throughout the research process enact their identity in a similar process of negotiation. As suggested, the way in which the participants of each club actively negotiate their identity in relation to the game's capitalism, tradition and their expectations for fandom is the commonality between the participants and the theme that binds my research. Taking this into account, I argue that my research has provided me with a framework to analyse the ways in which consumer fans establish their identity, which can subsequently be used in further research to explore the ways in which fans of different clubs, or indeed fans with different conceptions of their self-identity, enact fandom.

It was my acknowledgement of this framework, coupled with the recognition that my work focuses on a specific type of fan experience within the modern stadium, that encouraged me to apply my framework of analysis to pub fandom, engaging with self-identified traditional fans. I was keen to assess the way in which traditional fans enact identity, to see if they engage in similar discursive negotiations and to assess whether their identity is similarly shaped by their expectations of what it means to be a specific 'type' of fan.

As suggested, I opted to conduct research within the pub around the screening of England's Euro 2012 matches. The tournament was selected explicitly to test the application of my framework in relation to a different fan experience, but also for the way in which screenings of international matches are said to attract a diverse range of fans with different conceptions of their self-identity (see Carrington 1998; Bondy 2010; Brown 2014). The research around the tournament supported my assumption that the identity of the self-identified traditional fans was similarly enacted in negotiation, with the fans' expression of collective identity tempered by the presence of 'casual' fans within the pub. Indeed, Chapter 7 indicates that the presence of 'casual' fans within the pub compromised the traditional fans' expectations of the pub as a 'traditional' venue, emphasising the way in which their expectations for fandom had been constructed in a specific way.

I maintain that the inclusion of Chapter 7 operates to further explicate the nuances of identity within contemporary football culture, exploring the ways in which different agents influence fans' expectations of how they *should* constitute their identity as a specific type of fan. In doing so I believe that the chapter similarly demonstrates that my framework of analysis can be successfully applied to the analysis of different fan experiences within contemporary football culture and to the analysis of different fan identities.

To continue to develop a more nuanced understanding of contemporary football culture, I maintain that it is vital to 'shatter the aura' surrounding traditional football culture. While I do not consider this book to have achieved this objective, I believe that it has started to chip away at its aura, providing consumer fans with an opportunity to articulate their identity and negotiate the discourses operating upon them within football culture. I intend to continue this pursuit and encourage other researchers to chip away at the aura associated with traditional football culture, analysing the way in which fans of other football clubs throughout the football league negotiate their identity as consumers.

A good place to start would be with fans of a team in the northern part of the country. To refer to Sands (2002) again, he states that successful ethnography depends upon the selection of the right populations. I maintain that I have selected the right fan groups and the right clubs as cases to enable me to address my research questions and make perceptive generalisations about contemporary football culture. Having said that, I am conscious that I am only able to make generalisations in relation to fans from the southeast of the country. My research conducted within the pub indicates that my framework of analysis can be successfully applied to different fan experiences and to fans with different self-identities and I am keen to apply my framework to fans from different regions of the country. At present I am aware that my research 'colours in only a small section of territory' and subsequently has 'lesser value in navigating through the territory at large' (Sandvoss 2005: 6). As indicated in Chapter 3, my initial pilot studies were conducted with clubs throughout the football league situated in both the north and south of the country. As suggested, the final case studies were selected irrespective of their geographical location due to the way in which the culture of each club corresponds with different characteristics of the game's modern capitalism.

As outlined, the different marketing strategies and cultures of each club attracted different demographics: Norwich City attracted a significant number of family groups, MK Dons attracted a sizable number of middle-aged, middle-class fans, while Chelsea appealed to a global fan base from around the world. The clubs were selected as case studies for analysis in the recognition that the fans shared a communality of identity. When considering the data obtained from my pilot studies conducted at clubs from the northern part of the country, Northampton, Scunthorpe and Bolton, I was unable to identify a discernible communality between the fans that would act as an index for analysis. In hindsight, I failed to recognise that fans of northern clubs are bound by geography. In 2012, the year in which I conducted my ethnographic research, *The Economist* (2012) argued that the gap between the south of the country and the north, in life expectancy, political inclinations and in economic trends, was growing to the extent that they could be considered as separate countries.

Stuart Maconie (2007) can be used to develop this idea, arguing that, like a separate country, the north of England has a different cultural and political landscape to the rest of Britain. Maconie (2007) argues that the majority of the country can be considered as centre-right in political orientation whereas the north of England has a strong history of socialism, a divide that he suggests corresponds to the economic divide between the north and south of England. He continues arguing that the different economic conditions and different political orientation of the north have led to the development of a folk culture indiscernible to the south: 'The north means home, truth, beauty, valour, romance, warm and characterful people, real beer and proper chip shops' (Maconie 2007: 2).

It is significant that Maconie (2007) mobilises the same discourses associated with traditional football culture, which in both instances are associated with the integrity, authenticity and community of the working-class in opposition to the soullessness of capitalism. Taking this into account I speculate as to whether fans of northern clubs would be receptive or accepting of modern football culture, a culture that is fundamentally opposed to the folk culture of the region. It is important to remember that cultures are constantly in flux. My research was conducted around the 2011/2012 football season. Subsequently my analysis can be considered a valid interpretation of the participants' identity at that moment in time. The categories of identity that I associated with fans from clubs in the south of the country were abandoned after it became clear that the themes were not concomitant with the way in which the participants articulated their own fan identity. While it would be interesting to assess whether the shared geography of the north had a more significant impact on the participants' fan identity, it is important to remember that my research focuses on a small sample of fans associated with each club and this is not to suggest that the way that they articulate their fandom is constitutive of the club's wider fan base. With this in mind I think that it would be beneficial to return to conduct further research at each club to see if different participants constitute their identity in relation to my initial themes of analysis, gender, class and ethnicity, to analyse whether these characteristics of identity contribute to the fans' negotiation of the culture of their club or similarly influence their expectations for fandom.

It would be fascinating to return to the clubs to assess whether the changes that have happened within the culture have impacted upon the way in which the fans enact their identity. This would serve as a fascinating counterpoint to this research, providing me with further data to consider the ways in which consumer fans constitute their identity in negotiation of the culture of their club and the game's traditional culture. It would be fascinating to discover whether the changes that have happened at each club encourage participants to enact different types of identity, enabling me to analyse the way in which consumer fans constitute their identity at different cultural moment in their club's history.

Bibliography

Bale, J (1998) 'Virtual Fandoms: Futurescapes of Football.' Cited in Brown, A *Fanatics: Power, Identity and Fandom in Football*. London. Routledge.

Barker, C (2004) *The Sage Dictionary of Cultural Studies*. London. Sage.

Bondy, F (2010) *Chasing the Game: America and the Quest for the World Cup*. Boston. Da Capo.

Brimson, D (1998) *The Geezers Guide to Football: A Lifetime of Lads and Lager*. London. Mainstream Publishing.

Brown, O (2014) Football Fans Ticket Price Protest Doomed to Failure. *The Telegraph* [Website] Available from: http://www.telegraph.co.uk/sport/football/competitions/premier-league/11032422/Football-fans-ticket-price-protest-doomed-to-failure.html (Accessed 20 November 2014).

Burgess, C (2005) What on Earth Has Happened to Football? *The Guardian* [Website] Available from: http://www.theguardian.com/football/2005/feb/09/sport.comment (Accessed 16 November 2012).

Carrington, B (1998) "Football's Coming Home,' but Whose Home? And Do We Want It?' Nation, Football and the Politics of Exclusion.' Cited in Brown, A *Fanatics: Power, Identity and Fandom in Football*. London. Routledge.

Conn, D (2005) *The Beautiful Game? Searching for the Soul of Football*. London. Yellow Jersey Press.

Fiske, J (1992) 'The Cultural Economy of Fandom' Cited in Lewis, L *The Adoring Audience*. London. Routledge.

Hills, M (2002) *Fan Cultures*. London. Routledge.

Imlach, G (2005) My *Father and Other Working-Class Football Heroes*. London. Yellow Jersey Press.

Jameson, F (1991) *Postmodernism or the Cultural Logic of Late Capitalism*. London. Verso.

Lash, S (2007) 'Power after Hegemony: Cultural Studies in Mutation?' *Theory, Culture and Society* 24 (3) 55–78.

Maconie, S (2007) *Pies and Prejudice: In Search of the North*. London. Ebury Press.
Sands, R (2002) *Sport Ethnography*. Illinois. Human Kinetics.
Sandvoss, C (2005) *Fans*. Cambridge. Polity.
The Economist (2012) The North of England: The Great Divide. *The Economist* [Website] Available from: http://www.economist.com/node/21562938 (Accessed 18 May 2014).
Thornton, S (1995) *Club Cultures: Music, Media and Subcultural Capital.* Cambridge. Polity.

Appendix A

The cost of being a fan of each club selected for analysis for the 2011/2012 season.

Norwich City

Season ticket in the Aviva Community Stand – £423.43
Under 17s season ticket in the Aviva Community Stand – £281.50
Match day programme – £3.50
Replica shirt – £45
Child's shirt – £35
Pie – £2.50
Pint – £3.50

MK Dons

Season ticket in the East Wing – £324
Under 17s season ticket in the East Wing – £24
Match day programme – £3
Replica shirt – £40
Child's shirt – £33
Pie – £3.20
Pint – £3

Chelsea

Season ticket in the Shed End Upper – £880
Under 17s season ticket in the Shed End Upper – £425
Match day programme – £3
Replica shirt – £55
Child's shirt – £45
Pie – £3.60
Pint – £3.50

Index

Abramovich, R. 20, 39, 96, 98, 100, 105–106, 111, 112, 115–119
Aden, R.C. 116
AFC Wimbledon 72, 83, 86–88, 92
After Empire: Melancholia or Convivial Culture? (Gilroy) 11–12
Alcock, C. 17
American football 10–11
Ancelotti, C. 98–100
Ang, I. 80
Argonauts of the West Pacific (Malinowski) 37
Arsenal, founder of 17
Austin, S. 21
authoritarian conformity 57, 64
auto-ethnographic reflection 42

Bakhtin, M. 61–62, 68
Bale, G. 50, 51, 79, 126, 131, 136
Barclays Bank 1–2, 3, 4, 6
Barker, C. 5–6, 7
Barnes, S. 27–28
Bates, K. 19, 28, 51, 123–124
Baudrillard, J. 26, 27
BBC 29
Beckham, D. 136
Benitez, R. 117–118
Boas, A.V. (AVB) 98–107, 109–110, 112, 118
Brimson, D. 11, 129, 130, 134
Burke, P. 62

capitalism, phases of 21
carnival 61–62, 64, 68, 126
'carnival fans' 52, 66–67
Carrington, B. 125
case studies, selection of 39–40
Cavicchhi, D. 82, 83, 84, 92, 138
chav culture 116
'cheering for self' 96–98, 103, 106–108, 112, 116
Chelsea: description of 39; selection of 38, 40–41, 154; study of 96–119
Cherry, B. 75
Cole, A. 112–115
collectivity 128–130, 131, 134–135, 139, 140
commodities, ideological meaning of 5–6
'community building' approach 39, 72, 74, 76–83; *see also* Milton Keynes Dons
consumer fan: articulations of identity of 6–7; conception of 1–3; 'othering of' 149–150; self-identification as 49–51; traditional fan versus 3–5, 150–151
consumer-oriented cultural studies approach 5, 6, 7, 152
Cook, J. 116, 143
'core identity' 40–41
Crampsey, R. 18, 20
cultural hierarchy 36
cultural reorientation of football 2
Culture of the New Capitalism, The (Sennett) 22

de Certeau, M. 81
de Garis, L. 37
Dein, D. 28
de-territorialisation 75–76
Devine, T.M. 16, 22
Di Matteo, R. 104–112, 116–118
discursive negotiation 6, 48, 122, 142, 150–153
Doncaster, N. 74–75
Doyle, P. 98
'drop the Dons' campaign 89–92
Dyer, R. 97

Eastham, G. 24
Eco, U. 116
emotional engagement 56
'entertainment' approach 39; *see also* Chelsea
ethnographic research 36–38, 41–42, 153

FA Cup 17–20
Falcous, M. 74, 76, 83
false consciousness 149
'family club' 38–39, 46–47, 49–58; *see also* Norwich City
family fans 48–58
'fantasy frame' 100
Fay, B. 37
Ferdinand, A. 112
Finney, T. 24
Fiske, J. 80, 82, 86, 92
Flynn, A. 29
football: bureaucracy of 20–28; commercialization of 10–11; as escape 16–17; history of 14–20; modern culture of 28–31; professionalisation of 20–23; standardization of 15–16; *see also individual clubs*
Foust, C. 61
'franchise football club' 71
'friendlies' 17–18
Fromm, E. 57
'futeball' 14–15

Gasper, P. 52, 79
gate receipts 21
Gelder, K. 36
Gilroy, P. 11–12
Giulianotti, R. 30
grounded theory approach 40

Hall, S. 25
Hammersley, M. 36
Harvey, D. 28
Hawksbee, P. 87–88
Hayward, K. 116
hegemony 73
Heysel disaster 26–27
Hillsborough disaster 27, 29, 73
Hill-Wood, S. 17
Holding, J. 17
Holt, G. 65
hooligan culture/hooliganism 13, 23, 25–27, 47–48
Hopcraft, A. 29, 124, 129, 131
Hussey, A. 25–26, 27
Hutchinson, R. 22–23, 24, 63

Imlach, G. 10–11, 14, 22, 23, 47, 74
Inter City Firm (ICF) 47
interview methodology 42–43

Jenkins, H. 60
Juventus, Heysel disaster and 26

King, A. 3, 11, 38, 73

Lancaster, K. 63, 91, 100
Lash, S. 73
Liverpool 17, 26
local representation 47

Maconie, S. 154
Malinowski, B. 37
Mandel, E. 21, 29
Mansour, S. 20
Marcuse, H. 4, 5
matches, costs of 2
McKinley, E.G. 60
McNulty, P. 105
melancholia 11–12, 13
methodology overview 35–44
Millwall 93
Milton Keynes Dons: appropriation and 151–152; description of 39; selection of 38, 40–41, 154; study of 71–93
mimesis 143
MK Dons Sport and Education Trust 74
monopoly capitalism 21
Moon, J.D. 37
Moore, B. 47
Morley, D. 30
Moses, V. 65–66
Murray, B. 14–15, 16, 18–19
My Father and Other Working-Class Football Heroes (Imlach) 10

Neville, G. 96
Newcastle United 22–23, 24–25, 63
'No one likes us and we don't care' 93
Norwich City: description of 38–39; selection of 38, 40–41, 154; study of 46–69

'On the ball, City' 64–65

participant centrism 37–38
participant selection 42
participatory research: caution regarding 39; inclusivity and 35; principles of 7
Pearson, G. 48, 52, 60, 64, 67, 128, 131

pilot studies 38, 39, 40, 154
pubs and pub fans 122–146, 152–153
purposive sampling 42

Radway, J. 80, 81
Rafferty, J. 14, 16–17
re-branding 71, 73
'retain and transfer system' 21–22, 23–24
Rose, C. 74, 76, 83
Rosenberg, A. 36
Ross, D. 17–18, 18, 24–25

Sands, R. 38, 40, 153
Sandvoss, C. 6, 12, 13–14, 35, 39, 41, 54, 56, 61, 78, 82, 91, 103, 106, 130, 137, 142
Scholar, I. 28–29
Schrijvers, J. 42
Scott-Jones, J. 37
Sennett, R. 22
shin pads 18
Slater, M. 21
Snake Pit 58–68, 145
Stallybrass, P. 68
Symanski, S. 25

Taylor, M. 22
television 25, 26, 29, 123
terraces 2–3, 5, 28–29, 48, 65, 67, 124, 126–127, 129–132, 138–140, 142–144
Terry, J. 112–115
Thatcher, M. 26
Thornton, S. 36, 38, 79–80, 152
Tottenham 29
traditional fan: consumer fan versus 3–5, 150–151; self-identification as 61, 66–67
Transparency of Evil, The (Baudrillard) 26

Van der Riet, M. 35
Vass, J. 96–97, 103

wages, maximum 21–22, 23–24
Wagg, S. 18
Walsh, A. 30
Watt, S. 37
Weed, M. 79, 123, 130, 140, 143
West Ham United 46–48
White, A. 68
Wilson, P. 29–30
Wimbledon, MK Dons and 71–93
Winkelman, P. 39, 71, 72, 73, 74, 80–81, 85, 87–89
women in football culture 79–80
World War II 12–13, 17

Yar, M. 116

Zimbalist, A. 25

For Product Safety Concerns and Information please contact our EU
representative GPSR@taylorandfrancis.com
Taylor & Francis Verlag GmbH, Kaufingerstraße 24, 80331 München, Germany

www.ingramcontent.com/pod-product-compliance
Ingram Content Group UK Ltd.
Pitfield, Milton Keynes, MK11 3LW, UK
UKHW020206200926
475702UK00004B/642
9780367142650